The Untouchables

The Untouchables

The people who helped wreck Ireland – and are still running the show

SHANE ROSS AND
NICK WEBB

PENGUIN
IRELAND

To Ruth and Rebecca

PENGUIN IRELAND

Published by the Penguin Group
Penguin Ireland, 25 St Stephen's Green, Dublin 2, Ireland (a division of Penguin Books Ltd)
Penguin Books Ltd, 80 Strand, London WC2R 0RL, England
Penguin Group (USA) Inc., 375 Hudson Street, New York, New York 10014, USA
Penguin Group (Australia), 707 Collins Street, Melbourne, Victoria 3008, Australia
(a division of Pearson Australia Group Pty Ltd)
Penguin Group (Canada), 90 Eglinton Avenue East, Suite 700, Toronto, Ontario, Canada M4P 2Y3
(a division of Pearson Penguin Canada Inc.)
Penguin Books India Pvt Ltd, 11 Community Centre, Panchsheel Park, New Delhi – 110 017, India
Penguin Group (NZ), 67 Apollo Drive, Rosedale, Auckland 0632, New Zealand
(a division of Pearson New Zealand Ltd)
Penguin Books (South Africa) (Pty) Ltd, Block D, Rosebank Office Park,
181 Jan Smuts Avenue, Parktown North, Gauteng 2193, South Africa

Penguin Books Ltd, Registered Offices: 80 Strand, London WC2R 0RL, England

www.penguin.com

First published 2012
001
Copyright © Shane Ross and Nick Webb, 2012
The moral right of the authors has been asserted

Set in 12/14.75 pt Bembo Book MT Std
Typeset by Jouve (UK), Milton Keynes
Printed in Great Britain by Clays Ltd, St Ives plc

A CIP catalogue record for this book is available from the British Library
ISBN: 978–1–844–88277–9
www.greenpenguin.co.uk

Penguin Books is committed to a sustainable
future for our business, our readers and our planet.
This book is made from Forest Stewardship
Council™ certified paper.

ALWAYS LEARNING **PEARSON**

Contents

Prologue   1

1. The Department   7

2. Zombie Bankers   38

3. Access All Areas   60

4. Land of 999 Quangos   91

5. Fingers in Every Pie   112

6. Your Future Is in Their Hands   139

7. The Property-Pushers' Bailout   157

8. The Judges: JAABs for the Boys   184

9. The Directory   234

Epilogue   277

Acknowledgements   281

Index   283

Prologue

Not even an untouchable is immortal.

It was a cold Friday morning in January 2012, the twelfth day of Christmas, when they came to bid farewell to Alex Spain. Mourners gathered at the Church of the Assumption in Dublin's Booterstown Avenue. The service was packed with the great and the good of Irish business. Alex Spain was by all accounts a decent man. The mass was celebrated by the local parish priest, Monsignor Seamus Conway. Predictably, he lauded Alex Spain's business successes. Afterwards, mourners followed the hearse to Shanganagh Cemetery, ten miles south of Dublin. Finally, they headed to Alex Spain's beloved Milltown Golf Club for refreshments.

The obituaries in the newspapers followed. They told the story of a man blessed with many advantages in life. He was born in 1932 into the well-heeled Dublin professional classes: his father had been master of the National Maternity Hospital in Holles Street, and his mother was an architect who later ran an antique shop in the prosperous suburb of Ranelagh. Alex Spain ticked all the right boxes. He attended the up-market Blackrock College, where he captained the rugby team. From there he headed for University College Dublin, took a first-class degree in commerce and was again captain of rugby, a post held by his father before him. He became an accountant, soon joining Stokes Kennedy Crowley (SKC).

Spain was no doubt as brilliant an accountant as the obituaries said. So brilliant that he was prepared to open the most controversial of all bank accounts – of the infamous Ansbacher variety – for his Stokes Kennedy Crowley clients, back in 1972.

Offshore Ansbacher accounts had been used for tax evasion by a number of Ireland's untouchables. Not every account was illegal, but all prompted awkward questions and the unwelcome interest of a High Court inspector. Spain was listed by the inspectors as being in a category of people whose sole involvement was the establishment of Ansbacher trusts to which they never transferred assets. The inspectors also stated that Spain had revealed in a letter that he himself was the 'potential beneficiary' of an Ansbacher trust.

One of the Ansbacher accounts Spain had opened was for the late property developer Phil Monahan, the chairman of Monarch Properties. In 2012 Monahan was named by the Mahon Tribunal as having been 'likely to have known about' what it deemed 'almost certainly corrupt' payments made by Monarch Properties to councillors to secure land rezoning.

Spain also opened an Ansbacher account for Neil McCann of Fyffes banana fame. And he opened one for himself. Despite Spain's letter to the High Court inspectors insisting that his own Ansbacher account was never activated, they were satisfied that 'this constituted the carrying out of business for him by Guinness Mahon Cayman Trust', the offshore vehicle used by none other than Charlie Haughey and his own bent accountant, Des Traynor.

For some reason, unexplained to this day, no prosecutions have ever been brought against Ansbacher account holders. Secret settlements were made with the Revenue Commissioners but not a sinner was taken to court. Ansbacher account holders were untouchable.

In 1979, Spain succeeded SKC's legendary Niall Crowley as managing partner, and served in the position for five years. The obituaries told of when Spain was sent in by the government as a consultant to reorganize B&I, the troubled semi-state shipping company. He was credited with removing a burden from the state when the company was sold to Irish Continental in 1992. In line with a pattern of uncanny coincidences that marked his post-SKC career, KPMG (as SKC was renamed following a merger in 1987) were accountants to B&I.

He combined his passion for rugby with another sport where businessmen establish useful connections – golf. Besides Milltown, his club memberships included the elite, all-male Portmarnock and the legendary Royal and Ancient in St Andrews, Scotland.

In the mid-eighties, when Spain was at the height of his powers, a joke did the rounds. The joke had Spain and two SKC partners, the brothers Conor and Laurence Crowley, being kidnapped by the IRA.

The guerrillas take them into the Wicklow Mountains and demand a ransom, but it is refused. All three are granted a last wish before being shot. Conor Crowley, drawn to be the first man for the IRA firing squad, asks for a stiff drink and some Havana cigars. Spain, due to be shot second, merely wants to deliver his own epitaph to the assembled company – a one-and-a-half-hour eulogy of his achievements in SKC. Laurence Crowley, third in line, thinks for a moment and then declares that his wish was to be shot before Spain began his eulogy.

In 1988 Spain was made chairman of Xtra-vision, the video rental company. In May 1989 it was floated on the stock market with a value of IR£24.3 million, a massive figure at the time. The shares nearly doubled on the first day's trading, eventually hitting a peak value of £102 million. But Xtra-vision expanded recklessly at home and abroad, burning cash at an unsustainable rate. The share price collapsed from a peak of £1.03 down to less than 10p. In late 1990 the company was sold to the financial services group Cambridge for just £5.5 million. Xtra-vision's auditors were none other than SKC's successor firm, KPMG.

Among the mourners at Spain's funeral was David Dilger, another accountant from the SKC/KPMG stable. Later in his career Dilger had become a link with another of Spain's more controversial business associates – Larry Goodman. Dilger was chief executive of Goodman's Food Industries when Spain was chairman. The auditors, once again, were KPMG. They were also auditors to Larry's flagship company, Goodman International. Spain shared the board of Food Industries not only with Goodman himself but also with the dodgiest of Fianna Fáil TDs, Liam Lawlor.

Goodman International went into examinership when Spain was chairman of Food Industries. The banks insisted that Goodman's stake in Food Industries be sold to Greencore in 1992. Spain again somehow escaped unscathed from his association with the beef baron, of whom he had been a favourite.

Also among the mourners were the former governor of the Bank of Ireland, Laurence Crowley, and the former chief executive of AIB, Michael Buckley. The presence of these two giants of Irish banking served as a reminder that Alex Spain was not just an ace accountant. He had been chairman of a major bank himself.

Spain had chaired National Irish Bank at an embarrassing time. In 1998, High Court inspectors had been sent in to probe accusations of overcharging and tax evasion.

Much of the blame in the eventual inspectors' report (2004) was heaped on the shoulders of NIB's chief executive, Jim Lacey. Many years later – in 2011 – Lacey was disqualified by the courts from any involvement in the management of any firm for nine years, as a result of the findings regarding his management of NIB.

Spain had been a strong supporter of Lacey, but he managed to escape much of the ignominy attached to Lacey's activities – even though he was chairman of the board, and of the audit committee, at the time the scandals broke. The High Court inspectors merely delivered a token rebuke in his direction, branding his audit committee as 'remiss' for failing to ask management to quantify the possible liability arising from NIB's non-collection of DIRT tax.

Many years earlier, after Spain had been called before the Dáil's Public Accounts Committee to explain why NIB had been cheating on DIRT tax, the PAC's report pointedly headed the section about Alex Spain 'Mr Spain's Lack of Knowledge'. The former chairman had simply pleaded that he knew little or nothing about non-compliance with DIRT. Somehow, it had worked. Spain slipped away from the NIB chair in 1999, after ten years at the helm, virtually untouched.

Laurence Crowley was just one of four former SKC/KPMG managing partners at Spain's funeral – John Callaghan, Ron Bolger and Jerome Kennedy were there as well, as was the current managing partner, Terence O'Rourke. National Irish Bank's auditors, who had failed to question NIB's DIRT liabilities, were none other than KPMG. The blue-blooded accountants were not spared from criticism in the report. A pattern had been established. In the eighties and nineties, Spain became chairman of three companies audited by KPMG. His old firm did the audit. He chaired the board. And the companies landed in trouble.

Jim Flavin, deposed chief executive of conglomerate DCC, was another of the mourners paying their last respects to Alex Spain on that chilly January morning. Flavin's career path and background were strikingly similar to Spain's: both men had been at Blackrock

College, both were at UCD and both qualified as chartered accountants. Flavin's chairman at DCC was none other than Spain, who
served thirty years in the post – a longevity of service that presented
an open challenge to the code of corporate governance.

Flavin will forever be known as the guy whom the Supreme Court
found guilty of unlawful insider dealing in the shares of Fyffes. His
sale of DCC's shares in Fyffes was carried out in February 2000,
when Spain was chairman. In 2002 Fyffes sued DCC over the sale,
alleging insider dealing. A High Court verdict of not guilty was
given in December 2005. The case lifted the veil on some of the less
savoury activities in Irish corporate life, neither side emerging with
credit. At all times Spain backed Flavin to the hilt.

Fyffes appealed the High Court decision to the Supreme Court,
which overturned the High Court's judgement. DCC was forced to
pay Fyffes more than €37 million in compensation. Spain had by this
time vacated the DCC chair, but the DCC board, stuffed with stars
of the 'golden circle', brazenly resolved to eyeball the Supreme Court
and to back Flavin as chief executive despite the adverse finding of the
highest authority in the land. At the end of the day, a specially
appointed High Court inspector – barrister Bill Shipsey – stunned the
corporate world when he pronounced that Flavin 'genuinely believed'
he was not in possession of inside information when he sold the Fyffes
shares. Although Alex Spain had retired by the time the Supreme
Court gave its final verdict against Flavin, he was in the chair at the
time of Flavin's offending transaction, and he had stood by him.

What was it that made this man – who had been associated with
Jim Lacey, Larry Goodman, Liam Lawlor, Jim Flavin, Ansbacher
account holders and the disastrous Xtra-vision – an untouchable and
a pillar of the Irish business establishment?

How could a man with such sulphurous associations rise to the top
of KPMG and secure the chair of so many Irish public companies?

How could one of his obituaries have described him as 'a rock of
reason' who 'achieved all that he did through hard work and a belief
in considered, rational decision-making'?

Welcome to official Ireland.

1. The Department

In January 2010, having served three and a half years as secretary general of the Department of Finance, David Doyle retired from the civil service. Doyle's tenure as the head of the department had seen a catastrophic collapse in the Irish economy and in the public finances. The state had guaranteed the liabilities of the banking system, and then nationalized it, incurring obligations it might never be able to discharge. Before the end of the year, as a result of these developments, Ireland would no longer be able to borrow money on the open market, and would require an onerous bailout from the EU and the IMF.

You might think that everyone concerned would agree that the next secretary general of the Department of Finance should be a man or woman who had not had any part in the comprehensive failure of policy and regulation that had created the disaster. You would be wrong. There were three second secretaries in the department (the most senior officials after the secretary general). Doyle's replacement was the second secretary who ran the taxation and financial services division. His name was Kevin Cardiff. The departmental press release announcing Cardiff's appointment noted: 'As the financial crisis developed over the past 18 months' – in other words, since the summer of 2008 – 'Mr Cardiff was asked to concentrate solely on financial services matters.'

Doyle meanwhile retired with a gold-plated pension package, made up of a €343,000 lump sum and a €115,000 severance 'gratuity' payment. His annual pension is worth €115,000 per year.

The then Minister for Finance, Brian Lenihan, later revealed that the three secretaries general who had retired from the Department of Finance since 2005 had been paid a combined total of €386,478 in 'severance gratuities'. These payments were on top of chunky retirement lump sums of between €260,000 and €343,000 each. The department also shelled out €2.5 million in lump sums and other pay-offs to eight other high-ranking civil servants who retired over the same period.

The national economy was shot, the public finances were in ruins, but they were untouchable. Kevin Cardiff, the new secretary general, with his salary of €303,000 per year, was also untouchable.

To get a true sense of how the most important of the government departments operates, it is useful to look back to the good old days when the economy was booming and the state's coffers were brimming over.

In March 2002 the government appointed Tom Considine as secretary general of the Department of Finance. Fianna Fáil's Charlie McCreevy was minister at the time. Considine's predecessor, John Hurley, had just become governor of the Central Bank. It was something of a tradition for former secretaries general of the Department of Finance to make the move to the big building on Dame Street. With a top-grade salary of €348,000, lots of foreign travel and excellent nosh at some of the continent's top restaurants, there was plenty to like about running the Central Bank.

Considine was a 'lifer' at the Department of Finance, having joined in 1974, when he was in his twenties. His career had seen him serve as secretary general of the Public Service Management and Development branch of the department from 2000 until 2002. This was the part of the department that drove the flawed strategy of benchmarking during that period, which led to cavalier pay hikes for the public sector and has left Ireland in the unsustainable situation whereby the head of our 13,000-strong defence forces earns €189,114 – almost as much as the chairman of the Joint Chiefs of Staff of the US military. Or where the Garda commissioner takes home €185,000 a year – some €29,000 more than the chief of police in New York City. Wage increases of 5.2 per cent in 2001 and 5.1 per cent in 2002 were running at more than double the Eurozone average, and Ireland's competitiveness suffered. Considine was also part of an Implementation Advisory Group which proposed the creation of the ill-fated Office of the Financial Regulator – a semi-autonomous offshoot of the

Central Bank that would sit idly by while the country's banks ran themselves into the ground at an eventual cost of tens of billions to the public.

Now, as secretary general, Considine had even more responsibility. As well as serving on the board of the Central Bank, Considine was also appointed to the Top Level Appointments Board, which determined which candidates got the most important civil service jobs. He also joined the board of the National Treasury Management Agency (NTMA). Considine was at the absolute centre of the finances of the country. He was the most powerful civil servant in the country.

In the twelve months to May 2003, Irish property prices jumped an incredible 14.2 per cent, fuelled by madcap bank lending. Residential mortgage lending increased by a frankly insane 23 per cent in 2003 alone. Red lights should have been flashing about an overheating market. However, these issues were overshadowed by the fact that the economy was growing at a phenomenal rate. Ireland appeared to be flying. But it was hopped up on artificial stimulants. Ireland's manufacturing trade surplus, which had grown from the mid-1990s onwards, began to decline from 2002, with imports rising sharply. The growth in the economy was becoming more and more dependent on the domestic construction market and on consumer borrowings. The three years up to 2006 marked the craziest period of growth, with loan assets increasing at a rate of nearly 28 per cent per year. The Nyberg Report into the banking crisis reported how the Central Bank Financial Stability Report of 2005 pointed to potential issues over soaring property prices. An internal Department of Finance briefing note for Brian Cowen concluded that 'all evidence is that systemic risk . . . to the financial system from a downturn in the property market is relatively limited'.

Considine's four-year term ended in July 2006. He left with his head held high. The top-line figures suggested that the Irish economy was one of the best performers in the world.

The following February, the *Sunday Independent* revealed that Considine had joined the board of Davy Stockbrokers. There was no public announcement, just a discreet regulatory filing in the Companies

Registration Office. This was the same Davy Stockbrokers that was overseen by the Financial Regulator he had helped establish, and the same Davy Stockbrokers that made massive profits as one of the primary dealers in sovereign bonds issued by the NTMA, on whose board Considine had been serving.

The move was contrary to the rule specifying that civil servants could not take jobs in the private sector for at least a full year after leaving the service of the state. The purpose of the rule was to prevent potential conflicts of interest, and to put the brakes on a revolving door between the regulators and the regulated. But Considine had been given a special exemption, granted by the Civil Service Outside Appointments Board. At the time, the board was made up of Considine's former colleague Eddie Sullivan (who had replaced him as secretary general of Public Service Management and Development), Dermot McCarthy (secretary general of the Department of the Taoiseach), Peter Malone (of the National Roads Authority) and Breege O'Donoghue (a top executive at Primark and Penneys). O'Donoghue also served on the board of drinks group C&C, which was headed by Tony O'Brien – who also chaired the Review Body on Higher Remuneration in the Public Sector.

Considine was allowed to join the masters of the universe at the state's largest stockbroking firm, but only 'on condition that for the following six months, he would not engage in any matter in respect of which a state or state-owned body was a client'. The special dispensation for Considine was, as far as we can tell, unique – the one and only time we have uncovered when the rules have been waived for a top-level civil servant joining the private sector. The Department of Finance declined to say whether or not other similar exemptions have been granted.

In 2009, following the collapse and nationalization of the Irish banking system, Brian Lenihan appointed Considine as one of the public-interest directors on the board of Bank of Ireland. His job was to bat for the taxpayer as the bank received billions in state funding – money that could have gone to schools or hospitals instead. Considine joined the bank's audit committee and chaired its risk committee.

He resigned from the board of Davy to take the position, which paid well: Considine received €90,000 in 2010.

Since the fateful night of the bank guarantee in September 2008, Bank of Ireland has received €7 billion in state support to save it from going bust. It has not shown much gratitude in return. Just before receiving €3.5 billion from the state in 2010, the bank told Lenihan that it hadn't paid any bonuses in 2009. Not a cent. The Minister for Finance stood up in front of the parliament of this country and told us that no bonuses had been paid. Except they had: Bank of Ireland later confessed to having paid €66.4 million in bonuses. Here was a bank (that had been kept alive by the state) pulling an outrageous fast one. A subsequent report found that the bank had 'a restrictive and uncommon interpretation of what constituted a performance bonus'. In other words, it was playing fast and loose with the truth. Hardly in the public interest. Considine and his fellow state-appointed director – former Agriculture Minister Joe Walsh – should have walked in protest.

Considine's replacement as secretary general of the Department of Finance in May 2006 was David Doyle. The workmanlike Doyle had joined the department in 1976, after a stint at Texaco and four years at the Department of Education. After twenty years in the trenches, he made it to the elite levels of the department, becoming an assistant secretary in 1996. He spent three years in the budgetary and economic division before moving over to the banking, finance and international division. Then he moved into the public expenditure division at the Department of Finance before bagging the top job.

Civil servants are paid in various salary bands and grades. Doyle was the only secretary general in the country with his very own pay grade. He was given an annual pay package of €303,000 when he took the job – almost ten times the average industrial wage. (Dermot McCarthy, then head of the Department of the Taoiseach, was subsequently moved up to this super grade in late 2007.)

Doyle's tenure as the civil servant with the most influence over the economy will go down in history as an absolute catastrophe. While he was at the wheel of the Department of Finance, the property bubble hit new heights before bursting, the banking sector collapsed, the state got bounced into a poorly thought-out blanket guarantee of the banks' liabilities, a misguided tax strategy emptied state coffers and the country's disastrous economic situation saw it forced to seek help from the IMF and EU. The mandarins would be quick to point out that the government of the day is directly responsible for fiscal policy and ultimately responsible for regulation and everything else. But there is no evidence that the Department of Finance made any serious attempt to guide the government towards less ruinous policies.

The economy was heading for the rocks but there was still time to change direction. Brian Cowen's December 2006 Budget threw petrol on the property market with the introduction of more tax reliefs and the decision to remove further low earners from the tax net. These changes meant that the Exchequer was even more dependent on VAT, stamp duty and other demand taxes. Social welfare payments were upped, with child benefits, pensions and other benefits increased. It was a naked exercise in vote grabbing. The 2007 general election was looming. The economy began to splutter in 2007, property prices stopped rising and then started to fall, and a global credit crunch posed a direct threat to the business models of the Irish banks, which were crazily dependent on interbank lending. This is where the Department of Finance should have stepped in; contingency plans and worst-case scenarios should have been examined, and the economy prepared for a shock. It didn't happen.

When he stepped down, aged sixty, in February 2010, David Doyle was given a pension top-up worth €725,000 in added years. The Department of Finance confirmed that Doyle, who had worked for thirty-eight years in the civil service, was given the maximum pension available to those who had served forty years in the civil service. A departmental spokesman described the top-up as 'fairly small'. Tell that to the tens of thousands in negative equity, or those facing HSE cutbacks.

One would be forgiven for thinking that officials should have seen the crash coming. In June 2005, the *Economist* warned that Ireland had a major property bubble. We know that the department paid €7,050 a year for 42 subscriptions to the magazine in 2010 – one for every

15 members of staff. Surely someone of consequence in the department was reading it in 2005? And yet, the department's record for economic forecasting and reading the tea leaves was hopeless. During the boom years, it was a source of mild amusement that the highly paid civil servants couldn't get within an ass's roar of correctly forecasting tax revenues. In 1997 the department predicted that Ireland would have a budget deficit of around €113 million for the following year. Twelve months later, Charlie McCreevy announced a surplus of €1.06 billion. McCreevy just laughed it off. Mistakes like that didn't matter if the economy was flying.

When the economy stalled in 2001 and 2002, the Department of Finance was caught with its pants down. By the start of the summer, it emerged that tax receipts were looking much weaker than expected, but the department still insisted that things would pick up later in the year. In June 2002, Richard Bruton, then the Fine Gael finance spokesman, accused McCreevy of 'covering up' his department's inability to forecast correctly. Five months later, the department admitted that there would be a hole in the country's budgetary projections of €700 million or more for the year, due to an unexpected drop in tax receipts. The mini-recession of 2001–2 should have been a massive wake-up call for the department, revealing how dramatically a changing economic situation could affect the public finances and highlighting the need to prepare for the unexpected.

Instead, they went out to lunch. The economy heated up again, and Ireland entered the ruinous second phase of its boom, a period when the economy was driven almost solely by the construction and property sectors. The growth was dramatic and unsustainable – but as late as June 2007, the Department of Finance was still predicting a 'soft landing', with Finance Minister Brian Cowen spouting terrible guff in his Dáil speech on the Finance Bill: 'Our economy is set fair to enjoy strong growth rates over the medium term, albeit at a lower level than enjoyed over the past ten years. By accepting that more moderate outlook now, we can make it a reality and enjoy the much talked of "soft landing".' The mood was so buoyant that the department spent €3,227.75 on a 'post budget function' at Doheny and Nesbitt's pub in December 2007.

The department's forecasting was merely embarrassing. Its failure to recognize or react to icebergs looming on the horizon was catastrophic. There was no shortage of warnings: in 2005 the Department of the Environment wrote to the Department of Finance expressing concern over 100 per cent mortgages, which were being introduced by the likes of Ulster Bank and Permanent TSB. It feared that a fall in house prices could leave borrowers exposed. But the Department of Finance pooh-poohed these concerns, according to correspondence released to the *Irish Times* under the Freedom of Information Act in October 2011. An official replied claiming that many first-time borrowers were already getting 100 per cent financing from a variety of sources, including top-ups from the credit unions or from parents. The Merrion Street civil servants decided that moves to try to restrain the provision of 100 per cent mortgages would not be 'appropriate'.

Robert Pye, now a retired assistant principal at the department, wrote and circulated not one but seven papers in 2004 and 2005 warning, as he put it in one of them, that 'a major global shock could have a devastating impact on both our fiscal position and our banking system'. Pye also met with three assistant secretaries of the department in October 2004 to highlight his fears. He suggested that the Department of Finance should build up a stockpile of cash through the boom years to be used in case the economy crashed or slowed substantially. Pye was told that his concerns were 'legitimate' but 'simply untenable on political grounds'.

In January 2007, Pye sought to have an article published in the *Irish Times* warning about what would happen to Ireland if the country was faced with a sudden outside shock from the global economy. It was just two months before the first BNP hedge funds imploded in the US, signalling the onset of the global banking crisis. Pye's article brought an instant smack on the knuckles from his superiors. He received an official written notification from the department censuring him and ordering him not to submit the final article.

According to a 2011 story by Harry McGee in the *Irish Times*, in July 2007 the Department of Finance 'rejected' the UCD economist Morgan Kelly's published warnings of an impending property collapse. In a memo to Finance Minister Brian Cowen, John McCarthy, an economist in the department, prepared 'speaking points' for Cowen, including the assertion that people 'must be careful that we do not overreact to the current easing from the very high levels of activity' in the housing market.

According to McGee: 'The two-page document is the only record held by the department that deals with a spate of warnings about a property bubble made by a small number of economists during 2006 and 2007.' In other words, the documentary record suggests that the department did not take the issue seriously – except insofar as the warnings might affect public opinion.

In April 2012, *Sunday Independent* reporters Danny McConnell and Tom Lyons revealed how Maria Mackle, a mid-ranking official in the Department of Finance, had consistently raised serious concerns over the property market from 2005 onwards. She had compiled official responses to parliamentary questions submitted by TDs in which she outlined the real risks posed to the economy by an overheating property market. These responses were suppressed or seriously watered down by her superiors in the department. Emails from Mackle to her superiors were contained in a file submitted to the Public Accounts Committee. In January 2005 she emailed her immediate superior, Barra O'Murchada (who has since retired):

> Barra, I have reservations about the minister ignoring the possibility of a housing crash. I do have reservations about the final reply but am doing as directed in accordance with procedure.

In 2006, Mackle also raised concerns about the government's tax strategy, which was unwisely skewed towards property and other demand-related taxes. She pointed to criticism of Ireland's tax policy by the ESRI, the IMF and the OECD. Departmental principal officer Ronnie Downes responded:

> As regards the recommendations of the OECD and others about tax policy, I would recommend against making any reference to this issue in the PQ [parliamentary question]. It does not appear germane to the question and it is a sensitive policy area in any event.

In May 2006, Mackle was involved in preparing responses to a parliamentary question that had been submitted by Paul McGrath, a Fine Gael TD. In email correspondence with assistant secretary Derek Moran and assistant principal Paul Shannon about the McGrath query she told her superiors at the Department of Finance:

> Two replies have been drafted. The first contains material from Paul [Shannon] which is as close as I can get to the official position. The second represents what I perceive to be a more accurate reply but may be unacceptable to the department. I have serious doubts and reservations about the past official position on the housing market.

Derek Moran would later email her telling her to leave her personal opinions out of any future responses. A month later, Moran would instruct Mackle how to respond to a query from Labour's Joan Burton about the economy.

> Go back to them and say this . . . the large increase in new housing supply will restore equilibrium to the market . . . There is a broad consensus amongst commentators that the most likely outcome for the housing market is a 'soft landing'. The government continues to run a prudent, stability-orientated budgetary policy . . .

A speech Mackle drafted for Finance Minister Brian Cowen that year drew upon the ESRI's medium-term forecast, which warned of spiralling house-price inflation that heightened the risk of 'default on residential mortgages, thereby exposing the banking sector'. Senior civil servants were horrified by these forecasts. A more senior official than Mackle wrote:

> Marie,
>
> This type of material is not appropriate or suitable for a ministerial speech. It is positively alarmist in tone in some areas . . . Similarly, I don't see why we want the minister to make a statement to the effect that house-price inflation may continue to accelerate in 2006.

The department's main concern here was not with the accuracy of the ESRI's projection; it was with the supposed danger of alarming the public. Mackle has claimed that her career suffered because of her constant questioning of the departmental line. Her superiors continued to prosper, though, despite their utter failure to recognize the iceberg approaching.

The 2008 bank guarantee was the most disastrous financial decision ever undertaken by an Irish government. The move to make the taxpayer liable for the debts run up by out-of-control bankers has cost some €62 billion to date. The guarantee was conceived in haste by people who seem to have had no conception of how expensive it would prove.

A banking crisis had been coming up fast in the rear-view mirror for two years. Property prices had been falling at a dramatic rate, and the global credit crunch was causing serious liquidity problems at the credit-hungry Irish banks. In September 2007, there had been a run on Northern Rock with panicked British customers queuing for hours in an attempt to withdraw their life savings from the shattered bank. It didn't take long to freak out Northern Rock's thousands of Irish customers, and soon RTÉ was broadcasting images of long queues snaking around the corner of Northern Rock's Irish branch at the top of Dublin's Harcourt Street. Northern Rock's troubles had begun because the bank could no longer get the interbank funding it needed to keep its mortgage-lending business going. The implications for the Irish banks ought to have been obvious.

That year ended with Brian Cowen's Budget forecasting 'reasonably impressive' economic growth of 4.75 per cent for 2008. The Department of Finance figures led Cowen to announce a huge increase in government spending. According to the minister's speech: 'We need nearly 5 per cent more in 2008 compared to 2007 just to stay where we are.' This was simply nuts. Was no one watching what was happening out in the real world? Even before the collapse of Bear Stearns in March 2008 and the global crisis caused by the failure of Lehman Brothers in September of that year, the Irish banks were in serious trouble.

Once Lehman's went, the Department of Finance and advisers ranging from Merrill Lynch, Goldman Sachs and Arthur Cox started burning the midnight oil. Civil servants were even working on weekends. By the end of September 2008, the bank guarantee had been announced, with the state backstopping €440 billion in deposits and bonds. Four months later, Anglo Irish Bank had been nationalized and AIB, Bank of Ireland, Irish Nationwide and the EBS would be rescued by the state. A crippling recession, massive unemployment and a yawning gap between tax revenues and government spending would flatten the country, ultimately leading to the IMF/EU bailout and the loss of economic sovereignty.

Where had the Department of Finance been?

The role of David Doyle, Kevin Cardiff and other Department of Finance officials in the decision, at the end of September 2008, to guarantee the liabilities of the six Irish banks is highly obscure. As was their role in the department's failure to head off the catastrophic economic crisis. Two reports were compiled into the near collapse of the banking sector – one by former Finnish central banker Peter Nyberg, the other by former Canadian civil servant Rob Wright – which focused on the performance of the Department of Finance. The Nyberg Commission's report stated:

> A majority of the people interviewed by the Commission indicated that they saw no major problems except lack of liquidity until the end of 2007, at the earliest, and autumn 2008, at the latest. The reasons given were usually very similar, the most prevalent being: property prices in Ireland had never decreased markedly; everybody expected a 'soft landing' at worst; loan portfolios appeared sound; property credits were diversified by country or county or class; peer banks abroad did the same thing; and 'nobody told them' there was a potential problem.

The Nyberg Commission's efforts to determine what happened on the night when the bank guarantee was hastily agreed were:

> . . . complicated by the general lack of written records as to what transpired during the official discussions. While . . . there is some documentation available on various broad approaches that were examined in general terms in the course of 2008, the Commission is not aware of any official record of specific alternative options or

policy preferences presented to the Government on September 29 by the three main authorities involved (the Central Bank, the Financial Regulator and the Department of Finance).

The absence of a paper trail detailing how and why the infamous decision was taken may have been prompted by the 'pressure of events', according to Nyberg:

> . . . but is nonetheless regrettable, since it seriously complicates allocating specific responsibility with respect to a major policy decision with far-reaching financial consequences for Ireland.

This is one of the understatements of all time. We still do not know for certain how much pressure was put upon the government and the Department of Finance by the bankers or whether other approaches – such as a more limited guarantee or nationalizing Anglo Irish Bank – were considered in detail.

In October 2008, the Department of Finance became aware of a series of unusual deposits between Anglo Irish Bank and Irish Life & Permanent after an NTMA official noticed a reference to it in a report on the banking sector by PricewaterhouseCoopers. The net effect of the transaction was to make Anglo's balance sheet look €7.5 billion healthier than it actually was. Kevin Cardiff was informed and the Financial Regulator was informed. But Cardiff's boss, Finance Minister Brian Lenihan, wasn't told. Testifying at a hearing of the Public Accounts Committee, Cardiff said there 'wasn't a red flag' raised on the transaction. Lenihan later said that he hadn't read the passage in the PwC report and that he was only told about the transaction several months later. PAC chairman Bernard Allen described as 'incredible' the fact that all this had been allowed to go on without 'the controlling hand of the department'.

The Department of Finance's failure to grasp the significance of the Anglo/IL&P transaction – or see that the banks faced a solvency crisis rather than mere liquidity problems – shows that it was miles out of its depth. The failure to understand the nature and extent of the banks' troubles, even after the guarantee had been agreed, translated into a failure to recognize the shocking costs that would be borne by the public. Cardiff gave a private briefing that autumn to officials from the US embassy in Dublin. Confidential cables from the US embassy back to Washington later published by WikiLeaks revealed that Cardiff told the officials that the banks would not have to be bailed out. A 'herd mentality' based on 'rumour and innuendo' had, according to Cardiff, created the urgent need to backstop the banks and guarantee deposits. Cardiff also 'pointed out that auditors contracted by his department to look at the books of at least two of the institutions came away with "a favourable impression of the loan books".'

The US official sending details of the meeting back to the State Department in Washington noted that Irish authorities might be 'a bit optimistic' about the financial sector's prospects and would have their 'work cut out' to rebuild it. That a diplomat from another country – without access to the data – had a better idea of what was going on in banks than the top people in the Department of Finance pretty much says it all.

In July 2009, the Department of Finance revealed that tax receipts for the full year would be €3 billion less than it had reckoned at the start of the year. Two months later that figure was revised to a €5 billion shortfall. The increasingly sweaty bean counters had another stab at the data in October when they estimated that tax receipts would be €6.5 billion down on estimates. The final year-end totting up revealed how dismally inaccurate their predictions had been: tax receipts ended up being €8 billion short of expectation. It was the most inaccurate economic forecast ever produced by a government department in the history of the state – and that is saying something.

There are clearly some very smart and extremely able people in the Department of Finance. They just didn't have their hands on the tiller. Some civil servants consistently warned about the prospect of a property bubble, but their fears were rejected by more senior officials. We'll never know what would have happened if the top civil servants had experienced a moment of clarity and actually recognized the problems facing Ireland. Even as late as 2007, genuine awareness and decisive action would have made a difference. At the very least, if the department had understood what was going on, it – and the government – would not have been caught in the head-lights in September 2008. It would have understood the scale of the disaster about to hit the banks' balance sheets, and surely would not have countenanced a blanket guarantee of liabilities worth hundreds of billions of euros. Without the guarantee, and the massive state debt it has brought, it's far less likely that we would have needed an IMF/EU bailout. If the brakes had been put on the property market before the crash, fewer people would be stuck in the prison of negative equity. Ireland might be in a recession, but not a generation-crushing recession. But the red flags were ignored.

Finnish central banker Peter Nyberg's report into the banking debacle, after a series of hearings in March 2011, contained some use-ful findings but pulled its punches. The disaster wasn't anyone's fault in particular. 'The Commission has not and could not assess the actions or inactions of particular individuals in the authorities and did not think it was appropriate or fair to do so,' it noted. Nyberg was advised by a special committee of fourteen specially selected individuals ranging from banking and the civil service. Two mem-bers of the committee came from the Department of Finance itself.

Nyberg found that the Department of Finance's greatest flaw was that it was just too meek.

> The Central Bank (CB) and the Financial Regulator noted macro-economic risks and risky bank behaviour but appear to have judged them insufficiently alarming to take major restraining policy meas-ures. Among all the authorities a very limited number of individuals, either in boards or among staff, saw the risks as significant and actively argued for stronger measures; in all cases they failed to convince their colleagues or superiors. Thus the authorities largely continued to accept the credit concentration in the property market and avoided forcing action on the failings in the banks. The Government actively supported the market over an extended period against the apparently fairly weak but clear opposition of the Department of Finance.

Rob Wright's report also let the Merrion Street mandarins off the hook: 'We have been direct in our analysis and advice, but do not accept the notion that the Department is not fit for purpose.'

Wright echoed the views of Nyberg in saying that while the Department of Finance had warned about future pitfalls, it had done so in an extremely low-key way.

> The Department of Finance should have done more to avoid this outcome. It did provide warnings on pro-cyclical fiscal policy and expressed concern about the risks of an overheated construction sector. However, it should have adapted its advice in tone and urgency after a number of years of fiscal complacency. It should have been more sensitive to and provided specific advice on broader macro-economic risks. And it should have shown more initiative in making these points and in its advice on the construction sector, and tax policy generally.

Translated into English, Wright was saying that Fianna Fáil politicians don't react well to gentle or obscure hints; they need to be grabbed by the scruff of the neck and told that they are driving the country over a cliff.

Wright found that the department was severely lacking in technical skills. It employed plenty of people who could lunch for the country, but not enough who actually understood how the economy worked.

> The Department needs to increase substantially its numbers of economists trained to Masters level or higher and add other technical capacity, especially accounting, banking and financial markets expertise. Over the next two years the Department should double its number of economists trained to Masters level. It should organize itself to engage more University recruits at that level every year.

Wright also found that the department was 'poorly structured in a number of areas, including at the senior management level' and 'poor on human resources management'. The department was top-heavy and bloated with middle managers, Wright found.

> The Department of Finance is unique among Civil Service Departments in that Assistant Secretaries do not report directly to the Secretary General. There is an additional level of management – Second Secretary

General – between the Secretary General and the Assistant Secretaries in the Department of Finance. This arrangement blurs accountability, under-utilizes the expertise of Assistant Secretaries and helps to inhibit effective internal communications. The consequences of the neglect of this area are evident in a number of ways: insufficient commitment across the Department to performance management, skills shortages in critical areas and reporting structures at senior and middle-management levels that are far from ideal.

Wright also pointed to the insular mindset of the officials in the Department of Finance, noting 'it does not have sufficient engagement with the broader economic community in Ireland' and that it 'often operates in silos, with limited information sharing'. If compiling and then understanding economic data is crucial for the management of a country's finances, the department was snoring soundly at the wheel.

Submissions to the Wright Commission by the department emerged in the *Sunday Times* in June 2011. They revealed that the department was concerned that it did not have 'a whole economy overview' when making key decisions and that it was restrained by bureaucracy and 'poor communication'. The department conceded that it had a 'serious skills deficit in economics, policy analysis, accountancy and related professional competencies'. But having been so badly managed and unprepared for the economic crisis, it's reasonable to assume that the department has put on its game face and rectified those failings in the years since the economy began to suffocate.

Not so. A presentation in September 2010 by assistant secretary William Beausang together with Eamonn Kearns, director of the financial services division, revealed that the Department of Finance still needed to put systems in place to allow 'the exchange of information' between its civil servants and the other key players in the Financial Regulator and Central Bank.

David Doyle stepped down as secretary general of the Department of Finance in February 2010 as he reached his sixtieth birthday. Kevin Cardiff, who had been handling the department's response to the banking crisis from summer 2008 onwards, was appointed to succeed Doyle. The northside Dubliner has been compared to 'Forrest Gump' by the influential blog NAMA Wine Lake. This was not a tribute to his table-tennis skills, ability to run fast or bravery under fire. It was because he was present at most if not all of the key moments in the death spiral of the Irish economy and public finances. Cardiff was Lenihan's point man for banking and held key meetings with bankers when it became increasingly clear to the stock markets that the jig was up. He was the man who received the email from Merrill Lynch listing possible options on the night of the guarantee. He was in the room when the IMF/EU bailout was agreed in November 2010 – in fact, he was the guy that nobody recognized at the press conference announcing it.

Cardiff's upper lip must have got quite sweaty when a resurgent Fine Gael made noises about cleaning out the top levels of the mis-firing civil service as the 2011 general election approached. Michael Noonan is known to have had 'a heated exchange' with Cardiff in December 2010 over the level of information being provided to him about the Budget when he was the Opposition spokesman on finance. A slapdash briefing by Cardiff and his lieutenants on the state of the economy to Noonan, Phil Hogan, Joan Burton and Brendan Howlin as the new government was being set up also went down very badly with Noonan.

Three weeks after becoming Minister for Finance, Noonan pulled the rug from under Cardiff's increasingly well-padded posterior. He brought John Moran – a former banker with Zurich – into the department to head up its core banking policy unit. It was a clear sig-nal that the existing mandarins were not up to the job of restructuring the banks and that the new government was not afraid to recruit from beyond the confines of Merrion Street. The ten-strong team of bank-ing experts at the NTMA, headed up by former Ulster Bank chief finance officer Michael Torpey, transferred to the Department of Finance. Under the transfer arrangement the NTMA specialists retained their pay and bonuses but reported directly to Cardiff. Michael Noonan told the Dáil that the new arrivals were to 'enhance the oversight of the Banking Division'.

The appointments led to widespread speculation that Moran was being lined up to take Cardiff's job. But Cardiff wasn't ready to retire, and it's not easy to shift a secretary general. Firing civil servants is simply not done. Only one person has been kicked out of the Department of Finance since the economic crisis began – and it was a foot soldier, not a general. The top civil servants are untouchable. If Michael Noonan and the new government wanted to replace Cardiff and bring in someone new, they'd have to feather his nest.

Luxembourg is only marginally more exciting than Banagher. But it has more Michelin-starred restaurants per capita than anywhere else in the world. It is also the home of the European Court of Auditors, which is not a court at all but a somewhat flaccid institution that maintains the ledger for the vast spending of the European Commission. The Court of Auditors has one member from each EU member state, and nominations are in the gift of the government. The post tends to be a reward for political services rendered. Accountancy skills are not necessarily required: former trade union head and Labour minister Barry Desmond was a government appointee, as was former teacher and Fianna Fáil minister Máire Geoghegan Quinn. Former Fianna Fáil media adviser Eoin O'Shea took over Geoghegan Quinn's seat for the remainder of her term when she was appointed as a European commissioner in November 2009. O'Shea, at least, was an accountant.

In October 2011, with Kevin Cardiff still running the Department of Finance and O'Shea's term on the Court of Auditors coming to an end, the government made noises about moving Cardiff to Luxembourg. But it soon became clear that it wouldn't wash. Cardiff had made a fatal mistake. He'd broken rule number one of the civil service: people now knew his name. David Doyle had been utterly anonymous, and had got out of the department before his period in charge came under serious scrutiny. With the department's performance now in the spotlight, Cardiff became a publicly recognized figure.

The government wanted to get rid of him with minimal fuss. Taoiseach Enda Kenny, Tánaiste Eamon Gilmore and Michael Noonan railroaded his nomination to the Court of Auditors through

Cabinet without debate. They were going to drown him in Luxem-bourgeois gravy.

Public anger at his proposed move to a cushy job in Europe inten-sified when Nick Webb reported in the *Sunday Independent* that Cardiff stood to earn up to €1.6 million over his six-year term in office, through a lucrative package of wages and perks. Apart from the 'basic' salary of €203,000 – slightly more than his revised wage at Finance – Cardiff was entitled to a 'housing allowance' worth €27,000 per year (or €162,000 for his term in office). There was also a 'family allowance' of €5,400 to run a house. On top of this there's a special payment of up to €6,564 for each school-age child to cover the cost of education and other bills. On top of that, Cardiff was in line for a €30,000 'installation payment' on taking up the job. Travel expenses, insurance and removal bills are also covered.

The gravy will still pour even after the term in office ends. There's a €15,000 'resettlement allowance' for each member of the Court of Auditors on their departure from the post, and they can claim special 'transitional payments' too. If Cardiff serves a full term he will be in line for a payment of 50 per cent of his salary for three years after leaving the post – assuming he doesn't get another job in Europe. There's also a bumper pension entitlement of up to 70 per cent of the final salary at the court, which could be worth up to €126,000 per year. Sinn Féin TD Mary Lou McDonald described Cardiff's proposed appointment as 'reward for failure'.

The government closed ranks and united in their support of the civil servant – probably not what the electorate put them in power to do. Labour's Pat Rabbitte was asked if Cardiff was being pushed out by the government. 'There's no truth in it. A vacancy came in the Court of Auditors and the Minister for Finance has made the appoint-ment. It is the first time the question has been put to me. The mistakes of the past are made. We have had to contend with those mistakes, but that is not true.' Rabbitte was asking the public to believe that in the midst of the biggest financial crisis in the history of the state we were sending our most powerful civil servant off to Luxembourg – and there wasn't a nudge going on.

But the scheme to move Cardiff out to Europe was becoming

increasingly bumpy. Caroline Twohig, a reporter with TV3's sister station 3e, was having a drink with some friends in the Shelbourne bar when she landed a scoop. She told RTÉ's John Murray that she hadn't been eavesdropping, but that 'the conversation came up in my company about some money that had been miscalculated, and immediately my ears pricked up when I heard the figure'. It seemed that the national debt had been miscalculated to the tune of €3.6 billion due to a civil service snafu. 'I didn't really believe it at first, to be honest – who would? – and after choking on my drink I asked a few follow-up questions to the tune of, "What! What did you just say?" '

Cardiff was called in front of the Public Accounts Committee to explain. The red-faced mandarin told the committee that the department had 'no idea' why the gaffe had not been uncovered earlier and reported to him or other senior departmental civil servants. Emails given to the committee show that the subject of borrowing by the Housing Finance Agency – a quango that makes housing-related loans to local authorities and voluntary housing bodies – was first raised with the Department of Finance by the NTMA on 23 August 2010. The department was told that under new arrangements the NTMA was now doing all the borrowing on behalf of the agency and that general government debt figures should take this new arrangement into consideration. This would avoid the possibility of double-counting of Housing Finance Agency debt on the state ledger. Michael McGrath, secretary of the Department of Finance's budget and economic section, told the PAC that there was no record of any response to this initial email.

The issue was raised six times by the NTMA between August 2010 and the end of October 2011, but it never reached a level higher than middle management in the department and nothing was done. In the meantime, official government figures overstated the national debt by €3.6 billion as a result of the double-counting of the Housing Finance Agency debt.

It also emerged in the PAC hearings that Michael Noonan was not told about the error for five days after it had been pointed out to Michael McGrath. This was because McGrath was abroad and it was a bank holiday weekend. One can only wonder how bad a mistake would need to be for the minister to be told immediately. Noonan described the lapse as a 'humiliating schoolboy error'. Tánaiste Eamon Gilmore said this kind of accountancy mistake was 'unacceptable' and all safeguards would be in place to ensure that it would not happen again. A departmental investigation was set up. It was headed up by Michael McGrath. That's how the civil service works.

Members of the Public Accounts Committee ripped into Cardiff during the hearings. The grilling prompted a bizarre admission from the stressed civil servant. 'The Court of Auditors will be a doddle compared to this job,' he told Mary Lou McDonald.

The process of Cardiff's nomination to Europe continued. Enda Kenny said that Cardiff was 'technically well qualified for the job', and Public Expenditure Minister Brendan Howlin denied that there was anything untoward about Cardiff's nomination. 'There was a serious mistake made in the department . . . in relation to accounting. We will get to the bottom of that. There is no whiff of scandal.'

Perhaps. But in the private sector, overseeing an accountancy department that somehow erred by €3.6 billion would be the quick route to a P45.

As the Irish nominee to the Court of Auditors, Cardiff had to be interviewed by a committee of the European Parliament to see if he was suitable for the job. This gave rise to much behind-the-scenes lobbying. Arms were twisted. Ears were whispered into. Fine Gael leaned on the European People's Party – of which it is part – to back Cardiff's nomination. But Labour Party MEP Nessa Childers had had enough. She spoke out against Cardiff, saying that he was unsuitable for the job. For this she received a bollocking from fellow Labour MEP Proinsias de Rossa, who warned her that she could face party discipline if she continued to voice her opposition to the government's nomination. Childers said, 'I was threatened with expulsion from the Labour Party. The party, in the shape of a number of people, made very trenchant and, in some cases, highly aggressive phone calls which were an attempt to stop me talking about Mr Cardiff. The issue is much bigger than these people, the issue is about interference with my work as an MEP.'

Cardiff was interviewed by the committee. He looked back on his career positively, but noted 'that's not to say that I haven't made enormous mistakes. In the middle of a crisis you make very big mistakes and you make very big gains sometimes.'

The very big mistakes were easy to catalogue; the very big gains are less clear. He was asked by UK Independence Party MEP Derek Clarke if his work in charge of banking policy at the time of the guarantee had driven the state to bankruptcy. 'I've explained that I'm not entitled to say exactly how I advised the government but I've explained that I gave the government in my job, from my position, a range of options,' he retorted angrily. 'Frankly I don't accept that I therefore led the Irish people to bankruptcy. I certainly didn't and I was far from being the only person who was giving advice on that evening. The guarantee was introduced at a time of great pressure.'

Cardiff's nomination came to the vote. In a stunning rejection, the MEPs voted against his appointment. Even Fine Gael's allies opposed the move. Once again foreign diplomats could see what was wrong – but those in power in Ireland were utterly blind to it. What should have been a simple rubber-stamping exercise turned into abject humiliation for the civil servant and the Fine Gael-led government.

But Enda and the government weren't finished with Cardiff. There was a new reason why they couldn't turn back. Cardiff's job in the Department of Finance had just been advertised.

Then they got a break. The day after the dramatic vote against Cardiff, an otherwise sleepy Oireachtas European Affairs Committee meeting was jolted into life. Eoin O'Shea, the outgoing Irish member of the Court of Auditors, was ambushed by Labour Party TD Colm Keaveney, who brandished a series of private emails that O'Shea had sent to two of the MEPs on the nomination committee. In the emails, O'Shea linked Cardiff to the bank collapse and the Anglo/IL&P window-dressing transaction. O'Shea told the committee he had written the emails to the MEPs in 'a moment of madness'. His lobbying of the nomination committee against his proposed successor gave the government a chance to seize some sort of moral high ground. Fine Gael and Labour pulled in some favours and

Cardiff's nomination was voted through by a full meeting of the European Parliament.

Operation Luxembourg had finally achieved its aim.

While getting Cardiff out of the Department of Finance was bloody hard, it's nothing like the difficulties outsiders face when trying to get senior jobs in Merrion Street. Just one out of 314 applicants from the private sector was successful in landing a top job in the department between 2005 to 2010 – and the one successful candidate had formerly worked in the department before moving to the private sector for a while. One other candidate was offered a job but turned it down.

Being alive for a long time seems to be a key requirement for successful candidates in the civil service. Seniority counts for more than being any good at your job. The Commission for Public Service Appointments found that the Department of Justice had appointed civil servants to jobs where they hadn't even been on the internal shortlist for promotion. In a 2009 audit of appointments made by the Department of Finance, the commission found that one in four of principal officer grades had been given out on the basis of seniority. The fifty-one-page audit report also noted that the department applied the 'seniority rule' when it came to making promotions.

> With regard to appointments made using the seniority/suitability approach, it is the case that once the most senior officer was not deemed unsuitable then he/she would be promoted. This approach fails to meet the merit principle and indeed all principles of the Code.

In other words, if the most senior officer up for the job was deemed 'suitable' for a job, he or she would get it over more junior applicants of greater merit. At the time of the audit, just two of the top eighteen officials in the department had come from the private sector, with most of the key Sir Humphreys having been in situ for as many as forty years.

When Kevin Cardiff joined the department in 1984, his number two – secretary general for public service, Ciaran Connolly – had been in the finance division since October 1970. Donal McNally,

Ann Nolan and Jim O'Brien, three second secretaries at the department, had been there since the 1980s. Eight of the nine assistant secretaries had served in Merrion Street for over two decades, with John O'Donnell having put in more than thirty-three years at his desk, according to documents released to Nick Webb in April 2011. Only one of the four director-level civil servants had been there for less than a decade, with Eamonn Kearns – a director of the financial and banking services division – joining in 1977.

When filling the senior jobs in the civil service, it would be useful to know which candidates were actually up to scratch. But the system that exists to ensure this has been proven to be about as useful as a chocolate teapot. The Performance Management and Development System (PMDS) was introduced in 2007 as a way to gauge the productivity of civil servants. Each and every civil servant must undergo an annual assessment by their superiors which rates their work on a scale of 1 to 5 (with 5 being the best). Under the original system, staff who scored 2 were entitled to receive a standard pay increment; scores of 3 and more opened the door to promotions, bigger pay hikes and other perks.

But accountability isn't something that is welcome in the civil service, and the new system was soon rendered almost useless. In 2010, a total of 17,728 officials across all government departments were tested. Just nine scored a level 1. That's just one in 1,970. The consequence of being in the bottom twentieth of 1 per cent was not instant dismissal, but merely the denial of a pay increase. A mere 172 scored a level 2, which means 'needs improvement': so just 1 per cent of civil servants, apparently, need to raise their game. Details of the scheme released to the *Sunday Times* in November 2011 under the Freedom of Information Act revealed how a female clerical officer who was late for work twenty-six times in 2007 was awarded a score of 2. The following year, she was late twenty-six times again but was awarded a score of 3. Her manager noted that she had met all her work requirements and cooperated with changes to work practices.

A booklet entitled *Guidelines for Managing Underperformance in the Civil Service*, produced by the Department of Public Expenditure in March 2011, notes: 'A rating of 3 reflects that a good level of performance has been achieved.' A score of 4 means that a worker 'exceeds required standard', with the top score of 5 indicating 'outstanding' performance. Mercer, the human resources consultancy that designed the system, had initially forecast that 40 per cent of civil servants would score 4 or 5. In 2010, around 65 per cent of all civil service workers scored 4 or 5. Either our civil servants are simply marvellous or there's a systematic and deliberate ticking of the wrong boxes going on across government and other departments. The performance of the state over recent years, not to say decades, suggests the latter is the case.

Sean Aylward, secretary general at the Department of Justice, wrote to Ciaran Connolly in the Department of Finance in December 2009, raising concerns about the lack of poor scores in the testing. 'Clearly there is a persistent fear in the Irish character of confronting people,' he noted. A year later, he wrote to Connolly again; there was 'no doubt' that staff ratings were too high.

> There are many reasons for this, not least our almost congenital disinclination to confront our colleagues with the truth about their performance . . . It is bewildering that any rating higher than 'one', a rating that would cover total non-engagement with work, entitles [a worker] to an increment and by definition must represent satisfactory performance.

The Department of Finance scores show particular contempt for the marking system and highlight the institutionalized arrogance at play in Merrion Street: a staggering 83 per cent of its staff scored 4 or higher. The department aced the test – surely these couldn't be the same bozos who screwed up the economy?

Not every department rated itself so highly. The scoring patterns across the civil service prompted the Director of Public Prosecutions, James Hamilton, to write a snotty letter to his masters complaining that just 28.6 per cent of his staff had received a score of 4 or higher. Hamilton said that his staff were aware that ratings for the Department of Finance and the Taoiseach's Department 'start at four'. He warned that these extraordinary high scores at other departments were 'the single biggest problem' for his office when it was trying to make the performance management system actually work. The scores at the Department of Finance and the Taosieach's Department were simply unbelievable and completely undermined the whole exercise. He called for a 'forced distribution' of ratings across the whole civil service. Hamilton added that tackling underperformance of civil servants was critical and that his office was one of the few to have actually awarded a dud staff member a score of 1.

In November 2011, Public Expenditure Minister Brendan Howlin told the Dáil that he was 'fully aware that there are serious deficiencies in how the system is being implemented in the Civil Service'. New guidelines on assessing civil servants under the scheme were introduced in March 2012. Three months later, the scores for 2011 were released. Just 30 out of the almost 30,000 civil servants rated didn't perform well enough to get a pay rise. That's just 0.1 per cent of the entire civil service. Meanwhile, 64 per cent of the civil service received scores of 4 or 5 under the performance rating scheme.

The system is broken. It'll need more than a few woolly guidelines to repair it.

Poor performance is not a barrier to a good wage in the civil service. While the economy they managed was gradually turning blue, top civil servants decided that it would be a good time to reward their collective performance with higher salaries. Some of the fattest cats at the top of the civil service got enormous pay rises in December 2007. Four of the most senior mandarins in the country got double pay rises worth close to €60,000 after the body awarding salary hikes was lobbied by them (or on their behalf).

Three secretaries general – Julie O'Neill of the Department of Transport, Brigid McManus of the Department of Education, and Geraldine Tallon of the Department of the Environment – trousered pay rises of €58,000, bringing their salaries up from €212,000 to €270,000. Dermot McCarthy, the Taoiseach's secretary general, snagged a salary increase of €61,000; his salary jumped from €242,000 to €303,000. David Doyle was already being paid €303,000 at the time – more than the US President, the UK Prime Minister and the German Chancellor.

A harsh dose of reality was coming around the corner. By the end of 2008, it was painfully clear that the country was in massive financial trouble. Pay cuts of 10 per cent were introduced across the top tiers of the civil service. David Doyle and Dermot McCarthy saw their pay cut to a mere €272,700 – still more than Angela Merkel and Gordon Brown were making. Second-line departmental secretaries general – mostly on packages of €221,929 a year – saw their pay cut to a piddling €200,000.

In June 2011, the Fine Gael-led government capped pay for secretaries general at €200,000 per year. This was a 30 per cent drop on the September 2008 peaks – but it still meant that a secretary general of a government department was paid about €3,000 more than David Cameron in 2012 and €45,000 more than UN Secretary General Ban Ki-moon.

In April 2011 it emerged that some fancy footwork by the Department of Finance had helped mandarins escape some of the cuts. The Financial Emergency Measures in the Public Interest Act, introduced by Brian Lenihan in December 2009, meant that public servants pocketing over €200,000 per year faced a new 15 per cent levy on their wages; those below €200,000 saw their wages hit by 12 per cent. However, some high earners were allowed by the department to reduce their salaries to €199,999 in order to get into the lower bracket and thus end up taking home more money. Similarly, civil servants earning just over €165,000 were allowed to have their pay reduced to €164,999, thereby taking an 8 per cent cut instead of 12 per cent.

In December 2010, following a truly savage Budget in which dole and social welfare payments were cut and taxes rose, it was revealed that the civil servants who had helped draft much of that Budget were still doing quite nicely indeed. In response to a question from Fine Gael's Fergus O'Dowd, Brian Lenihan told the Dáil of a series of bumper bonuses paid to some of his officials over the previous three years. He outlined that 19 Department of Finance staff members at principal and assistant principal level had received 'special service' payments for 2008 in the amount of €53,394. The following year, 27 staff members at principal and assistant principal level received 'special service' payments of a cool €55,670. In 2010, 52 staff members at principal and assistant principal level received 'seniority allowances' of €115,395.44. Not bad going for key officials in the department that had played a central role in the near collapse of the country. It was payment for failure on a grand scale.

There are still lucrative nixers to be done, too. Across the civil service, government departments spent millions rehiring former staff members on lucrative consultancy deals. The Comptroller and Auditor General revealed in 2010 that the Department of Finance had paid €161,512 to hire four former staff members back on a consultancy gig. The practice was widespread across the entire bureaucracy. Many had retired ahead of a deadline in order to avoid major tax increases on their 'lump sum' received on retirement. Almost 7,900 public sector workers and civil servants retired at the start of 2012 to avoid new rules that would have seen their pensions cut. The chief medical officer in the Department of Social Protection, who retired at the start of the year, was rehired, bagging a salary of about €102,152. Richard Bruton, the Minister for Jobs, Enterprise and Innovation, gave jobs to a few recently retired civil servants, including a former Department of Transport secretary general. Eamon Gilmore's Department of Foreign Affairs brought back Frank Cogan, a former assistant secretary, to head a taskforce for about €70,835 per year. Former deputy secretary Padraig Murphy was also rehired at a fee of €62,450 to serve as Gilmore's special representative on the Organization for Security and Co-operation in Europe. Despite the massive unemployment queues, hundreds of former public servants – principally teachers and medical staff – were rehired on lucrative contracts by the state. The public sector knows how to look after its own.

Senior civil servants are a slippery adversary for any minister, especially one who wants to remove some of their perks. In his Budget speech in December 2009, Brian Lenihan took the chopper to the cosy performance-related bonus scheme for top civil and public servants, which over recent years had been worth an extra 10 per cent of some civil servants' salaries. Behind closed doors, 150 of the country's top civil servants raised hell. Incredibly – considering how weak their hand ought to have been – the scheme was actually watered down. The new pay drop saw the civil servants suffer a disproportionately smaller cutback, on the basis that they'd already

suffered some discomfort because a previous performance bonus
scheme had been downsized.

Economist Karl Whelan told the *Sunday Independent* that senior
civil servants appear to be the only group in Irish society that gets to
count earlier cuts as part of the current cuts.

> For instance, the cuts to social welfare payments announced in the
> Budget are in addition to the 2 per cent cut related to the elimination of
> the Christmas bonus. Would the government consider changing its cuts
> in social welfare rates to take account of this?

Over the last decade the civil service has developed a much bigger
ass to cover. The size of the so-called 'permanent government' has
mushroomed at a far faster pace than employment in other sectors –
and nowhere more clearly than in the top ranks. From 1998 to 2009
there was a 462 per cent increase in the number of principal officers
across government departments. The numbers jumped from 60 to
337. There was a 339 per cent hike in the numbers of higher assistant
principals, rising from 171 to 751. Meanwhile, the number of executive officers more than doubled from 2,429 to 4,889. The lower grades
of the civil service couldn't keep up: the number of counter-minders
or fax-carriers rose by a mere 14 per cent. But what were all of these
top-ranking civil servants doing?

Replacing Kevin Cardiff as secretary general of the Department of
Finance took time. External candidates were made even less welcome
when the department announced that it would not be paying any
travel expenses for applicants based abroad. In January 2012, Paul
Cullen's story in the *Irish Times* reported that a public sector candidate was the most likely winner of the plum job.

> Appointing an external candidate to 'shake up' the department would
> serve only to further demoralize staff, according to one source familiar
> with the process.

There were just three external candidates among the twenty-one finalists for the job. Given the circumstances, the appointment made in March 2012 could almost be described as refreshing. The top job went to John Moran, who had been Michael Noonan's point man on banking within the department, having been brought in from the Central Bank in 2011. The floppy-haired Moran had actually worked in the private sector – he headed up Zurich Financial Services before donning flip-flops to run a juice bar in the Languedoc between 2005 and 2010.

At least he'll have practice telling which mandarins might actually be lemons. But if he intends to bring fresh thinking and approaches to a department staffed by lifers with a dismal record, he'll be up against it.

2.   Zombie Bankers

Whatever became of the four amigos?

Remember the quartet of cowboys who rode up to fortress Finance in Merrion Street on 29 September 2008? The most powerful bankers in Ireland carried a numbing message to the government: Ireland Inc was about to collapse; its banks were bust.

It was a stick-up. On that night the raiders demanded that they be pulled back from the precipice. A shell-shocked government unlocked the doors of the treasury and wrote them a blank cheque. That episode should have been the bankers' last hurrah. As players in the most catastrophic decision in modern Irish history, a move that led directly to the humiliating and draconian EU/IMF bailout of November 2010, the famous four might today expect to be sidelined, impoverished, shamed, ostracized.

Far from it. They are ex-bankers, members of a select gang. No matter how dismal their track records, former bankers are on the pig's back.

Why did Richard Burrows, Dermot Gleeson, Brian Goggin and Eugene Sheehy not slink off into the sunset after delivering the news of Armageddon to Taoiseach Brian Cowen and Finance Minister Brian Lenihan? The fate of the four highwaymen tells us much about Ireland today.

Richard Burrows, the governor of the Bank of Ireland, was the most battle-hardened businessman of the four. There is no evidence that Governor Burrows, on his €500,000 salary, ever screamed 'stop' to Bank of Ireland's unfolding lending madness. Indeed, he was an enthusiast for the bank's policies and cocksure about its prospects. In May 2008, barely four months before he and the others made their pilgrimage of doom to the Department of Finance, he wrote to shareholders:

Bank of Ireland ended its financial year to 31 March 2008 with a strong capital base, good continuing access to funding and strong asset quality.

Burrows' letter also sought to put clear water between the Bank of Ireland and the 'global financial crisis', insisting that management had operated 'prudently and conservatively to ensure that the Group remains in robust condition'. Burrows laid it on with a trowel to his shareholders:

> Asset quality at 31 March 2008 remains strong. We have minimal exposure to those asset classes most associated with dislocation of financial markets and we hold appropriate provisions against these exposures.

The governor concluded with a token tribute to his chief executive, Brian Goggin, the man destined to accompany him cap-in-hand to the government just four months later. He boasted:

> Our management, ably led by Chief Executive Brian Goggin, rose to the challenges we faced. Brian, his management team, and all staff throughout the whole organization, have the gratitude and appreciation of the Court for their hard work in difficult circumstances.

The script had all the marks of a chairman who was asleep at the wheel.

Richard Burrows was born in Dublin in 1946, was educated at Wesley College and trained as an accountant. He joined Irish Distillers in 1971 and, with astonishing speed, became managing director in 1978 at the age of thirty-two. When Irish Distillers was taken over by the French spirits group Pernod Ricard in 1988, Burrows was retained as chief executive and then as chairman.

In March 2000, he was made a non-executive director of the Bank of Ireland. His credentials as one of Ireland's top business insiders made him a front runner to succeed the incumbent governor, Laurence Crowley. It will have done him no harm that he had begun his career in Crowley's old firm, Stokes Kennedy Crowley, now

KPMG. He was appointed deputy governor in 2002. When Crowley retired in 2005, Burrows was appointed governor of the bank – what any other bank would call chairman of the board.

Six months after he joined the Bank of Ireland board, he was promoted to joint managing director of Pernod, a full-time post based in Paris, which he held until 2005. Burrows' rise to the top of every tree he climbed seemed effortless. His sailing connections, his social graces, and above all his careful nurturing of contacts ensured that even when living abroad he remained an insider in Ireland's business world. While chief executive of Irish Distillers he accepted the presidency of the Irish Business and Employers Corporation (IBEC) in 1998. It was strange that such a supposedly busy man aspired to hold a position in such a toothless outfit, but his appetite for networking was voracious.

While Burrows' ascent to the top seemed unstoppable, his career had suffered at least one surprise setback. He was a fine sailor, but must have come to believe he could walk on water when, in 2001, he tried to topple the long-time incumbent, Pat Hickey, for the chair of the Olympic Council of Ireland. Opponents of Hickey persuaded Burrows that he could oust him. Burrows swallowed the bait, allowed his name to go forward, and conducted a very public campaign. But he was trounced by 27 votes to 10.

From that day on, Burrows stuck to the sort of contests he understood best – picking up directorships. These included such lucrative numbers as CityJet, Britvic and Rentokil. His time at the top of the Bank of Ireland delivered the regular good news of steady dividends and a rising share price to satisfied shareholders – until the property boom turned into a bust. For a while – even after the government bailed out the entire banking system – it looked as though his calm, affable manner might carry him through the storm. He was coasting along, untouchable, until May 2009. He had announced apocalyptic figures for the Bank of Ireland for the previous year. Its bad-debt forecast soared from €4.5 billion to €6 billion in the space of just three months. It was only a year since he had reassured shareholders with promises about the bank's 'strong capital base' and 'strong asset quality'.

Finance Minister Brian Lenihan finally lost patience with him. The governor issued a grovelling apology, accepted the blame for the collapse in the bank's share price, and resigned. By any normal standards Burrows' career should have been over. At the age of sixty-three, having presided over the staggering meltdown of a bank, he had no future. Surely that was the end of Richard Burrows. Boardroom watchers expected him to retire quietly, fade into the background and live on his riches. He would probably be asked by other boards not to stand for re-election. Or worse.

This view was naive. It arose from a basic misunderstanding of Irish – and, indeed, global – boardrooms.

Barely two months after Burrows had resigned from his perch at Bank of Ireland, British American Tobacco (BAT) issued a press release. A Mr Richard Burrows was joining the board as a non-executive director. He would be taking the £525,000-a-year chair in November. Sceptics wondered if the BAT board had been smoking the wrong stuff. Had none of them read the Irish papers or even the *Financial Times*? They had, but they still wanted Burrows. They cared not that they were enlisting a man whose bank had been bailed out by the state and whose shareholders were marooned. Bank of Ireland's share price had been €13.30 on the day he became governor. On the day he announced his resignation, it was trading at €1.34. During that period he had trousered more than €2 million in fees from the bank.

There was some token opposition to Burrows' elevation. The BAT share price dropped 1.6 per cent on the day his appointment was announced. According to the *Financial Times*, Guy Jubb of Standard Life Investments – one of BAT's top ten shareholders – dissented mildly, stating that 'at a time when stewardship is in sharp focus, it is questionable whether this appointment will enjoy unanimous support'.

Nils Pratley in the *Guardian* was more outspoken. Noting that 'BAT is Britain's ninth largest company', he wrote:

> The appointment sends a terrible message about accountability in boardrooms . . . It is hard to believe that Burrows, after his BoI years, still carries the authority required of a FTSE 100 chairman. Is he a big

enough figure to sack the chief executive if necessary? Would he command the support of shareholders in a crisis?

Terry Macalister revealed in the same paper that PIRC, the corporate-governance consultancy, had serious reservations about the appointment. BAT responded by nervously describing support for Burrows as 'sufficient', and at the subsequent AGM the resistance was nominal. As always, at the end of the day, the big corporations held the institutional shareholders' proxies in their pockets. On 28 April 2010 Burrows got more than 99 per cent of the vote.

The directors' recommendation to shareholders had been cunningly crafted. They told investors that their candidate for the chair had been a director of a string of companies including CIÉ (which they omitted to mention is a chronic basket case), chairman of the National Development Corporation (now a failed political entity) and a director of P. J. Carroll, an Irish member company of BAT. They said he'd been governor of the Bank of Ireland 'during a difficult period in that bank's history'. No hint was given of the extent of the bombsite he had left behind.

Since his appointment, Burrows can sometimes be spotted on the red-eye flight from Dublin to London City Airport on Monday mornings. He is met in London by a chauffeur who takes his suitcase and leads the way to his beautifully upholstered car.

Perhaps BAT was a one-off? Perhaps the Irishman's frantic networking over the years had led British companies to turn a blind eye to his failure in the financial quagmire, but to recognize the great sailor's skills in the food, drink and tobacco sector?

Perhaps.

Yet an even bigger shock was to follow. The man who played a leading role in the destruction of the Bank of Ireland had landed another plum position. This time the insiders were mocking the gods. In 2009, the same year that Richard Burrows left the Bank of Ireland in tatters, he was named a director of the IMF's Regional Advisory Group: Europe. Members of the group were described by IMF head Dominique Strauss-Kahn as 'prominent experts'. It was an astonishing appointment. The IMF is the rescuer of last resort for governments in financial trouble. It is a fire brigade and an ambulance – but it is also a policeman. It demands repentance and reform. It imposes harsh medicine on those nations that have acted recklessly.

Ireland, of course, is one such country.

There is little dispute about the reason for Ireland's economic collapse. Its reckless bankers were principally to blame for the entry of the IMF in November 2010. Burrows had been in the front line of offenders. The same man who played such a prominent part in fuelling the furnace was now on the side of the firefighters, policemen and paramedics. His leap from the ranks of the rogues into the ranks of the righteous was breathtaking. As with nearly all of Burrows' boards, he was quietly invited, not elected, to join the IMF group. Somebody influential must have asked him. Today the IMF is mum about how they co-opted the chairman of one of the errant banks in Ireland on to the board of its European advisory group. After all, the IMF has had to rescue Ireland from Burrows and his ilk. What on earth were they doing, clasping him to their bosom?

It turned out to be a short-term appointment. The IMF European Regional Advisory Group was abandoned in 2011.

Burrows' gift for networking goes well beyond Ireland, or even Europe. Little known to the Irish public, the miracle survivor of the destruction of Irish banking has since 1994 been a member of possibly the most exclusive business club in the world, the highly secretive political/business group known as the Trilateral Commission.

The Trilateral Commission is a club of people who rarely hold overt political power but exert serious influence in global business and politics. The European branch reads like a 'who's who' of continental oligarchs. It includes top brass from UBS, BP, the European Commission, the Rothschild Group and the British House of Lords. It includes bankers galore, along with former European cabinet ministers and prime ministers. These are people who can pick up the phone to heads of governments and bend their ears.

The small Irish membership of this exclusive club includes former AIB chairman and Goldman Sachs boss Peter Sutherland, former Taoiseach John Bruton – now tsar of Ireland's International

Financial Services Centre – and Digicel chairman Denis O'Brien, who was deputy governor of the Bank of Ireland under Burrows. They would not like to be reminded of it, but at one point the Irish membership also included the corrupt Fianna Fáil TD Liam Lawlor, who was jailed three times for refusing to cooperate with the Flood Tribunal.

Another of the handful of Irish members of the Trilateral Commission is none other than Dermot Gleeson, Burrows' one-time opposite number at AIB, who accompanied him on that fateful mission to Merrion Street on 29 September 2008.

Gleeson came to commerce far later in life than Burrows. A Blackrock College boy, his decision to head for the Law Library was a natural consequence of a stint as a flamboyant debater in the Literary and Historical Society in UCD. He was appointed a senior counsel less than ten years after going to the Bar, becoming reputedly the youngest 'silk' in the common law world. As a senior counsel he took on high-profile clients including supermarket king Ben Dunne and civil servant Matt Russell. But his most celebrated client was another untouchable, the beef baron Larry Goodman, possibly the most controversial Irish businessman of his generation, who came before a tribunal of inquiry into the industry in 1991. Gleeson emerged from the Beef Tribunal with his reputation enhanced. He had defended Goodman with a brilliance that stunned and infuriated the meat magnate's enemies.

Like so many barristers, Gleeson had planted deep political roots: he was a long-time donor to Fine Gael. After the party lost the 1992 general election, party leader John Bruton came under political pressure from party rival Michael Noonan. Bruton appointed a Commission on the Renewal of Fine Gael, which was widely seen as a device to buy time for the beleaguered leader; Gleeson served on the commission. After the commission had reported, Bruton clung on to the leadership long enough to tumble into power when the Fianna Fáil–Labour government suddenly fell in 1994. Gleeson was appointed Attorney General in Bruton's new government, a position he held until Fine Gael lost power in 1997.

Gleeson's stellar performance in defence of Larry Goodman made him a natural choice when AIB came to seek a top-notch barrister to defend it after the revelation of the DIRT tax scandal in 1999. Although Gleeson lost the battle to persuade the Public Accounts Committee that AIB had been granted a tax amnesty after it facilitated clients in tax evasion, he stole the show in many of the public hearings. In May 2000, Gleeson was invited to join the most prestigious – and one of the best-paid – boards in Ireland. He later ascended to the chair of AIB, in 2003. Gleeson was a fitting successor to Lochlann Quinn, who had an uncannily similar background. Both men had been educated at Blackrock College and University College Dublin. They lived within a stone's throw of each other in Ballsbridge. Both were at various times members of the secretive Bilderberg Group, an annual conference of the sorts of people who also pop up on the Trilateral Commission. Gleeson also attracted the attention of Sir Anthony O'Reilly, who invited him on to the board of Independent News & Media in 2000.

In 2003, Gleeson had the world at his feet. Within five years, the biggest bank in Ireland was on the brink of going bust. The scale of the destruction over which he and AIB chief executive Eugene Sheehy had presided was even greater than what happened at Bank of Ireland; but, as with Burrows, Gleeson proved to be untouchable. At the end of his first year as AIB chairman, Gleeson reported that the bank was in 'good shape and good heart'. At the time the share price stood at €12.05. When he left, it had collapsed to €1.73. Two years after that, as a final indignity, it was to lose a full quote on the stock market.

For his first five years in the chair, as the property market overheated courtesy of AIB and other banks, Gleeson reported to shareholders with the self-satisfied tone so typical of top bankers. By 2007, when the storm was obviously brewing, Gleeson was in denial. In that year's annual report he wrote of the 'success' of AIB, while attempting to justify a reckless dividend increase of 10 per cent. He congratulated the group on its ability to 'enhance its risk management processes in 2007'. Oblivious to the danger signs in the domestic property market, he parroted the Cowen government's mantra that 'the economic fundamentals remain solid and growth is expected to pick up again in 2009 and beyond'. He reassured us:

> Ireland is still growing at the same rate and the fundamentals of our economy, including our public finances and demographics, remain good ... Our asset quality is expected to remain good, our capital position is excellent and our level of funding support is strong.

Like Richard Burrows, within months of mouthing such reassuring mumbo-jumbo Gleeson was making his way to Merrion Street to eat his words.

Gleeson hung on to the AIB chairmanship until July 2009. His 2008 annual report blandly blamed 'adverse economic conditions' for the tanking AIB share price and the need for the government's bank guarantee. When Gleeson finally resigned, no tears were shed for the ex-chairman. AIB's investors were incensed. He was even the target of two eggs from an irate shareholder at his final meeting. Nor did the board stand behind him. After his resignation Dan O'Connor, his successor as chairman, nailed him to the cross. In his first annual report (2010) O'Connor described AIB's 2009 performance under Gleeson as 'highly unsatisfactory. Our shareholders deserve an explanation.' And in case the blame had not been clearly apportioned, he pointed the finger unambiguously at Gleeson and the former chief executive, Eugene Sheehy, noting that, 'We made a significant contribution to our own problems.' He was specific:

> We set up teams to lend money to developers in the property and construction sector. With the benefit of hindsight, it is obvious that many banks, including AIB, lent too much money to this particular sector. It is also clear, in retrospect, that our credit management processes and our oversight in this area failed to prevent this from happening in AIB.

Pointedly, he added:

> Our new management team, headed by our Group Managing Director Colm Doherty, is now in place. I firmly believe Colm has the strategy, the vision and the ability to rebuild trust and confidence in AIB.

His announcement of board changes failed to offer even the customary token thanks to the departed chairman. Gleeson's business career, it might have seemed, was in tatters. The former Attorney General was widely expected to return to the Bar Library nursing his commercial wounds. He was unlikely to land a seat on the bench – often regarded as a right by ex-AGs – as he had blotted his copybook in AIB. But Gleeson had been building a wider business portfolio and profile. His private investments betrayed an appetite for business – and sometimes for raw speculation. He had taken several big bets. In 2001, he had joined a syndicate that included high-flying property investor Derek Quinlan and former Anglo Irish Bank director Lar Bradshaw to invest in the Four Seasons Hotel in Ballsbridge. It was eventually sold for just €15 million, about a quarter of what it had cost to develop. In another deal, he partnered with others to invest €20 million in a corner property on Dublin's Dawson Street. Eyebrows were raised when it became known that Gleeson had been keeping such exotic company as Quinlan and Bradshaw, both big bulls at the sharp end of the property market.

Gleeson seemed an unlikely candidate for instant recruitment by the City of London's talent spotters after the AIB disaster. A lengthy period of decontamination might have been expected. And yet, just six months after extricating himself from AIB, Gleeson got into bed with another dodgy colossus, taking the chair of Travelport, a travel company seeking a flotation on the London Stock Exchange. The €2.1 billion share sale was billed as the largest to hit the market in two years.

Gleeson was in line for a huge chairman's salary, comparable to the one he had just lost at AIB. Speculation that he might even be given share options surfaced in the media.

Like Richard Burrows at Bank of Ireland, the man who had presided over AIB's demise somehow managed to float away into calm international waters. Perhaps Gleeson's membership of the Trilateral Commission had impressed Travelport's majority owners, Blackstone. This private equity group had bought Travelport for £4.3 billion in 2006. Its advisers included blue-chip City names such as Barclays Capital, Citigroup, Credit Suisse, Deutsche Bank and

UBS. Gleeson, still mixing in exalted company, was on the come-back trail. When asked what Gleeson could bring to the party, a spokesman for Travelport responded robustly: 'For those of us at Travelport who know him, it is quite clear that he is the best person for the job. He is a strong adviser and we believe he has the right skills to successfully chair Travelport as a newly listed company.'

Perhaps the principal reason for Gleeson's appointment was that Travelport's corporate headquarters were due to be based in Ireland. The proposed nine-member board included no fewer than three Irish directors: chairman Gleeson, Google chief John Herlihy, and a name strangely familiar to Gleeson from his AIB days, Gary Kennedy.

Gary Kennedy had served on the board of AIB under Gleeson. He was group director of finance and enterprise technology from 1997 to 2005. He lost out to Eugene Sheehy for the chief executive post in 2005. His old job was then split into two, while he was offered a new post within the bank. According to Gleeson at the 2006 AGM, he turned it down and negotiated his exit. Kennedy was awarded a breathtaking severance package: a €579,000 payment for loss of office, plus €2.01 million for his pension fund. At a time when Gleeson was in the chair, the bank agreed that Kennedy would additionally become a 'special adviser to the group on finance and risk' at a five-figure fee until 2008. His legal fees of €150,000 were paid by the bank. One shareholder at the AGM described Kennedy's package as a 'platinum' rather than a golden handshake.

Now, here was Kennedy popping up as a director in Gleeson's latest exploit. The familiarity of either man with Travelport's busi-ness was not immediately obvious. Their familiarity with each other was well documented. Nor were John Herlihy's great skills in the travel business apparent. He did, however, sit on the board of another Irish company, Greencore, alongside none other than Gary Kennedy.

Kennedy had been busy networking. He had already landed on the board of Elan just before jumping from AIB, and following his departure he picked up non-executive directorships at Greencore (2008) and Friends First (2009).

Gleeson and Kennedy suffered a nasty reverse when the Travelport flotation was pulled in February 2010 due to 'lack of investor appetite'.

'Market conditions' were given as the reason. These were indeed unfavourable, but prospective investors seem to have suspected that Gleeson and his fellow directors were attempting to use the market as a dumping ground for Travelport's heavy debt. According to the *Financial Times* the promoters of the flotation had hoped to halve Travelport's massive debt, reducing it to the still formidable figure of $2.3 billion.

Kennedy's posting to the board of Travelport may have raised a few eyebrows, but even by Ireland's incestuous standards of corporate governance his next appointment – as a well-paid director of the nationalized Anglo Irish Bank, in May 2010 – was stunning. It was a breathtaking restoration for one of the old guard at the toxic AIB, resurrected at the top of the zombie Anglo. Old bankers, it seems, never die. They take a short breather, then resurface. The state itself, the taxpayer, was offering Kennedy further rewards for his advice – on risk. Besides being a full board member, Kennedy had been the director at AIB in overall charge of finance and risk management, until he left in 2005. Suddenly yet another AIB old-boy could point at these trophy boardrooms and claim that he had been vindicated by his peers.

Despite the disastrous collapses of the banks of which they were chairmen, Dermot Gleeson and Richard Burrows have carried on, bruised but unbowed, as if nothing untoward had happened. The same cannot quite be said of the other two men who accompanied them to Merrion Street on the night of the guarantee: former AIB chief executive Eugene Sheehy and former Bank of Ireland chief executive Brian Goggin. Neither has resurfaced in any significant business role. They are no longer masters of the universe. But, in their own less conspicuous way, Sheehy and Goggin too are untouchables.

Today Eugene Sheehy is completing a degree in history at Trinity College Dublin. At the same time he is reaping rich rewards for long service to a toxic bank. Sheehy retired from AIB at the age of fifty-five with a pension of around €450,000 a year, while Goggin will be paid €650,000 per annum for the rest of his life. The two ex-bankers may not be lording it over the business world in the manner of their former chairmen, but they are poverty-proofed.

The story is much the same for other ex-bankers. After it emerged that Irish Life & Permanent had cooperated with Anglo Irish Bank in a window-dressing exercise intended to make Anglo's balance sheet look better at its financial year end, Denis Casey, the IL&P chief executive, reluctantly resigned along with two subordinates. On top of a pretty soothing €4.57 million pay package in his final year, Casey walked away with a severance payment of €1.25 million and a €2.93 million sweetener to his pension pot. He receives an annual pension of €430,000. Ex-bankers never starve.

After Casey, Goggin and Sheehy stepped down in quick succession, the chance to open a new chapter in Irish banking presented itself. All three of the banks they had run could have hired untainted successors to restore confidence. Bank of Ireland was the first to be offered the opportunity. After Goggin announced his retirement in February 2009, it was assumed that, with the state keeping the bank afloat, Finance Minister Brian Lenihan would insist upon an outsider. But less than two weeks after the news of Goggin's exit broke, Burrows revealed that the board had unanimously agreed to appoint an arch-insider, Richie Boucher, to the chief executive's job. Burrows insisted that the decision was made after 'an exhaustive process in Ireland and internationally, involving internal and external candidates'. Nobody believed a word of it. Boucher was the favourite son. He was installed in haste, just over a month after Brian Goggin resigned. In a lukewarm endorsement, Lenihan told *Business & Finance* magazine that 'there never was any lack of confidence expressed by the government in the appointment of Boucher'. He told the Oireachtas Finance Committee that Boucher was 'the best candidate available'.

Already a member of the board of the Bank of Ireland, Boucher had been a key decision maker in the bank during the property frenzy (when he was chief executive of its retail division). He oversaw development loans soaring to €7.1 billion. He was a friend of high-profile property developer Sean Dunne. His appointment caused consternation, and was opposed by billionaire Dermot Desmond, Ireland's most influential entrepreneur. Desmond, a substantial shareholder in the bank, wrote to Burrows expressing his dismay at the appointment of Boucher. Desmond's letter reached the media. In it he demanded to know whether 'Mr Boucher had a major involvement in the bank's exposure to property lending'. He went on to state that, as the chief executive of retail financial services, Boucher 'must have been responsible for fatal errors of judgement, including advancing loans to developers on the strength of overstated land values and insufficient security'. Despite such powerful opposition, Boucher survived. Bank of Ireland brazened it out.

Lenihan was a bit more robust when AIB tried to pull the same stunt after Eugene Sheehy's departure. The minister's insistence on giving serious consideration to an outsider was met with resistance from the AIB board. They procrastinated, peddling the standard feeble line that no decent external candidate would accept such a low salary as the €500,000 on offer. For several months the board pushed the claims of Colm Doherty, who had been a senior AIB executive for over twenty years and a board member since 2003. Lenihan, aware that public opinion would resist another insider taking the helm at a state-controlled bank, wriggled for months. The AIB board was not for turning. Doherty was their only candidate. Once again, the minister blinked: two–nil to the banks.

Irish Life & Permanent refused to buck the depressing trend of broken banks appointing insiders. After Casey left in early 2009, they went through a process of selection that resulted in the appointment of one of the bancassurer's own directors, Kevin Murphy. Murphy had been in the company for thirty-seven years. Like Boucher and Doherty, he was a perfect choice to preserve the sick culture in the Irish banks.

AIB and Bank of Ireland were the biggest banks in the country, and they were radioactive. But two smaller banks, Anglo Irish Bank and Irish Nationwide Building Society, each of which was led by a single figurehead – Sean FitzPatrick and Michael Fingleton, respectively – were even more catastrophically overexposed to property, and took the prize for toxicity.

In July 2012, three ex-Anglo bankers – FitzPatrick, former finance director Willie McAteer, and former head of Irish lending Pat

Whelan – were charged in connection with loans allegedly made to Anglo clients for the purpose of purchasing Anglo shares. The Office of the Director of Corporate Enforcement was continuing to investigate a number of other aspects of the bank's conduct. The Gardaí had openly signalled their interest in former chief executive David Drumm, but he was refusing to come back to Ireland from the United States.

Three and a half years earlier, in January 2009, the toxicity of Anglo had caused some of the bank's former directors to resign their seats on other companies' boards. Gary McGann, chief executive of packaging group Jefferson Smurfit, was obliged to give up his bed of nails as chairman of the Dublin Airport Authority (DAA), and Anne Heraty left the board of state-owned Bord na Móna. But neither resignation could be regarded as a great sacrifice. Heraty continues as chief executive of recruitment firm CPL, which she founded, while McGann remains boss of Smurfit Kappa and retains his place on the boards of United Drug and the insurance firm Aon McDonagh Boland. Ned Sullivan, who joined the Anglo board in 2001, retained the chair at Greencore despite the Anglo connection. None of the three had opposed Sean FitzPatrick's elevation from the chief executive's job to the chair, a power grab thoroughly discouraged by all codes of corporate governance.

Even the names of the replacements for those removed from the Anglo board reinforce the impression that, in Ireland, ex-bankers never die. The government's appointment in 2009 of Maurice Keane, former chief executive of Bank of Ireland (and supporter of Jim Flavin during his long insider-dealing battle at DCC), signalled a paralysis, an unwillingness to shake up the old bankers' club.

If Keane's comeback to the Anglo board was a dig into the distant past, the appointment of Richard Burrows' successor as governor of the Bank of Ireland a few months later smelled of desperation. Finance Minister Brian Lenihan again took advice from precisely the wrong people – his top civil servants and the Bank of Ireland itself. Pat Molloy – the predecessor of Maurice Keane – had retired as chief executive in 1998. A Bank of Ireland lifer, Molloy had finished up with a three-year lap of honour on the board in 1998 until he was finally put out to grass on a healthy pension in 2001 after forty-four years' service. Eight years later, at the age of seventy-one, he was being recalled to take the reins. Like Keane, he was the choice of politicians, banking insiders and discredited mandarins, all still in the old loop.

Molloy took the job at a salary of just under €400,000 a year. Since his first retirement from the bank he had enjoyed years of board-hopping, including a dark spell at Eircom (1999–2001) and a difficult period at Waterford Wedgwood (2002–9). He also took the chair at CRH (2000–2007) and at superquango Enterprise Ireland (1998–2008). Molloy's main selling point was that he had not been in banking during the years of property madness.

When Molloy retired in 2012, the board's choice of his successor was staggering. They opted for a Scotsman by the name of Archie Kane, who had left Lloyds TSB in a boardroom cull in 2011. Kane had been the director in charge of Lloyds' insurance division when it mis-sold payment protection insurance (PPI) on a stunning scale. By August 2012 Lloyds had been forced to set aside £4.8 billion to cover claims from victims of this scandal. Kane was one of five directors to have parts of their 2010 bonuses clawed back as a result. The Lloyds board was careful to note that the decision to cut the bonuses was 'based entirely on the principle of accountability and in no way on culpability or wrongdoing by the individuals concerned'.

Nobody better exemplifies the story of Ireland's ex-bankers than Peter Denis Sutherland.

Long before he was made chairman of Allied Irish Banks in 1989, Sutherland had already dazzled the Irish establishment. After his term at AIB ended in 1993, he headed into the global stratosphere. His status in Ireland was just short of godly.

In 1989, Sutherland had the normal qualification required for the chair of any Irish bank: he knew little about banking. He knew a good deal about other unconnected matters, though.

Sutherland was possibly the luckiest Irish businessman of his generation. Educated at Gonzaga, the upmarket secondary school in Dublin's Ranelagh, he graduated from UCD before heading for the

King's Inns to train as a barrister. Contemporaries say he was a good front-row forward but not particularly bright at school, and only an average legal studies student at UCD. In 1973, at the age of twenty-seven, Sutherland got down and dirty with Fine Gael, standing for the Dáil in Dublin North-West. He received only 6.2 per cent of the vote and retired hurt, never to involve himself in electoral politics again. He did not need to. Sutherland floated effortlessly up the ladder of life for most of the next forty years.

In 1981, his political patron and friend Garret FitzGerald plucked him from a promising career at the Bar to make him Attorney General and a cabinet member at the age of thirty-five – much as John Bruton would haul his own pal Dermot Gleeson into the Cabinet in 1994. Suds served two terms as Attorney General, both of them brief. The first was ended abruptly by the fall of FitzGerald's first government in late 1981. Sutherland returned to the AG's office in 1983, but once again his term was cut short, this time by a promotion. In 1984 the Taoiseach offered him the most prestigious post under his patronage: Sutherland became Ireland's European commissioner.

Suds took up the competition brief, and was seen as a strong commissioner. He received fawning press coverage from the media at home, especially from his adoring fans in the *Irish Times* and RTÉ. His urbane demeanour guaranteed him a platform in both media outlets whenever he wished. They were proud of him because he was part of what they saw as the emerging, self-confident Ireland; he could mix it with overseas opponents. No Irish public figure in modern times, with the possible exception of John Hume or Mary Robinson, rivalled Suds in the uncritical media he enjoyed.

His spell as Europe's competition commissioner was the making of him. When he retired from the European Commission in 1989, a casualty of a change of government, to be replaced by Fianna Fáil's Ray MacSharry, it was natural that offers of board memberships back home would be showered upon him. Sutherland took to the world's boardrooms like a duck to water. In 1990 he became a director of BP. Apparently the oil giant's board had been impressed by his effectiveness when, as competition commissioner, he slammed a fine on them, and resolved to snap him up as a director if he ever became available.

In 1989, he joined the board of Guinness Peat Aviation, which also included Garret FitzGerald, businessman Sir John Harvey-Jones and Nigel Lawson, former UK Chancellor of the Exchequer. GPA founder Tony Ryan felt that decorating the board with politicians and celebrity business leaders would inspire investor confidence when he took the aviation company to the stock market. Ryan was hopelessly wrong. The flotation went belly up in humiliating circumstances. Most of the directors, including FitzGerald, exited with egg on their faces and holes in their pockets. Suds, the media darling, escaped flak for his part in the flotation.

Sutherland joined the board of the building-materials giant CRH at a time when it had an astonishing seven directors who held Ansbacher offshore bank accounts. His chairman, Des Traynor, was Charlie Haughey's bagman, an eighteen-carat crook who used CRH headquarters to run a private bank without a banking licence. CRH's corporate governance standards were a long way from the ideals of Haughey's arch-enemy and Sutherland's mentor, Garret FitzGerald. Suds' departure from CRH in 1993 came nine years before the worst excesses of his fellow directors were exposed in the Ansbacher Report. Similarly, his colleagues on the board of AIB turned out to be less than angelic. But he was long gone to much higher callings before the culture at the bank he had chaired was exposed as rotten.

Suds' successor in the chair at AIB was none other than Jim Culliton, another CRH director and Ansbacher account holder. Other associates on the board included Tom Mulcahy, later to resign as chairman of Aer Lingus over tax issues, and Ray McLoughlin, the author of the infamous 'note to John Furze' – a document that was produced in the High Court in September 1999 as evidence that Ansbacher (Cayman) marketed its services in Ireland as a way of hiding hot money from the taxman.

In 1994, Sutherland was widely tipped as a possible president of the European Commission to succeed Jacques Delors. Sympathetic articles in support surfaced from the usual Irish suspects, and in the *Financial Times*, the *Wall Street Journal* and the *Economist*. Sutherland was not thought to be discouraging the speculation, but his political patrons in Fine Gael were out of office, so it was not a runner.

Sutherland soared into a different league in 1993, when he accepted the job as director of the General Agreement on Tariffs and Trade (GATT). He was the lead player in the Uruguay round of global trade talks, and was widely applauded for brokering one of the biggest trade agreements in history. The triumph of the Uruguay round opened new doors for Sutherland. Not only did he claim the chair at BP, but he also picked up directorships in globally recognized companies such as Ericsson and Delta Airlines. And it paved the way for his re-entry into Goldman Sachs. In 1990 – prior to his appointment to GATT – he had been made a European adviser to Goldman Sachs International, the UK subsidiary of the giant Wall Street investment bank. He had given up the gig when he went to GATT. Now he was made a partner – one of just 400 in a firm that employed 35,000 – as well as becoming chairman of Goldman Sachs International. Partners coin it in good times and bad. According to the *Wall Street Journal*, the typical Goldman Sachs partner was paid between $3 million and $5 million in 2011, and a great deal more in good years. A few years later, Suds was made a director of the Royal Bank of Scotland.

Peter Sutherland, the idealist who, according to the *Irish Times* in 1984, was clearly associated with the 'social conscience wing' of Fine Gael under Declan Costello and his 'Just Society' policy, was now an unstoppable pillar of capitalism. Peter Sutherland, the follower of Garret FitzGerald's liberal philosophy and his pluralist crusade for constitutional change, had, by the turn of the millennium, become the multinational plutocrat par excellence.

Although Suds' spell at AIB (1989–93) seemed uneventful at the time, the ghosts returned to haunt him. In 1999, when the DIRT scandal had come to light, the former chairman was summoned under subpoena before the Public Accounts Committee to tell them what he knew about the shenanigans at the bank on his watch.

Unaccustomed to being interrogated about his conduct, Sutherland was lofty and dismissive when challenged. He got right under the noses of his panel of TDs – including the chairman of the committee, Jim Mitchell, with whom he'd sat in the Cabinet. Mitchell is believed to have been particularly irked by a request from Suds to be excused from attendance for a day during the PAC hearings to jet off to a more important meeting of one of his overseas boards. The chairman is reported to have refused the request. Sutherland, the mighty globetrotter, was grounded in a Leinster House committee room, steam coming out of his ears.

He explained to the committee that when he had been informed about the systematic fraud on the state by AIB he referred it down the line, as 'the issue of non-resident accounts and DIRT was an issue which was essentially one for management. Management, as I understand it, believed that the issue was under control.' Then he insisted, astonishingly, that he 'did not intervene in any way'. The PAC report slated 'eminent' bank directors for not enforcing ethical standards. Suds was silent on the matter. And that, as far as Peter Sutherland was concerned, is where the issue ended for him. Ditto most of the Irish media.

AIB made a €90 million settlement with the Revenue Commissioners for its part in the DIRT tax scam, the biggest penalty ever imposed on any of the banks. No bank chief faced a penalty beyond the indignity of giving evidence in public before the DIRT inquiry. No guilty bank manager suffered punishment for leading clients down the path of non-resident addresses to evade tax.

Goldman Sachs' reputation has suffered considerably over recent years, with unsavoury revelations about the way it does business. A well-argued attack on Sutherland by Fintan O'Toole in 2010 highlighted the connection; but even more damaging to Sutherland's reputation have been his associations with BP and the Royal Bank of Scotland.

Suds' thirteen-year tenure in the chair of BP proved far too long. His later years there were dogged by boardroom rows and controversies about the oil giant's safety policy. He forced his one-time friend Lord John Browne out of the chief executive's job a year early, replacing him with Tony Hayward, who was later reviled for his mishandling of the massive Deepwater Horizon oil spill in the Gulf of Mexico.

The Deepwater Horizon spill was not the only major disaster to unfold on Sutherland's watch at BP. A massive explosion at a BP refinery in Texas in 2005 killed fifteen workers. Investigators found that safety measures had been postponed because of pressure to reduce expenses. In 2007, an independent investigation into the explosion headed by James Baker, former US Secretary of State, found that BP skimped on safety. It was a scathing report.

Nor has Sutherland's association with Royal Bank of Scotland enhanced his reputation: RBS has the distinction of being the bank that went belly up for the largest amount in history. It was bailed out at a cost of £45 billion by the UK government, leaving the rescues of Richard Burrows' Bank of Ireland, Dermot Gleeson's AIB and Sean FitzPatrick's Anglo in the shade. Suds' presence on the board since 2001 and his presence on the remuneration committee that awarded disgraced chief executive Sir Fred 'the Shred' Goodwin a €17 million pension pot prompted suspicions that Suds was no different from other greedy bank directors.

His final AGM at BP was interrupted by dissatisfied shareholders complaining of his role on the board of RBS. Sutherland refused to apologize. The BP investors had noticed that his old friend Sir Tom McKillop had been in the chair at RBS while Suds was a board member; at the same time, McKillop had served as a director of BP under Sutherland. It was an uncomfortably cosy picture, but a familiar one. Shareholders were equally irate about the high level of remuneration for BP directors and employees in a year when the shares had fallen by a third. Suds himself, who had earned £600,000 in the previous year, defended the high level of pay for the BP chiefs: it was the multinational's hundredth anniversary.

Sutherland's departure from RBS in 2009 was part of the unceremonious clearout following the nationalization of the bankrupt bank by the British government. The board had been savaged for allowing Sir Fred to embark on a reckless acquisition programme. Sutherland was leaving a year early after an eight-year stint.

Sutherland has an apparent weakness for honorary degrees, having been awarded at least fifteen doctorates, many of them from provincial universities. His CV lists baubles by the bucketful, medals galore, grand crosses, lifetime achievement awards, fellowships from those institutions wishing to touch his mantle or hoping to enlist him as a benefactor. Like Sir Fred Goodwin, he was awarded a knighthood by

Her Majesty the Queen. After Goodwin was stripped of his title for his excesses at RBS there were calls for 'Sir' Peter to be cut down to the same size. They were resisted. (Suds' title was only an honorary knighthood. He was an Irish citizen, and as such would have been obliged to receive permission from the Irish state to accept the undiluted version.)

Like his good friend Lochlann Quinn – a later chairman at AIB – he was a benefactor to University College Dublin. Where Quinn gave €5 million to the 'Quinn' School of Business, Suds gave €4 million to UCD's 'Sutherland' School of Law. The untouchables were becoming immortals. Today, despite his fall from so many high perches, Sutherland is still a master of the universe. He still meets movers and shakers at the World Economic Forum at Davos. He still networks at the Bilderberg Group and the Trilateral Commission. He still commands high fees in top boardrooms.

Although the wonder boy has become the fat cat, the Sutherland balance sheet in Ireland is still hopelessly lopsided in his favour. Peter Sutherland remains an idol in Irish business circles. Guests at the dinner tables of Dublin 4 still whisper his name with reverence in the hope that he may one day cross their threshold. The media still seek him out for soft interviews to hear the great man's ideas on how to solve the problems of Ireland, Europe and the world. Despite his unhappy career in banking, he still pontificates about economic policy and commands a hearing in any forum in Ireland.

The halo still sits comfortably on the head of the hero.

3.   Access All Areas

The Lobbyists, the PRs, the Donors and the Revolving Doors

Table 23 at the Dublin Chamber of Commerce annual dinner in the five-star Four Seasons Hotel in Ballsbridge, in February 2012, was hosted by Goodbody Stockbrokers. Members of Goodbody's corporate finance team – the unit that handles the buying and selling of companies and other such deals – broke bread with Robert Watt, the secretary general of the Department of Public Expenditure. Watt's department (newly created by the Fine Gael–Labour government to handle the public expenditure functions previously covered by the Department of Finance) had embarked upon a programme of selling off state assets such as Bord Gáis, Coillte, the ESB and the shareholding in Aer Lingus. Also at table 23 that night in February, as Ronald Quinlan reported in the *Sunday Independent*, were Coillte chief executive David Gunning and ESB finance chief Donal Flynn.

Why might a stockbroking firm wish to host officials of state-owned companies at the same table with the civil servant who has been charged with selling them off?

Goodbody is in the business of buying and selling assets, and winning one of the mandates to act for the state or a state entity in a major sell-off would be a lucrative gig. The Telecom Éireann stock market flotation in 1999 generated €74 million in fees for slick-suited corporate financiers, lawyers and assorted bean counters. The smaller Aer Lingus IPO in 2003 led to a €29.74 million payday for various corporate advisers. Goodbody had filled its pockets as one of the global coordinators of the Aer Lingus float, having been retained by the Department of Transport. Separately, it also advised Aer Lingus on a defence strategy against two Ryanair takeover bids. Goodbody had also worked with the ESB on the €450 million sale of a power station to Endesa and the buyout of a wind farm from DP Energy.

With a public tender for lucrative advice contracts looming for state sell-offs, it was all too easy to take a cynical view of Goodbody's motives in schmoozing the people who would help divvy out these contracts. The month after the Chamber of Commerce dinner, the *Sunday Times* reported that Goodbody had won a contract to advise Coillte on 'strategic options' including the potential sale of assets. We will never know whether anything that was said at table 23 had any bearing on this outcome. But it looked awful.

Ronald Quinlan's scoop about table 23 offered a relatively rare insight into the workings of corporate hospitality in areas where the public interest is at stake. The Standards in Public Office guidelines for Irish civil servants note that:

> All offers of hospitality from commercial interests which have or might have contractual relations with the Department/Office of the civil servant to whom the offer is made must be reported by that civil servant to his or her manager for direction.

However, the Department of Finance told the authors that there is no register of invitations or hospitality in operation: in other words, the guidelines are strictly informal, and attempts by Nick Webb using the Freedom of Information Act to track down details of hospitality or invitations received by ministers have not borne fruit. This means either that civil servants and ministers are not being invited to rugby matches, race meetings and gala dinners by corporate interests, or else that it's happening in a very underhand way, with no transparency about who is entertaining whom outside office hours.

Lobbying by big business interests also takes place in the literal corridors of power, but finding out who is trying to influence legislation and regulations for their own benefit is difficult. Attempts by the authors to use the Freedom of Information Act to find out which lobbyists had visited Leinster House and which politicians signed them in, from January 2009 until the end of 2011, were refused by the civil servants running the Oireachtas in March 2012. There were too many visitors over the period and it was impossible, they said, to give a breakdown of lobbyists visiting the centre of government.

However, we did obtain the appointments diaries of Enda Kenny and of the two secretaries general of the Department of the Taoiseach who have served him, Dermot McCarthy and Martin Fraser.

Apart from a large number of Mayo-related meetings and constituency events, and an early visit from Jerry Crotty of Mayo Renewable Power, Enda Kenny's diary was full of meetings with some of the most powerful business corporations in the country. Several of the companies that secured meetings with the new Taoiseach would have had very specific agendas; others were presumably there to remind the Taoiseach of the importance of Ireland's anomalous 12.5 per cent corporate tax rate, which helps them keep their tax bills so low.

Shell, which is advised by Q4 Public Relations, the firm set up by former Fianna Fáil general secretary Martin Mackin and former Fianna Fáil strategist Jackie Gallagher, got in to see Enda within five months of his election as Taoiseach. Shell's European chief, Greg Guidry, and the managing director of Shell Exploration and Production (E&P) Ireland, Terry Nolan, were listed as visiting the Taoiseach in July 2011, according to the diaries.

Also during his first six months in office, Kenny met three times with executives of drug company Elan and its spin-off Alkermes. Elan has a chequered history, with its blockbuster drug Tysabri having been withdrawn after being linked with a rare and fatal brain condition. Racy accountancy practices also saw Elan investigated by the US Securities and Exchange Commission. In 2010, the company agreed to pay a €147 million fine for having promoted the use of its epilepsy drug Zonegran by children, even though the drug is not approved for such use; its methods of encouraging unapproved uses of the drug included bringing doctors on all-expenses-paid junkets to the Caribbean and to ski resorts. Elan's payment was the biggest ever legal settlement by an Irish public company. Hardly a glowing example of the finest standards in corporate Ireland but, boy, was it well connected – as three meetings with the Taoiseach in six months can attest.

A delegation from the US Chamber of Commerce – advised by former Progressive Democrats insider Stephen O'Byrnes' firm

MKC – saw the new Taoiseach in May. Google's John Herlihy and Eric Schmidt also lobbied Kenny. Google, which is also advised by MKC, has managed to shave over $1 billion off its annual tax bill using slick tax schemes which shuttle profits through its companies in Ireland, the Netherlands and Bermuda.

Representatives of the computer giant Dell, advised in Ireland by Q4, met with Enda in June 2011, and the company's founder Michael Dell stuck his head around the door in September of that year. At the end of August, Kenny attended a private dinner for the board of powerful global drug company Eli Lilly at the Old Head Golf Club in Kinsale. Other early visitors who got time in the new Taoiseach's diary included Andrew Witty, the global CEO of GSK, Sarah Matthews of Dun & Bradstreet, John Cunningham of Arvato Bertelsmann and Carl Burger of Smith Root Inc.

US investor Wilbur Ross, who failed in a bid to buy the crippled Irish bank EBS at a knockdown price in 2009 before picking up a big chunk of Bank of Ireland in 2010, visited the Taoiseach in November 2011, days after a meeting with private equity kingpin Steve Schwarzman and his Irish lieutenant Gerry Murphy. Several weeks later, Murphy would be linked to the NAMA advisory board but ultimately wouldn't take the job. Elan got more face time with Enda in January 2012, when the Taoiseach met the drug company's chairman Bob Ingram and its board in the Merrion Hotel in Dublin. John Hourican, head of investment banking at Royal Bank of Scotland (and the son of former Bord na Móna chief executive John Hourican Sen.), visited along with Jim Brown of RBS subsidiary Ulster Bank.

The appointments diary of Department of Enterprise secretary general Sean Gorman and his successor John Murphy was also released to Nick Webb under the Freedom of Information Act. Before the government changed, the department's top mandarin was lobbied by some of the country's most influential businessmen and company bosses including Musgrave's Chris Martin, IBM's Michael Daly, Google's John Herlihy, HP's Martin Murphy, Aer Lingus's Christoph Mueller and Bank of Ireland's Richie Boucher. There was also a private dinner in the National Gallery of Ireland hosted by financial services giant Zurich in December 2010 and a lunch with IBEC's

Pat Ivory in Restaurant 41 on St Stephen's Green. After the installation of the new government, visitors included Vodafone public affairs head Paul Ryan, KPMG's Laura Gallagher, Google's John Herlihy and Microsoft's Paul Rellis.

The visitors' book at the Department of Enterprise for April 2011, the first full month of the new government, shows that one of the earliest visitors was Drury Communications public affairs chief Iarla Mongey. David Begg of the Irish Congress of Trade Unions wasn't far behind. There was also a private reception with waste company Indaver in the Hibernian Club in May 2011 and a private gathering with the Irish Banking Federation (IBF) in the Westin Hotel in June 2011.

There is nothing intrinsically wrong with meetings between business people and state officials. The two big problems with the way lobbying works in Ireland relate to access and transparency. Not everyone can pay the big bucks to hire a lobbyist. Not everyone who asks will get into Government Buildings to meet the Taoiseach or a top civil servant. And there is a serious shortage of transparency about meetings between key civil servants or politicians and big business. The schmoozing of politicians and civil servants is a job for an insider. Political careers invariably end in failure, but former politicians and party hacks often use their extensive contacts from within the bowels of government to carve out lucrative careers on the other side of the revolving door.

Tom Parlon has passed through the revolving door in both directions. Parlon headed up the Irish Farmers Association from 1997 to 2001 before parachuting in as a Dáil candidate for the Progressive Democrats on the eve of the 2002 general election. He won a seat in Laois–Offaly and was promptly rewarded with an appointment as the Minister for State at the Department of Finance with special responsibility for the Office of Public Works. The OPW is in charge of handling government procurement and advising on public construction projects ranging from flood defences to new Garda stations. Handling the nuts and bolts of the decentralization policy was also a key OPW responsibility. During the heady days when

Parlon was the junior minister in charge, it also had a role in consulting on multimillion-euro public–private deals to construct schools, government buildings and the €380 million National Conference Centre, built by Johnny Ronan and Richard Barrett's Treasury Holdings.

Parlon had bucketloads of money to spend on building stuff – and not all of it was well spent. In 2005, the Public Accounts Committee accused the OPW of wasting millions of euros in taxpayers' money when it spent €19 million on accommodation for asylum seekers that was never used. The OPW was also involved in the controversial Thornton Hall prison project. In 2005, the state spent €30 million to buy land in north Dublin as the proposed site of a new super-jail to house 2,200 prisoners, which was to replace Mountjoy Prison. The price for the land was vastly in excess of the going rate for land in the area. The Department of Justice and its advisers accepted that they had been 'seen coming', and new guidelines came into force enabling the state to use intermediaries when buying assets on the public market. But at the time of the deal, money wasn't seen as a problem for the state; in January 2006, Parlon claimed that the twenty-acre Mountjoy site was worth around €2 billion. Another €13.3 million was spent by the state on security, drainage and landscaping for the project by the end of 2010, bringing the total outlay to over €43 million. The financial crisis saw the prison project mothballed.

By the time of the 2007 general election, the public was sick of the sight of the Progressive Democrats and Parlon lost his seat after a very expensive campaign. His political career was over. Seven weeks later, he announced that he was going to take a job as the head of the Construction Industry Federation – the lobby group representing the building industry in Ireland – at a salary of €250,000 per year. Its members ranged from giant civil engineering groups John Sisk & Son and John Paul Construction to some of the wealthiest property developers in the country, including Gerry Gannon's Gannon Homes and Sean Mulryan's Ballymore Residential. Parlon was moving from the nerve centre of government spending on construction right over to the guys who wanted all the government contracts. And he was doing it with a ministerial pension worth €31,192 per year in his back pocket.

The Labour Party kicked up stink about the appointment, point-
ing out the quite obvious potential for conflict of interest: Parlon had
a wealth of knowledge about the OPW and the government's plans.
Parlon told RTÉ in July that he had 'no ethical questions to answer'
and that he was clear that he had 'acted in a proper manner'.

Parlon was exceptionally effective. He worked relentlessly behind
the scenes for his new employers, who were facing a dramatic drop in
demand for their services due to the bursting of the property bubble
and the collapse of the public finances. One of his bigger successes
came in October 2008, when it emerged that his former colleagues
in the government had ignored their own guidelines – following
intense lobbying – by failing to ensure that a number of lucrative
state projects were awarded using newly introduced fixed-price
contracts intended to ensure that the state got value for money.
These guidelines had been brought in after major state contracts for
the Luas and Dublin Port Tunnel had spiralled wildly over budget.
The new contracts meant that builders were to be paid a sum
agreed at the beginning of work and any cost overruns would come
out of their own pockets. But just ahead of the introduction of
these new fixed-price contracts, Parlon persuaded the government
to allow up to €150 million worth of contracts to go ahead under
the old rules.

As Michael Brennan reported in the *Irish Independent*, a letter from
Parlon to Finance Minister Brian Lenihan in May 2008 warned of the
'expense and disruption' that builders would face if water service
contracts were changed in keeping with the new contract rules. The
former politician – who, as Brennan pointed out, had described
fixed-price contracts as a 'key reform' when in government – pushed
all the right buttons, warning that the creation of 150 jobs in Waterford and flood prevention at Carlow could also be threatened by
delays caused by the roll-out of the contracts. The following month,
according to Brennan, Lenihan wrote to Environment Minister John
Gormley and to Education Minister Batt O'Keeffe 'saying he had
decided "on balance" that there should be some "flexibility" on the
issue to avoid delaying the projects'.

Parlon blamed the affair on the fact that local authorities had not made the switchover to the fixed-price contracts, and claimed, 'It would have taken 12 to 15 months to re-tender.' He may have had a point. But not every individual, community or industry is able, when inconvenienced by the inefficiency of public administration in Ireland, to secure a high-level ministerial intervention to sort the problem out. In hiring Parlon, the CIF had got itself the sort of access and influence that the rest of us can only dream about.

Wilson Hartnell Public Relations – part of the global WPP group controlled by one of Britain's best-known businessmen, Sir Martin Sorrell – has also seen the logic of hiring prominent figures from the world of politics. From 1999 to 2002, WHPR's public affairs division was headed up by former Labour Party insider Fergus Finlay, who had helped overhaul Mary Robinson's image from a stuffy and high-brow academic lawyer to an unbeatable presidential candidate in 1990. (Two years earlier, Finlay had started to present a bizarre political chat show on RTÉ with Frank Dunlop; the show was dropped in 2000 after revelations emerged at the Flood Tribunal about Dunlop bunging councillors.) Finlay left WHPR in 2002 to advise Pat Rabbitte. The revolving door between politics and the private sector just kept spinning. WHPR signed up Alan Dukes, former Fine Gael leader and ex-finance minister, the following year. He would become a director of the company in May 2006.

Dukes' public role at WHPR saw him produce a series of rather dull reports for various influential groups, including a lengthy volume about the bloodstock industry, which was facing questions over its tax-free status. In December 2009 he was appointed as a public-interest director of Anglo Irish Bank, becoming chairman the following year. Anglo's single biggest customer and largest shareholder was Sean Quinn. WHPR held the lucrative PR contract to advise Sean Quinn and his businesses. With Quinn and his family owing Anglo €2.8 billion and fighting to retain control of their empire, the relations between bank and client were highly sensitive. Clearly there were questions that needed to be answered about Dukes' positions at Anglo and WHPR. Kathleen Barrington of the *Sunday Business Post* emailed some queries to Dukes after his Anglo appointment. Dukes replied tetchily:

I am not a 'lobbyist': representation of clients' legitimate interests
is a minor and infrequent aspect of my work as a public affairs
consultant with WHPR. I normally engage with clients at a much
earlier and more fundamental stage of their policy process. The
following answers should not be construed as indicating that
I accept your assertion that I am a 'lobbyist'.

The former Fine Gael politician told Barrington that he did not
see a potential for conflict between his proposed role as a chairman of
Anglo Irish Bank and his role with WHPR. Dukes said that he had
never lobbied on behalf of the Quinn Group, Quinn Insurance or
Sean Quinn. Asked to supply a list of clients on whose behalf he had
acted since becoming a consultant to WHPR, he wrote, 'This is
none of your business. It is a matter between WHPR and its clients.'

Anglo ultimately took control of the Quinn empire and the former tycoon was declared bankrupt. A vicious legal battle between
Anglo and Quinn over the ownership of €500 million worth of foreign property assets kicked off in early 2012. While Quinn was ousted
from his business, WHPR kept the lucrative consulting gig when
new owners Liberty Mutual took over Quinn Insurance.

Former Fianna Fáil general secretary Martin Mackin was appointed
to the Senate by Bertie Ahern in May 2002, a few days before the general election later that month. It was a shameless piece of cronyism
even by Fianna Fáil's low standards. The position gave Mackin the
keys to Leinster House.

Along with former Fianna Fáil insider Jackie Gallagher, Mackin
set up Q4 Public Relations in 2003. Operating from a fine Georgian
townhouse on St Stephen's Green, the PR and lobbying firm's client
list included Dell, Microsoft, Tesco, Coca-Cola and Shell. Apart
from the blue-chip corporate accounts, Q4 also whispered in ears on
behalf of industry lobby groups including the Irish Spirits Association. The agency hoovered up state contracts during Fianna Fáil's
reign of error. In 2004, Q4 was awarded part of a €4.5 million contract to publicize the disastrous e-voting machines – machines that
would never be used. This led to a Fine Gael claim in the Dáil that

there was 'a suspicion that these consultancy jobs are for friends of Fianna Fáil'. Fianna Fáil minister Martin Cullen dismissed the allegation, adding that there was no partiality towards Q4 in the tendering process.

Q4 was paid €23,700 to provide advice for the Department of Finance in relation to the Ecofin conference in 2004. The following year, the Department of Justice paid Q4 €43,000 for two PR projects. The Department of Enterprise, Trade and Employment revealed that Q4 had earned €72,000 for PR and consultancy to Culture Ireland in 2008 and another €15,245 in 2007. Q4 landed the PR contract for the government when the state was floating Aer Lingus in 2006. The firm also won the lucrative deal to advise on the Transport 21 infrastructure programme from the Department of Transport. Gallagher and Mackin's firm even acted for the Association of Higher Civil and Public Servants. This is the organization run by the country's top civil servants, the people who have a major say in which PR firms win state contracts.

The potential for conflict of interest within firms doing so much business related to matters of public interest is great. Chinese walls would need to be extraordinarily high and covered in razor wire to prevent the transfer of sensitive information related to clients who held opposing interests. Although it employs just a handful of consultants, Q4 acted for the pharmacy lobby group the Irish Medication Safety Network – and for the Pharmaceutical Society of Ireland, which regulates pharmacies. Other uncomfortable bedfellows have included Channel 6, a privately owned TV station, and the Broadcasting Commission of Ireland, which regulates the television sector. Q4 was advising the poachers and the gamekeepers.

In 2005, Q4 won one of its most high-profile accounts – to spin for the National Consumer Agency. The quango already had its own internal PR unit, but it clearly felt the need to spend taxpayers' money on external advice, too. Q4 held the contract on an 'interim' basis for three years despite the lucrative fee earner never being put out for an open tender. In 2008, the contract was finally put up for tender and Q4 was successful, winning a gig worth €200,000 per year. It subsequently emerged that Bertie Ahern's former girlfriend

Celia Larkin had proposed Q4 at a board meeting of the agency. Q4 won again when the contract went up for public tender in 2011.

In 2009, it would emerge that Q4 was also advising Tesco. 'There's definitely a potential conflict of interest where you have Q4 representing the NCA, which is doing price surveys on Tesco products, and at the same time putting out ads telling you how cheap Tesco is,' said Fine Gael's Leo Varadkar. Q4 helped advise Tesco on announcing a range of price cuts at its border stores. At the same time it was spinning for the NCA, which put out a statement from chief executive Ann Fitzgerald calling for Tesco to make the price cuts in all its Irish stores, not just the border shops.

With Fianna Fáil dead and buried, spots have had to change to stripes. Ronan Farren, a former assistant of Proinsias de Rossa and son of SDLP's Sean Farren, stood as a Labour Party candidate in the 2009 local elections in Dublin South. He has been at Q4 since 2008. Damien Garvey was a Fine Gael policy director from 2002 to 2007 before becoming an associate at the firm. Following the 2011 general election he left to join Fine Gael minister Jimmy Deenihan's kitchen cabinet at the Department of Arts and Sport.

One of the biggest beneficiaries of regime change has been the fast-growing DHR Communications, chaired by former ICTU general secretary Peter Cassells and run by ex-Labour Party press officers Catherine Heaney and Tony Heffernan. The business also has links to Fine Gael: Martina Quinn worked in party headquarters and Cliona Doyle worked as a Fine Gael parliamentary assistant before moving to the PR firm. In October 2011, after a tender, DHR took over the plum role of advising the Broadcasting Authority of Ireland. The job had been held by Q4 for a number of years. DHR has also landed media consultancy gigs with state agencies such as Irish Aid and the Digital Hub Development Agency – where its chairman Peter Cassells had served as a director.

On the other side of St Stephen's Green from Q4 are the premises of Edelman Ireland – part of the vast Edelman Group, which is the world's largest independent PR company. It's less than a hundred metres from Doheny & Nesbitt's pub, where government ministers, key civil servants and lobbyists sink pints till the early hours. Edelman

Ireland is chaired by Jim Glennon, the former Ireland second row forward and a Fianna Fáil senator from 2000 to 2002 before being elected to the Dáil for Dublin North. Ryanair, the biggest airline flying in and out of Ireland, joined Edelman as a client eighteen months after Glennon became company chairman in November 2008. Michael O'Leary's airline is a constant demander of change on everything from airport charges to the travel tax, and its methods tend to be less subtle than having a whisper in the ear of a relevant civil servant. Glennon's experience as a member of the Oireachtas Transport Committee would have done Ryanair's cause no harm.

On 24 March 2011, the day before Fine Gael's return to power, the PR and lobbying firm Fleishman-Hillard Saunders won an €80,000 tender to advise FÁS. The previous October, the firm's head of consulting, Mark Mortell, had gone on leave to work as an adviser to Enda Kenny ahead of the upcoming general election. The former Fine Gael councillor is extremely close to the Taoiseach, and was appointed to the chair of Bord Fáilte in 1996 when Kenny was Tourism Minister. Following Fine Gael's election victory, Mortell returned to his day job. It emerged that Mortell would be working on the FÁS account, although not on a day-to-day basis. FÁS insisted that there was no political or other outside interference in the awarding of the two-year contract to the firm. In March 2012, Fine Gael came calling again, with Mortell drafted in to consult and advise on the European Fiscal Treaty referendum campaign.

Whereas Fleishman-Hillard Saunders was in a strong position, following the rise of Fine Gael, to benefit from its links to the party, other firms had to tweak their allegiances. Drury Communications was founded in 1989 by Fintan Drury, who would later become a board member of Anglo Irish Bank as well as being one of former Taoiseach Brian Cowen's most trusted confidants. Drury, who left Drury Communications in 2000, was part of the infamous golf game with Cowen and Sean FitzPatrick at Druids Glen that helped topple the government. Drury Communications also had connections to the Progressive Democrats: public affairs director Iarla Mongey was a former adviser to Mary Harney and a big cheese at the Government Information Services during the Fianna Fáil–Progressive Democrats government of 2002–2007. The firm had done well out of the Fianna Fáil-led government, securing major contracts with Telecom Éireann and the Department of Health. It was also a long-term adviser to Anglo Irish Bank and kept hold of the lucrative contract after the bank was nationalized in 2009.

But the winds of change were blowing through Leinster House, and with Fianna Fáil facing an electoral hammering Drury Communications had to reposition itself. One week before the 2011 general election was called, the firm announced the hiring of Gerry Naughton, who had been political director of Fine Gael from 2002 to 2007.

Edelman was another firm that needed Fine Gael blood, and they found it in Olwyn Enright. A former TD for the party, daughter of long-serving Fine Gael TD Tom Enright, and wife of Joe McHugh, the Fine Gael TD for Donegal North, she was the party's spokesperson on social welfare when, in June 2010, she backed Richard Bruton's powder-puff palace coup against Enda Kenny. Enright wasn't reappointed to Enda's front line, and two months later she announced that she would not be running in the upcoming election. She was going to spend more time with her young family. But in April 2011, just a month after her former colleagues in Fine Gael were swept to power, Enright joined Edelman's public affairs division.

Murray Consultants, set up by Joe Murray in 1974 and fronted for many years by Jim Milton, is best known for its blue-chip corporate PR business, with clients ranging from Kingspan and Grafton Group to Kellogg's and Coolmore Stud. But more recently Murray has muscled its way into the lucrative lobbying sector, too. Instead of hiring a former civil servant or politician, it chose ex-*Irish Times* chief political correspondent Mark Brennock to head up its public affairs operations in 2006. Public affairs clients of the company include the legal firm Arthur Cox and FBD Insurance. The firm was extremely active on behalf of Treasury Holdings after it launched legal proceedings against NAMA in February 2012. Brennock told *Business Plus* magazine in May 2009:

> Lobbying is not effective unless politicians are able to get the civil
> service behind them. A lot of what I do is breaking the administrative

logjam by finding out who my client needs to convince, then helping them to make their case. The private sector doesn't know how to work with the public one.

Former Progressive Democrats general secretary Michael Parker was a co-founder of Insight Consultants, along with former *Sunday Press* editor Michael Keane. Fine Gael chief strategist Frank Flannery joined the company as an adviser after the general election. In April 2012, Colm Keena of the *Irish Times* questioned Flannery about his new role. While Flannery confirmed that he was working for Insight, he declined to say which clients he represented and would not comment on whether or not he had lobbied any politicians or civil servants for clients. Flannery still does voluntary work for Fine Gael. His employers have acted for clients including Bord na Móna, An Post, Rehab, the Beacon Medical Group and the Catholic bishops of Ireland.

Former Progressive Democrats press officer Ray Gordon's firm Gordon MRM has many of the juiciest PR and lobbying consultancies in the state financial sector – including NAMA (€300,000 per year), the National Treasury Management Agency, the National Development Finance Agency and the State Claims Agency. The NAMA and NTMA roles must sit somewhat awkwardly with Gordon's continuing association with Irish Life & Permanent, which owns a chunk of the special purpose vehicle that was set up to take a 51 per cent stake in NAMA to keep its debts off the country's balance sheet. The NTMA has been involved with the failed attempts to sell off Irish Life, which were shelved in early 2012.

On 8 May 2012, Gordon's firm released three press statements. The first one was from NAMA announcing the launch of its new 80:20 pilot scheme to finance first-time buyers. The second one was from Permanent TSB expressing support for the NAMA initiative. The final press release was on behalf of the Society of Chartered Surveyors indicating a 'cautious welcome' for the new scheme. Other clients have included Bank of Ireland's corporate finance wing IBI, the Irish Stock Exchange and property website myhome.ie. The Chinese walls at Gordon's firm must be extremely robust.

Gordon previously worked at MKC Communications, which hired Fine Gael press officer Mike Miley as a client director after the 2011 election. MKC's chief public affairs elbow-tugger is Stephen O'Byrnes. A co-founder of the Progressive Democrats, unsuccessful candidate in the 1992 general election and party press adviser, O'Byrnes was appointed by the Fianna Fáil–Progressive Democrats government to the RTÉ Authority in 2000, after leaving politics.

It was quite a feat to represent the media, spin to the media and bend the ears of politicians, but not a unique one: PR man Tom Savage was appointed chairman of the RTÉ Authority in February 2009, while also running the Communications Clinic with his wife Terry Prone. In May 2012, as Savage was being grilled (in his RTÉ capacity) by an Oireachtas committee over the *Prime Time Investigates* libel of Fr Kevin Reynolds, Labour senator John Whelan claimed: 'The chairman of the authority himself has the most glaring conflict of interest with regard to his media communications company which is at the heart of the kind of programming we're talking about – we're not talking about a company that dwells on gardening programmes or cookery classes. The Communications Clinic specializes in political PR, spin-doctoring on public affairs.'

Savage rebutted the allegations. 'If the insinuation being made by the senator is that I have not got the highest standard of integrity, honesty and ethical approach to my work, I resent that deeply,' he responded. Savage added that he had never faced a conflict of interest during his time helming the RTÉ board. 'Not a single issue has cropped up on the board that I have had to absent myself.'

Lobbyists and publicists are generally fairly discreet about their activities and methods. Former Brian Cowen adviser turned spin doctor Paul Allen is one of the few lobbyists who actually publicize what they do. In a blog on the website of his company Paul Allen & Associates, Allen recounts his role in persuading the government to provide state funds for a car scrappage scheme to assist the motor industry.

> Following our intensive lobby campaign, the late Brian Lenihan took the initiative to introduce the car scrappage scheme in the 2009

budget, offering motorists a €1,500 government discount off the price of their new car, when trading in a vehicle aged 10 years or over.

The motor industry benefited greatly from this taxpayer-funded stimulus package. The trick was repeated the following year.

In 2010 ahead of the most talked about and difficult budget for generations, we lobbied the Government for a second time on behalf of the SIMI (Society of the Irish Motor Industry) to retain the scrappage scheme.

The scheme was extended. Another notch on Allen's corporate bedpost was a lobbying campaign aimed at securing more favourable treatment for microbreweries by classifying them as crafts. Brian Cowen subsequently chopped the rate of tax on exotic ales and beers in the 2004 Budget. The industry responded by brewing a special-edition ale called 'Brian's Brew', made with purest Offaly water.

The proposed €350 million incinerator at Poolbeg in Dublin has been the subject of a truly stupendous lobbying campaign by US multi-national firm Covanta, which won the contract to build and operate the rubbish-burning facility. However, the site chosen for the incinerator was bang in the middle of the Dublin South-East constituency of Green TD John Gormley. After he became Environment Minister in 2007, Gormley blocked the licence required for the project to go ahead.

Covanta hired MKC Communications in early 2010, and their campaign saw the US Ambassador Dan Rooney meet with Gormley and later Taoiseach Brian Cowen in July of that year – an unusual diplomatic intervention in a public row over state policy. In January 2011, the *Sunday Business Post* reported that senior Covanta executives had met with Fine Gael leader Enda Kenny and the local Labour TD, Ruairi Quinn. Jens Kragholm, European vice-president of Covanta, expressed the firm's opposition to the levy on incinerated rubbish championed by Gormley. Kragholm told the paper that Covanta hadn't received any assurances from Kenny or Quinn at the 'informal' meeting but that they had been 'sympathetic'. The US firm had indicated that there was 'no way' that the €350 million project would proceed if the threat of the levy remained.

In July 2011, soon after replacing Gormley as Environment Minister, Fine Gael's Phil Hogan scrapped the offending levy. It would later emerge that Kildare property consultant Arthur French, who was employed by Covanta, had played golf at a Fine Gael fund-raiser at the K Club in July 2010. French told the *Irish Times* that he had 'nothing to hide'. He insisted that he had not been hired because he knew Phil Hogan. 'I know an awful lot of politicians better than Phil,' he said. French added that he had never met Hogan over the Poolbeg project. 'There was no need to meet Phil Hogan, he had his mind made up and so had the government. I don't think there was any need for arm-twisting on that one.'

Bringing the US Ambassador into the fray is a nuclear option, but it's one that had been used before. In 2003, Environment Minister Martin Cullen commissioned a consultancy report on litter. The final report proposed an annual €5 million levy on chewing-gum makers, burger joints and ATM machine owners to help bear some of the cost of cleaning up litter. The levy on chewing gum was to be raised by a 5-cent consumer tax on every packet, which would fund the special equipment needed to remove chewing gum from pavements. The giant gum manufacturer Wrigley approached the US Ambassador to Ireland, James Kenny, who set up a meeting between the company, government representatives and himself. Shortly afterwards, the levy was dropped in a spectacular U-turn by Cullen's replacement Dick Roche. Instead of the levy, gum companies agreed to contribute €2 million to an 'information and education campaign' each year.

The education programme was completely useless – and the gum stains remain.

The banks also had a pivotal role in shaping policy related to their industry and challenged decisions that could have threatened the billions of euros they were making in profits before the crash. Former Fianna Fáil general secretary Pat Farrell was the banks' weapon of choice as he headed up the industry lobby group – the Irish Banking Federation.

The banks are savage lobbyists. During the boom, they leaned on the government to reduce regulation, so that they could grow and grow and lend more and more money. And when the economy collapsed and they were bailed out by the taxpayer, they fought tooth and nail to protect their patch. During the boom, the banks lobbied hard for changes in the definition of collateral that could be used as security against their borrowings from international money markets. The banks wanted to be able to issue bonds backed by commercial mortgages, but the Financial Regulator – not generally known for its resistance to the banks' wishes – was dragging its feet on the preparation of legislation, the Asset Covered Securities (ACS) Act, that would have allowed this. A March 2006 letter from the Regulator to the Department of Finance obtained by the *Sunday Business Post* warned that commercial property lending had 'greater inherent volatility by comparison with other asset classes in terms of valuation and default experience'. Anglo and the Irish Banking Federation kicked into gear to put pressure on the Department of Finance. Emails obtained by Kathleen Barrington of the *Sunday Business Post* revealed the red-hot intensity of the lobbying campaign.

Colm Breslin, a senior civil servant in the Department of Finance, fired off an email to Enda Twomey, Pat Farrell's number two at the IBF, on Friday 13 October 2006. 'The IBF is certainly an effective lobby coordinator; we are under seige [sic] from reps from banks about slippages in the ACS time path,' he wrote.

The email came just days after Farrell had written a personal letter to the then Finance Minister, Brian Cowen, expressing his 'disappointment' that the timetable for the legislation had fallen behind schedule. Cowen had also received a barrage of other letters from Anglo chief executive David Drumm, as well as from Austin Jennings, chief executive of Bank of Ireland Global Markets, David Kelly, managing director of AIB Mortgage Bank, and Michael Doherty, managing director of Germany's WestLB. The squeeze was on.

Other letters, released to the *Irish Times* under the Freedom of Information Act, show the intensity of the lobbying and the access the banks had to Cowen. In May 2006, Bank of Ireland boss Brian Goggin wrote to Cowen thanking him for coming to a private dinner at the bank's corporate headquarters and giving his views on the legislation. The banker wrote oleaginously:

> I can honestly say that I find it hard to remember when I have had as enjoyable, insightful and stimulating few hours' discussion. You raised a particularly interesting issue, indeed challenge, on the question of influencing or at least informing the debate on where and how we take forward this great project that is modern Ireland – a place that is so very different and has so much greater potential than earlier generations could have dreamed of.

Goggin described the legislation as 'enlightened and innovative' and a model for the political, public and private sectors. The legislation making it easier for the banks to borrow money was enacted in February 2007.

The banks also helped to kill off new guidelines regarding the fitness and probity of key executives working in the industry. New compliance codes for companies and directors were first proposed in 2000. Lobby groups including the Irish Taxation Institute and the Institution of Chartered Accountants of Ireland joined with the Irish Banking Federation in a move to see these new codes completely kiboshed, or at least watered down. The intensity of this lobbying was highlighted in a report by Central Bank governor Patrick Honohan into what went wrong with Irish financial regulation. The Honohan Report also noted that attempts to control the spread of 100 per cent mortgages being offered by the banks were stymied over threats that competition might suffer: 'Excessive weight was given to this aspect, probably in light of lobbying objections from institutions who feared a diminution in their market share.'

The banks continued to lobby hard even after the economy collapsed and most of the domestic banks came under state control. The issues of personal debt and insolvency were of huge importance to the banks, especially with close to 80,000 mortgages in arrears or being restructured at the start of 2012. The banks were dealing with personal debt problems on a case-by-case basis. In other words, they were taking their time. Any move for a widespread debt resolution system would mean that the banks would have to crystallize losses on their already fragile balance sheets.

Faced with massive losses on mortgages, the banks stepped up the pressure on the government. Stephen Hester, the chief executive of Royal Bank of Scotland (which owns Ulster Bank) travelled to Ireland in April 2012 to meet Finance Minister Michael Noonan and officials in his department. In March 2012, Simon Carswell reported in the *Irish Times* that the IBF had met with the Department of Finance twice and made seven submissions between August 2011 and January 2012, ahead of the proposed legislation on personal insolvency. The department refused to reveal details of the submissions and meetings, citing 'confidentiality'.

The new insolvency regime was expected to be introduced in February 2012, but the intense pressure from the banks saw the drafting of the new legislation delayed. As well as reducing the duration of bankruptcy from twelve years to three, the government's plans focused on the introduction of three types of out-of-court settlement for debtors. The banks wanted the proposed €3 million ceiling for insolvency agreements lowered and they also wanted secured mortgage debt to be left out of the legislation. A report by Deutsche Bank in May 2012, suggesting that Irish banks would need to be bailed out again to the tune of €4 billion due to mortgage defaults, was greeted with horror by the Irish banks. For the first time it was clear that the international markets understood that the banks and the government hadn't faced up to the personal and mortgage debt time bomb.

No amount of lobbying or lunching of key officials can disguise the fact that the personal debt crisis in Ireland is only going to get worse.

The horse-racing and bookmaking lobbies have been an extremely efficient player of politicians over the last decade. The gambling set had a sympathetic ear in Finance Minister Charlie McCreevy. He slashed betting tax from 10 per cent to just 1 per cent over a five-year period. In October 2008, faced with collapsing Exchequer receipts,

Finance Minister Brian Lenihan indicated that he was considering raising betting tax to a modest 2 per cent. The Irish Independent Betting Officers' Association (IIBOA) was in like a shot. Lenihan met with representatives the following month; afterwards he announced that the tax hike, initially scheduled to kick in on 1 January 2009, would be postponed until May 2009. There would also be a review of the industry which would examine how online and phone gambling could be taxed.

Before the May deadline, Lenihan was again buttonholed by the IIBOA. The deadline passed without much comment, and the following month the Department of Finance confirmed that plans to increase the tax rate would not progress that year. The U-turn on betting tax cost the Exchequer more than €30 million that year. That money could have paid for the roll-out of the cervical cancer vaccine, which had been shelved due to lack of funds.

The following year, betting tax was once again highlighted as a potential revenue source for the government. Taoiseach Brian Cowen indicated in May 2010 that betting tax was to be overhauled. A proposal for a 2 per cent levy on winning bets was floated. Paddy Power bookmakers, represented by Drury Communications, described the move as 'insane', and the Irish Bookmakers Association's Sharon Byrne warned that a third of bookie shops would close if the new tax was introduced. The scare tactic worked and the bookies escaped again.

The new Fine Gael–Labour government was less horsey than the last lot. Most of the Labour Party would probably have difficulty telling one end of a nag from another, and Fine Gael Agriculture Minister Simon Coveney told the MacGill Summer School meeting in July 2011 that 'the decision to effectively reduce what was once a 10 per cent betting tax down to 1 per cent, which has resulted in a significant decline in revenue coming from betting tax, was crazy, and I think it should be reversed'. But by the time the December Budget came along, the government's enthusiasm was somewhat weaker. Instead of raising the betting tax, the government decided to extend it to online and phone betting. The move was forecast to raise a modest €14 million.

★

Given that so many TDs in recent years have been publicans or associated with the pub industry, it should probably come as no surprise that Ireland's booze industry has so much clout when it comes to legislation. Companies such as Diageo, Irish Distillers/Pernod Ricard, Heineken and the C&C Group have deep, deep pockets and employ phalanxes of advisers to defend their business from interfering lawmakers.

Advertising booze to kids is clearly not a good thing. But the drinks industry here has been enormously successful at stalling or diverting moves to introduce a blanket ban on advertising. There's a system of self-regulation to make sure that Big Booze doesn't overstep the line. It sounds eerily like the same 'principles-based' regulation that the banks were supposed to be following. This self-regulation involves lots of worthy-sounding initiatives and education programmes, but you can still see Carlsberg ads when Ireland are playing football or during the ad break in *Iron Man*. You'd hardly throw a brick at those audiences without hitting a kid.

Moves to restrict drink advertising on television and cinema started in earnest in 2003, but it took almost two years for the Department of Health – headed by Mary Harney – to endorse the new regime. The government's Alcohol Strategy Task Force recommended major restrictions on advertising, as did a separate government-commissioned report. These were overlooked. In October 2005, John Gormley accused the government of 'kowtowing' to the drinks industry. 'Who calls the shots? Who has the power? Is it the elected representatives or the powerful lobbyists on behalf of the vested interests?' he asked during a heated Dáil debate. Gormley alleged that the recommendations were ignored 'at the behest of the drinks industry', adding that the Alcohol Products Bill had 'mysteriously disappeared' from the list of promised legislation.

The government argued that a complete ban was 'totally impossible', citing a lack of control over satellite television and a lack of consensus in Europe. The limp new voluntary guidelines meant that booze ads could be shown when the number of children watching a show was less than 25 per cent of the total audience. It was tweaked up to 33 per cent before being dropped back to 25 per cent during a review in 2008. The alcohol industry barely broke a sweat.

Speaking at the Sláinte Conference in Ballina in November 2011, former National Alcohol Policy adviser Dr Ann Hope gave her view of what happened when the legislation was being drafted.

> The drinks industry brought all the heavy hitters from America and around the world to Bertie Ahern's desk. They argued they would self-regulate if the legislation was not enacted. That legislation was passed by Cabinet twice, but it never saw the light of the Dáil or the Seanad. That is how powerful they are.

In his 2007 book *The Corporate Takeover of Ireland*, UCD academic Kieran Allen writes:

> The sharpest move that the drinks industry made was to hire MRPA Kinman Communications [MKC] as its lobbying agency . . . Junior Health Minister Sean Power, who happens to be a publican, claimed that the industry was told about the draft law and was asked their opinions. As they agreed to implement an improved voluntary code drawn up under the aegis of the Department of Health, it was decided to 'delay' the introduction of the Bill.

And so it lay, dead to all intents and purposes – until February 2012, when a special report from the National Substance Misuse Strategy Steering Group to the Department of Health recommended that booze advertising be completely banned before 9 p.m. and that a special 'social responsibility' levy be introduced. Lobby group MEAS – Mature Enjoyment of Alcohol in Society – flipped out. The group, which is funded by the drinks industry, withdrew from the final recommendations of the steering group's report and issued its own recommendations. It also claimed that members of the steering group were 'ideologically prejudiced' against MEAS. The report was despatched into the bowels of the Department of Health to be turned into concrete proposals by civil servants. It joins a long line of other reports sitting in civil service in-trays.

The drinks industry is spectacularly well connected with the government. In May, just before the start of Euro 2012, Foreign Affairs Minister Eamon Gilmore togged out for MEAS and its website Drinkaware.ie to launch a guide to healthy boozing at the football championships. Gilmore's high-profile association with the drink industry lobby group came three weeks before his party colleague Roisin Shortall – Minister for State at the Department of Health – announced her plans to ban the alcohol sponsorship of sport. Shortall admitted that the ban mightn't come into effect for five years or more. The government will face a general election before then, and the strength of lobbying from the industry is going to be a serious obstacle to her ambitious plans.

While at the *Sunday Tribune*, Matt Cooper uncovered an extraordinary situation whereby the Fianna Fáil-led government changed legislation to suit one man.

In the early 1990s property developer Ken Rohan was involved in a tax dispute with the Revenue over some splendid artworks in his stately home in Wicklow. The art had been bought by his building company and handed over to him as a benefit in kind. The Revenue challenged this arrangement and handed Rohan a whopper of a bill. He appealed it and won, but the Revenue indicated that it would be going after him for other years and would take the matter to the High Court if initial attempts were unsuccessful. Cooper suggested that the bill could have been as much as €1.5 million.

Rohan organized a comprehensive lobbying campaign and wrote to the then Finance Minister, Bertie Ahern, in October 1993, urging him to introduce an amendment in the upcoming Finance Act. Officials at the Department of Finance drafted a response explaining why Rohan's arguments had been rejected. Despite this advice, Ahern said he wanted an amendment introduced.

It was revealed almost a decade later that Bertie Ahern and the then Taoiseach, Albert Reynolds, had enjoyed a private dinner at Rohan's country home in the months before the 1994 Finance Bill. Another bombshell was that Fianna Fáil fund-raiser Des Richardson – a close associate of Ahern – had been on a lucrative retainer by Rohan for strategic consultancy advice up to 1997.

Revelations about links between lobbyists for Rupert Murdoch's News Corp and the British Culture Secretary Jeremy Hunt during

News Corp's bid to buy out the other shareholders in BSkyB high-lighted the worrying overlaps between big business and politics in the UK. British Prime Minister David Cameron had warned that crony capitalism and the links between powerful corporations and politics were a stain on politics. 'It is the next big scandal waiting to happen. It's an issue that crosses party lines and has tainted our polit-ics for too long, an issue that exposes the far-too-cosy relationship between politics, government, business and money,' he said in February 2010.

In January 2012, the British government announced that it was to introduce a statutory register that must be signed by political lobby-ists when entering the Houses of Parliament. Less imposing was a measure whereby lobbyists had to sign up for a code of conduct. The European Union also has a register that lobbyists must complete, with details of which companies they represent and where they receive funding from. By spring 2012, only a fraction of the key Irish lobby groups had signed up for the register.

The Irish companies or lobbyists that had registered included state agency Enterprise Ireland, which spent 'between €250,000 to €300,000' on 'estimated costs to the organization directly related to representing interests to EU institutions last year'. Also registered were Facebook Ireland, Kellogg's, Eddie O'Connor's Mainstream Renewable, Smurfit Kappa and Irish Ferries. Big Irish companies with pan-European interests such as Ryanair or CRH are not listed in the register, which either means they don't lobby, haven't filled in the forms, or don't lobby under their own name, preferring to use an industry-wide group.

Moves to regulate lobbying in Ireland and to provide some sort of transparency over who is being lobbied and by which vested interest have been unveiled with great enthusiasm by successive govern-ments – and then they've been quietly killed off. In 1999, the Labour Party put forward the Registration of Lobbyists Bill in the Seanad. It was voted down by the government on the grounds that insufficient research and consideration of the issue of lobbying had been con-ducted in the country – which has got to be up there with 'the dog ate my homework' as one of the lamest excuses of all time.

The appearance of Frank Dunlop at the Flood Tribunal led to noises about regulation of lobbyists – even from Fianna Fáil. In April 2000, former Fianna Fáil minister Michael O'Kennedy called for the creation of a register of lobbyists. The move was echoed by Labour's Ruairi Quinn, who offered to 'work constructively' with the government on his party's own Registration of Lobbyists Bill. That May, it emerged that the Attorney General, Michael McDowell, had started to draft legislation on the establishment of a register of lobbyists. The Cabinet had agreed at a pre-Easter meeting to move forward with the legislation. However, the Fianna Fáil-led government insisted on moving forward with the legislation on an all-party basis – a nice idea in theory, but a sure-fire way to bog it down in practice.

According to a government statement in December 2000:

> . . . it is the Government's intention to introduce a regulation and registration system for those who operate on a paid basis as lobbyists in one form or another seeking to exert influence on political and public service decision making.

But the legislation was mothballed ahead of the 2002 election.

In July 2003, Environment Minister Martin Cullen said he was considering proposals to regulate public relations consultants and lobbyists with access to the key decision makers in government and the civil service. The Institute of Public Administration was asked to investigate and produced a report in March 2004. The following year, an all-party committee of TDs and senators was asked to examine how the state should regulate lobbying activities. Death by all-party committee. The proposed legislation eventually lapsed when the government's term ended in 2007.

In 2006, DCU academics Raj Chari and Gary Murphy were asked by the Department of the Environment to examine the lobbying industry in Ireland and abroad. Their final report recommended the establishment of a register of lobbyists. In September 2006 a Department for the Environment spokesman said that the findings 'were still being considered'.

The Green Party's 2007 general election manifesto included a pledge to establish a national register of lobbyists, which would detail the company, clients and interests being represented. When Fianna Fáil and the Progressive Democrats were unable to form an overall majority, the Greens were invited into the tent. Following intense negotiations, a programme for government was introduced. On the very last page was a commitment to 'consider' legislation to regulate lobbyists. Within months of taking up office, leaks coming from John Gormley's Department for the Environment indicated that officials were working on plans for new regulation.

Labour had proposed legislation on lobbyists from the Opposition benches in 1999 (twice), 2000, 2003 and 2008, and in March 2010 Fine Gael's New Politics document included a proposal to register all lobbyists and to ensure that their activities were overseen by the Standards in Public Office Commission. With the greatest of respect to SIPO, it has as much clout as a ball of cotton wool. SIPO has no powers to sanction those who refuse to provide it with information or documents, and has no investigative powers of its own. Fine Gael's 2010 proposals included plans to remedy both of these glaring weaknesses in SIPO.

Within weeks of taking power, Enda Kenny promised 'decisive action' to sever the links between big business and politics, in order to restore public confidence in government. The report of the Moriarty Tribunal had raised all kinds of questions about Fine Gael's handling of a donation from Denis O'Brien in the 1990s, and Enda needed to regain the moral high ground for the party. Defending Fine Gael from Opposition barbs, Kenny said that the new government had committed itself to a range of measures designed to clean up politics. These measures included introducing the necessary 'legal and constitutional provisions' to ban corporate donations to political parties and to reduce the threshold of donations to election candidates. The new government also promised to introduce a statutory register of lobbyists and a set of rules governing the practice of lobbying. Other measures to be introduced included whistle-blower legislation and new rules to ensure that no minister or senior public servants could work in any area of the private sector involving a potential conflict of interest with their previous job for at least two years after leaving the public service.

Two months later, in June 2011, Labour Minister for Communications Pat Rabbitte told the Public Relations Awards dinner that new legislation to improve transparency by introducing a register of lobbyists was being considered by the government. Rabbitte said that he did not think that lobbying should be prohibited but that the public had a right to know who was lobbying the government, Oireachtas and public servants to change the laws. Brendan Howlin's Department of Public Expenditure opened a 'public consultation' on the registration of lobbyists, which closed in February 2012. The department asked for submissions about what should be in the new legislation. It wanted to know what kind of information should be disclosed by the lobbying firms and whether all the information should be made public automatically, such as by posting all contacts between lobbyists and officials or ministers online. The fifty-odd submissions made by lobbyists and lobbying companies were united on one fact – the legislation should not hinder contact between lobbyists and the people they seek to lobby.

The lobbyists spotted a number of opportunities to blur and confuse the issues. This is what they are paid good money to do. The phrase 'commercial sensitivity' is one of the great excuses for a lack of transparency. NAMA uses it with aplomb. It's a get-out clause for refusing many freedom of information requests. Lobbyists have also made sure that details of dealings with civil servants and politicians that are commercially sensitive will need to be considered carefully. In others words, kept quiet.

The spinners and elbow-tuggers also raised concerns over the definition of a lobbyist and the role of a lobbyist. The submissions to the Department of Public Expenditure included one from business lobby group Irish Business and Employers Confederation, which suggested that the term 'lobbyist' be scrapped altogether. IBEC also proposed a model whereby trade associations – such as IBEC – could be left out of any register 'on the basis that it is clear whom and what they represent'.

In any case, the creation of a register of lobbyists wouldn't guarantee transparency. Not by a long shot. Australia introduced a register of lobbyists in 1983 following a scandal involving a parliamentary lobbyist who was close to Labour government ministers. He was caught having an affair with a KGB spy, leading to fears that his close links to the top echelons of politics had created a national security risk. Lobbyists were required to notify the Lobbyist Registrar whenever they took on a new client and lobbied ministers or politicians. It soon became clear that the rules were being ignored. The register was abolished in 1996 by the Australian government. A new system, which put the onus on politicians to act ethically, was introduced instead.

What are the chances of such a system being introduced – and followed – in Ireland? The incoming new regulations to improve transparency over dealings between big business, lobbyists and key decision makers will have enough holes to drive a bus through them.

While hiring lobbyists is one way to get a foot in the door to influence policy, donating cash to political parties also buys access. Elections are expensive and the party with the most money invariably punches above its weight. When Enda Kenny got his hands on the Fine Gael joystick in 2002 he reversed the cash-strapped party's ban on receiving corporate donations. That stance was reaffirmed in 2010, when the party was preparing its proposals on political reform. Phil Hogan said that the party 'agree with companies being able to support political parties to the limits that they have been up to now'.

Then, suddenly, there was a dramatic U-turn. During the general election campaign, Fine Gael completely changed its tune, falling in behind the other political parties. Corporate donations were now not such a good thing. It was a cynical volte-face, but Fine Gael did what it had to do to get elected.

In early 2012, new legislation was brought in reducing limits on corporate donations from €6,350 to €2,500 for a party donation and falling from €2,540 to €1,000 for contributions to individual politicians. The threshold above which donations must be declared also fell, from €5,080 to €1,500 for a political party and from €635 to €600 for an individual. Incredibly, Fine Gael did not receive a single reportable corporate donation between 2002 (when Enda Kenny became party leader) and 2010 – according to its declarations to SIPO.

SIPO reported that:

> The total value of donations disclosed by parties during 2010 was €67,907.55, the lowest amount disclosed since the introduction of the disclosure requirement 14 years ago. None of the three main political parties (Fianna Fáil, Fine Gael nor the Labour Party) disclosed any donations in 2010.

A February 2012 investigation by the *Irish Independent* found that between 2001 and 2010, private companies made €725,000 in political donations to all the main parties, according to details contained in their accounts and annual returns lodged with the Companies Registration Office. Various well-known businesses had declared donations of €66,000 to Fine Gael in their company accounts between 2001 and 2010. Over the same period of time, just €228,000 in corporate donations was declared to SIPO by the various political parties. That's a gap of €497,000. While this gap in disclosures is presumably down to parties not having to declare donations from companies of less than €2,500 a pop, it highlights the problem of the regulations over political funding. There's very little transparency. We simply don't know which powerful corporate interests donated close to €500,000 to political parties over the last decade.

Some of the major donors have included details of the payments to political parties in their accounts. Developer Pat Doherty's Harcourt Group and its Airscape subsidiary donated €212,000 to political parties over the period, split between Fianna Fáil, Fine Gael, Labour and the Progressive Democrats. But if you'd only looked at the SIPO filings by the political parties you'd have gained a very different picture of Harcourt's largesse. The filings with SIPO only disclose donations of €20,000 by Harcourt. The remaining €192,000 was obviously donated in sums that were under the disclosable threshold.

Another developer, Sean Mulryan's Ballymore Group, donated €114,000 to political parties over the 2001–2010 period. The parties disclosed €22,000 of these donations to SIPO.

The fact that legislation to regulate lobbyists has been kicking around Leinster House since 1999 without ever seeing the light of day does not fill one with confidence about the fate of current efforts. The ambitious plans to reform politics proposed by Fine Gael and Labour while in Opposition will be stretched and spun. Transparency will become blurred. There'll be more 'consultation' and even a report or two. But in the long run these fine plans will be fudged.

It didn't take long: Fine Gael and Labour have already turned into Fianna Fáil.

4. Land of 999 Quangos

In June 2011, RTÉ reported that the average salary at the National Treasury Management Agency in 2010 – in the middle of a recession – had hit €100,000, and that bonuses in that year had totalled €2 million. The average bonus was €7,700. Fourteen staff at the agency, which borrows money on behalf of the state on international markets, were paid more than €250,000. In the face of public anger at the revelations, the nine most senior NTMA executives waived their bonuses. But the genie was out of the bottle.

Michael Somers, who had led the agency from its creation in 1990 until 2009, was asked by RTÉ's Aine Lawlor about having been paid over €1 million in 2008. He was uncharacteristically gauche: 'Well, what I'd say to that, in that regard, is I kept the country running and solvent for the nineteen years that I ran the NTMA.' He went on smugly, 'And if they didn't want me, they didn't have to have me. I mean I had plenty of other job offers and I could have gone off. As indeed could have the others that were working for me.' It was breathtaking, showing an arrogance hitherto unseen from the smooth-tongued Somers, who had always been skilled at handling the media. For years, his annual briefings about the performance of the NTMA were legendary, creating the impression that the state's sovereign borrowing was in the hands of a wizard. Now he was coming under harsher scrutiny – but he was an untouchable.

Somers was always strangely secretive about his own salary and jealously guarded the tradition that the pay packages of his legion of well-paid disciples remained under wraps. Traditional mandarins were deeply suspicious that the creation of a semi-detached agency to handle treasury functions previously covered by the Department of Finance was a wheeze aimed at facilitating the more ambitious public servants in the department to command private-sector pay without sacrificing public-sector benefits. That may explain why, to this day – apart from the chief executive – the details of the remuneration of the NTMA elite remains a closely guarded secret. The Minister for Finance answers parliamentary questions on the subject by restricting himself to spelling out the number of employees earning specified levels of pay within certain brackets.

Somers had reason to be secretive. His own pay rate was in the stratosphere compared with others in the public service. In 2008 he made a salary of €565,000, a bonus of €403,000, and €30,000 for his work as a commissioner of the National Pensions Reserve Fund. The NTMA itself was not subject to the Freedom of Information Act. Like the Central Bank, for years it had escaped proper media or parliamentary scrutiny. Somers' salary was revealed only because a freedom of information request had snared a piece of correspondence with the NTMA. When the Department of Finance eventually agreed to release the figures, Somers appealed the decision to the Information Commissioner, Emily O'Reilly.

O'Reilly blew a fuse. She was adamant that Somers' remuneration should be released. She was highly critical of the way Somers' package had been arranged, describing the process as 'extraordinary'. Apparently the Minister for Finance, Brian Lenihan, had met with the head of the agency's remuneration committee, David Byrne, and agreed a figure. O'Reilly was surprised that there was no paper trail supporting the discussion and that there were no officials present at the Byrne–Lenihan meeting. Worse still, the department could not release Somers' pay for 2007 because there was no record of it in their files. Questions began to be asked about this previously unexplored empire. Doubts arose about its constant pleas that commercial considerations meant it needed protection. More pertinently, observers began to ask whether Somers' frantic defence of information about his salary carried any message about the selectivity, the accuracy and the angles of other news being spun out by Auntie Mae.

The NTMA was set up to manage the national debt. Somers, its first chief executive, was an enthusiast for the project. He believed that an independent specialist outfit was needed to ensure that the Irish state secured the best possible interest rates on its borrowings, and low-risk diversification of currency exposure. It would need to be staffed by people who had, or could develop, sound global contacts in the securities industry and operate effectively in the global debt markets.

The Department of Finance was bitterly opposed to the proposal of a stand-alone agency. They wanted to keep debt management within their Merrion Street fortress. But Somers won the argument. The Taoiseach of the day, Charles Haughey, was convinced that there were savings to be made in tighter debt management.

Somers loved the limelight and became the agency's public face. He was brilliant at news management. Annually, around the turn of the year, he called a press conference. Almost inevitably, with a proud but puzzled Minister for Finance sitting beside him, he announced how Ireland and the NTMA had once again beaten its target on debt saving in the previous year. He had saved the nation millions by shrewd management of the debt. A grateful minister basked in Somers' reflected glory. A grateful nation nodded. The minister had been handed a few extra million to dispense.

Hardly anyone, and probably least of all the various finance ministers who gloried in Somers' performance at these media events, knew the difference between a derivative and a donkey. Somers held their hands, year after year, as he steered them through the maze of hedging, options, warrants and the jargon of the financial jungle. The cameras clicked, the hacks scribbled. The public had no notion what was going on. The media, starved for a story in the post-Christmas period, parked their critical faculties as Somers filled their empty news pages that had threatened to interrupt their seasonal celebrations.

After Somers stepped down from the NTMA, the state and the bankers looked after him royally. In January 2010 he was initially appointed a 'public interest' director of the newly nationalized AIB at a basic fee of €27,375 a year plus €3,000 for each committee meeting he attended. Six months later, he was made deputy chairman at a rate of €150,000 a year.

After the earthquake in Ireland's financial world, Somers' retirement from the NTMA was the ideal opportunity to hire a global hotshot to run the agency. Hell would freeze over first. John Corrigan, an ex-AIB man who had worked at the agency since the early 1990s, seamlessly sailed into Somers' shoes. The minister's announcement of Somers' exit and Corrigan's assumption into the job came in the same press release that announced Somers' arrival on the board of state-owned AIB.

In 2011, the state set up an agency called NewERA, under the aegis of the NTMA, to handle the selling of state assets. Corrigan recruited Eileen Fitzpatrick, another NTMA insider, to head it up. There was no competitive process. There were no interviews. Fitzpatrick's qualifications for the post were not immediately apparent.

When asked by Shane Ross, during a hearing of the Dáil's Public Accounts Committee, about Fitzpatrick's skills in the sale of state assets, Corrigan quietly exploded: 'The manner in which you have criticized the person personally, both in the Dáil yesterday and in your Sunday newspaper column, have been a source of great disquiet to me.' He did not mention that Fitzpatrick's skills were in investment management. The only person whom he admitted to having consulted about the appointment of Fitzpatrick to this lucrative post was none other than the king of the quangos himself, David Byrne, who, among other things, was the chairman of the NTMA's advisory committee. Byrne was the man who approved Somers' €1 million package. Byrne was the man who had approved Corrigan's original remuneration of €490,000 plus a possible €390,000 bonus. He was not likely to demur at the promotion of an insider.

David Byrne was the poor man's Peter Sutherland. Like Suds, he became a senior counsel before he hit forty; like Suds, he was hauled out of the Law Library to be Attorney General. His appointment after Bertie Ahern came to power in 1997 followed a report he wrote confirming that St Luke's, Ahern's constituency office in Drumcondra, belonged to the party, not to Bertie himself, as had been alleged. His findings would have been a relief to Ahern.

Like Suds, Byrne did not linger long in the AG's office. His patron had higher things in mind for his protégé. When a vacancy arose in the European Commission in 1999 with the retirement of Padraig Flynn, Bertie handed the position to Byrne.

Byrne made way for Charlie McCreevy after one term in Brussels.

Just like Suds, upon his return he saw the doors of Ireland's board-rooms opening for him. The offers came tumbling in. Byrne grabbed them with gratitude. One of the first was the boardroom of Irish Life & Permanent, a seemingly safe haven when he arrived in 2004, but a bed of nails by the time he departed in 2008. There is absolutely no sign that Byrne spotted the dangers looming for the company that today stands virtually worthless.

A year later, he picked up board membership of the building-materials firm Kingspan, which had strong Fianna Fáil connections – among its other board members was former cabinet minister Rory O'Hanlon. The third public company to offer him rich rewards was DCC, which he joined in January 2009 as deputy chairman at a fee of €103,000 a year. DCC was highly profitable, but still recovering from the debacle which had overshadowed it for several years – the insider-dealing case that had haunted its chief executive, Jim Flavin.

Meanwhile, since December 2007, Byrne had been chair of the NTMA Advisory Committee. Byrne was not involved in the day-to-day business of debt management or investment. His job was to decide matters such as the remuneration of the highly paid bosses of Auntie Mae. Like many chairmen, Byrne always seemed to be in a generous mood when presiding over the remuneration committee. Basic salaries for its senior executives would have made many bankers blush. Bonuses had ballooned over the years since the NTMA's launch in 1990. The beneficiaries regarded themselves as a public-service elite with skills unmatched by others. They had managed to convince the gullible public of their magical financial powers and persuaded politicians that they would steer the economy to shore in any storm.

David Byrne was not the only political protégé on the NTMA Advisory Committee. Beside him sat none other than Hugh Cooney, the chairman of Enterprise Ireland, another quango with an inflated reputation that tends to deflect criticism by accusing critics of national sabotage. Hugh Cooney was a retired accountant with credentials that certainly qualified him for the NTMA Audit Committee, but he was also an Offaly man and a donor to the election effort of Brian Cowen, who was Minister for Finance at the time of Cooney's appointment.

Cooney had succeeded a long line of Fianna Fáil supporters when he joined the board of the Aon McDonagh Boland Group, a financial services company that has shown a distinct preference for Soldiers of Destiny. Among Cooney's predecessors on that board were former Fianna Fáil Taoiseach Albert Reynolds, former Fianna Fáil Minister for Finance Ray MacSharry and Paddy Wright, the Smurfit boss with strong Fianna Fáil family connections.

So the Fianna Fáil party kept loyal nominees on Auntie Mae's board while stoutly protesting this giant quango's independence from government. It was theoretically working in the national interest and did not become openly involved in political controversies. However, in 2012 it entered the referendum campaign when Finance Minister Michael Noonan announced that the NTMA was advising that a no vote would cut the state off from borrowing at an affordable rate. Noonan insisted that the advice was 'independent' – but it happily coincided with his own views. According to the *Irish Independent* this was the 'first time that the NTMA has been brought into a European referendum campaign'.

Auntie Mae stood at the head of a big quango family. Its most important offspring was the National Pensions Reserve Fund (NPRF), created by Finance Minister Charlie McCreevy in March 2001. McCreevy directed that 1 per cent of gross national product be put into the fund annually. Fearing that future governments would loot the national nest egg, he made it illegal for any administration to raid the piggy bank. (McCreevy's mistrust of his successors proved prescient when Brian Cowen and Brian Lenihan legislated to plunder the fund when they needed to bail out the banks.)

McCreevy took appointments to state boards more seriously than many other politicians. Seeking credibility, he filled the National Pensions Reserve Fund's first board with civil servants and foreigners. Eyebrows were raised among his party colleagues when they spotted such juicy spoils of political war lost to non-combatants (mostly mandarins and experts). But McCreevy could not resist appointing the head of pharmaceutical company Elan Corporation, Donal Geaney, to the chair of the NPRF. Geaney was a Fianna Fáil supporter; he was also a director of the Bank of Ireland with ambitions for the governorship. His friendship with former Fianna Fáil government press secretary P. J. Mara was no secret in business circles. He had already enjoyed political patronage as chairman of the Irish Aviation Authority. Donal aspired to join the insiders. Guys with such ambitions rarely rock political boats. He ticked all the conventional boxes.

Geaney died young in 2005, by which time McCreevy had been exiled to Brussels. It was Brian Cowen's turn to appoint his successor. His choice for this highly sensitive €51,424-a-year job was Paul Carty. In 1990, Carty had been appointed to the inaugural board of the NTMA. Albert Reynolds was the minister responsible for the appointment, but such a crucial board would never have been approved without the imprimatur of the Taoiseach, Charles Haughey. And Carty and Haughey went way back. Between 1971 and 1987, Carty had been a partner in Haughey Boland, the accountancy firm founded by the former Taoiseach before it merged with Deloitte & Touche and dropped the controversial part of its name. Between 1985 and 1992, Carty was also a director of Haughey's son Ciaran's company Celtic Helicopters.

Carty would go on to be a star witness before both the McCracken and Moriarty Tribunals as they traced the way that Haughey Boland – later Deloitte & Touche – organized a bill-paying service for Haughey. Evidence was given that Haughey's bagman, Des Traynor, made regular and substantial payments to Paul Carty. Carty in turn used the funds to meet various bills due for the ex-Taoiseach. He told the Moriarty Tribunal that he had paid a total of €901,514 on behalf of Haughey between 1 August 1988 and 31 January 1991. His evidence at the tribunal had clashed with Haughey's when the ex-Taoiseach insisted that Carty had been acting 'in loco parentis' for the company. Carty denied it, declaring that he was merely taking instructions from a client. After Judge McCracken reported that there were possible misconduct cases to be answered, the Institute of Chartered Accountants of Ireland (ICAI) appointed High Court

Judge John Blayney to conduct an inquiry. Carty was initially informed that there was a prima facie case to answer. He subsequently successfully appealed the adverse findings against him. Accordingly, there were no findings against him personally. His firm Deloitte, however, was reprimanded for lack of objectivity in work for the Dunnes Stores group and censured for lapses in not seeking independent advice in the case of Celtic Helicopters.

Carty's high profile at the two tribunals and his closeness to Haughey and Traynor guaranteed that he was an audacious choice for the chair of the €14 billion pensions reserve fund, but Cowen was never one to worry too much about charges of cronyism. Carty's appointment was for five years. In 2010, when Cowen was still Taoiseach and Lenihan was Minister for Finance, he was reappointed for another five-year term. By the time he leaves office he will probably have scooped more than €500,000 in fees from Ireland's heavily depleted national pension fund.

Perversely, ordinary directors of the fund are even more generously rewarded than the board members of their parent, the NTMA, taking an annual fee of no less than €34,000 a year. They include a one-time Fianna Fáil TD and senator, Dr Brian Hillery, and a banker favoured by the Fianna Fáil government, Maurice Keane, the former Bank of Ireland chief who enjoys further state patronage with his €99,360 per annum directorship of Anglo Irish Bank. Professor Frances Ruane – the director of another quango, the ESRI – was appointed as one of the watchdogs over this fragile state asset despite her bruising experience with the German bank DEPFA. She had been a non-executive director of the IFSC-based outfit that had collapsed in 2008, costing the German taxpayer well over €100 billion.

The largesse of the NTMA is contagious. Frank Daly, the government's pet chairman, has graduated rapidly from the chair of the Revenue Commissioners – firstly to the chair of Anglo Irish Bank, then to the chair of the National Asset Management Agency (NAMA), yet another part of Auntie Mae's empire. NAMA and the NTMA inhabit the same home, the modern Treasury Building in Dublin's Grand Canal Street, and the NTMA is obliged to provide NAMA with staff and business support services as required. Daly commands

€150,000 a year in fees from NAMA. His colleagues on the NAMA board have seen a steep hike in their remuneration – up to €60,000 a year – despite the austerity being imposed elsewhere in the public service.

When the new government took over in 2011, the NTMA was crying out for change. Here was a state monolith combining bankers' salaries with a code of secrecy. It should have been top of the hit list for Enda Kenny's new government.

The Taoiseach's words about the NTMA in the Dáil did not suggest much of an appetite for surgery. He asserted – without a jot of evidence – that the NTMA 'has done a very good job'. He approved the appointment of Eileen Fitzpatrick, describing her as 'very eminently qualified'. He was singing from the same hymn sheet as Corrigan. Kenny had an opportunity, taking office at a moment of national crisis and austerity, to insist that there were no sacred cows among the quangos; that all salaries would be made public; that appointments to senior positions would be advertised; and that all state bodies would be subject to the Freedom of Information Act.

The new Taoiseach bottled it. A tribal politician to the last, he instinctively retreated. He stood four-square behind the old ways of doing things. We shouldn't have been surprised; but Fine Gael – even more than Labour – had fuelled high expectations of a full-frontal attack on waste and cronyism in semi-states and beyond. More than eighteen months before the election, at the MacGill Summer School in Glenties, Co. Donegal, Richard Bruton (Fine Gael's spokesman on enterprise) had flown one of those unnecessary, but memorable, kites that Opposition spokesmen tend to fly when seeking attention. Speaking to an astonished audience of influential opinion formers, Bruton promised that Fine Gael would replace the membership of all state boards within six months of taking office.

Bruton's kite came two years after the publication of a well-argued report written by another Fine Gael frontbencher, Leo Varadkar, that had examined the 'land of a thousand quangos', condemned the mushrooming of state bodies under Bertie Ahern, and proposed remedies. Varadkar promised that not only would Fine Gael initiate the abolition of some quangos and the mergers of others, but it would also make agencies submit prospective chairpersons and chief executive officers for questioning before Dáil committees. He identified 2,416 political nominees on the boards of state agencies, and he specifically singled out two NTMA offspring – the National Pensions Reserve Fund and the National Development Finance Agency – as not being covered by the Freedom of Information Act. His report promised root-and-branch changes.

Fianna Fáil looked upon such reformist zeal with tribal scepticism. They knew that they were destined to lose office, but suspected that the quangos would survive. So convinced were they that Bruton's threat was political sabre rattling that they repeated the cynical exercise practised by governments of all political colours since the state was founded. In their dying days in power in March 2011, they prepared for Opposition with a final gesture of defiance, stuffing the vacancies on the state agencies with party loyalists. According to John Drennan in the *Sunday Independent*, they fixed up over a hundred supporters in the last days of their regime. Former TD Dermot Fitzpatrick was one of the lucky ones, securing a seat on the Dublin Dental Hospital Board. Leitrim Fianna Fáil councillor Mary Bohan was rewarded with a seat on the Health and Safety Authority (HSA) while Donegal Fianna Fáil activist David Alcorn was given a term on the National Roads Authority (NRA). Fianna Fáil trustee Richie Howlin was reappointed to the chair of the National Building Agency. Minister Pat Carey appointed Jim Donlon, his own top constituency organizer, on to the NRA board. He facilitated outgoing Finance Minister Brian Lenihan when he named former Fianna Fáil TD Marian McGennis to the boardroom at Dublin Bus. Outgoing Taoiseach Brian Cowen would not have been displeased when Carey landed Offaly councillor Peter Ormond at the top table at An Post with a €16,000-a-year stipend. Fellow Offaly councillor Danny Owens hit the boardroom of the Irish Sports Council.

The governing bodies of institutes of technology were injected with fresh Fianna Fáil blood. Even Fianna Fáil's puritanical coalition partners, the Greens, joined in the orgy of patronage after they announced that they were leaving government. Of the first thirty-five appointments made by the government after the Greens had signalled their exit, twenty came from party leader John Gormley's Department of the Environment. Fianna Fáil and the Greens were throwing down a gauntlet to the new government: remove our legion of last-minute nominees or hold your tongues. They were calling the Fine Gael/Labour bluff.

Fine Gael and Labour huffed and puffed about the abuse of patronage by a government without a mandate. When, in early Dáil exchanges, the new Taoiseach was asked about the political appointments, he expressed his horror at what had happened. Yet, ominously, the solemn promises to reverse the Fianna Fáil cronies' appointments were conspicuously missing. Kenny took refuge in the old safety net of seeking legal opinion. He would ask the new Attorney General, Máire Whelan, for advice on the consequences of sacking the gang of late arrivals to the quango boards. He was wobbling.

The wobble was followed by the cop-out. The Attorney General's advice came back within a week. Kenny mournfully told the Dáil that long legal battles might ensue if he took such extreme measures. He condemned the naked cronyism with wild words, but no action. The Fianna Fáil nominees were safe for their full five-year terms.

Leo Varadkar made a gesture. The new Minister for Transport, the man who had led the anti-quango crusade, wrote to six of the Fianna Fáil nominees appointed by Carey asking them to step aside in the national interest. One poor innocent, the only non-political nominee, took him at his word and resigned. The others, more battle-hardened, held their ground. The minister is believed to have received some defiant replies.

The Fine Gael–Labour coalition, with its promise of a new politics, still had an opportunity to cleanse the system of patronage. It was open to them to introduce a new way of making appointments to state bodies. On Wednesday 13 April 2011, an innocent-looking press release was issued by the Department of Agriculture. The new Fine Gael minister Simon Coveney confirmed the appointment of a man called Phil Meaney to the €21,600-a-year (plus expenses) part-time gig as chairman of Bord na gCon, the Irish Greyhound Board. Coveney described Meaney as 'eminently well qualified'. He went on to outline Meaney's 'successful business background and his involvement in the greyhound industry over a period of twenty-five years, including his recently held position as chairman of the Kilkenny Greyhound Company'.

There was one big omission in Coveney's eulogy. Meaney was also chairman of something else. During the 2011 election campaign he was chairman of Fine Gael's strategy group in Carlow-Kilkenny, the constituency that had delivered three seats out of five to Fine Gael in the general election just seven weeks earlier. Fine Gael had good reason for showing instant gratitude to Meaney, as the party had only won a single seat in the constituency just four years earlier. Carlow-Kilkenny was also the stronghold of Fine Gael's Phil Hogan, arguably the most powerful member of the parliamentary party after the Taoiseach. Kenny was deeply in debt to Big Phil, who had stood by him during the attempted putsch within the party in 2010 and had played a crucial part in saving his skin. Hogan was in an impregnable position to ask for a payback.

Pat Deering, one of Fine Gael's elected TDs from the constituency, let the cat out of the bag when he admitted that he had lobbied for Meaney. Coveney admitted that he had been lobbied, but insisted unconvincingly that such tactics made no difference. Meaney's Fine Gael connections 'were not a factor', he insisted.

It was game on. Politics were back to normal.

In the autumn, Coveney promoted another familiar blueshirt to a key position. Brody Sweeney, the well-known sandwich entrepreneur, was made a director of Bord Bia, the Irish Food Board. The press release referred to six appointees; the name of the new chairman, Michael Carey, was buried in the middle. No explanation or biography was given for any of them, except a brief two-liner about the chairman. There was no reference to the fact that Brody Sweeney had been a candidate for Fine Gael in 2007, having joined the party two years earlier. His arrival in Fine Gael was a gesture of faith, at a time when Enda Kenny's fortunes and those of the party were at a low ebb. Enda was proud of his new recruit, parading him as living proof that successful business people believed in Fine Gael. He owed Brody big time.

Sweeney caught the political bug. He worked night and day to win a seat in Dublin North-East, but flopped at the general election, coming sixth out of eight candidates for the three-seater.

Brody's excursion into politics is widely believed to have caused him to take his eye off the ball of his once flourishing business, the O'Brien's Irish Sandwich Bars chain. Nevertheless it came as a major shock to Irish business when the company went into liquidation in 2009. Brody, on his uppers, was delighted to be appointed to the Bord Bia job. He openly admitted in a letter to the *Sunday Independent*, 'I lobbied everyone I knew in Fine Gael to get it.'

Among the other five Bord Bia appointees was a man named Gary Brown, of Below the Line Marketing. Brown had given a donation to Ruairi Quinn, now Labour's Minister for Education. Labour supporters needed to be looked after, too. No mention was made of Brown's generous support for the democratic process.

But perhaps the highest-profile piece of patronage among the early appointments of the new government was bestowed by Leo Varadkar, once the scourge of the quangos.

Ministers are not always masters of their own domains when it comes to appointments to bodies under their own department. Sometimes they are obliged to appoint someone else's cronies. All appointments are approved by the Taoiseach. And it was presumably at the behest of Enda Kenny that Leo Varadkar appointed Bernard Allen, a former Fine Gael TD and an old crony of Kenny's, to the Irish Sports Council. Allen had retired from the Dáil in 2011 after thirty years of loyal service to Fine Gael and two short periods as a minister of state. He had been chairman of the Public Accounts Committee in his final term. Above all, like Phil Hogan, he had rallied to Enda Kenny when the putsch against the leader was being plotted.

Allen was not a bad appointment. He had been a minister of state with responsibility for sport. He was amiable and popular. He had promised not to take any fees. He even came through the public applications process to win the prize. But no one would ever believe that – as the final decision rested with the Fine Gael minister – Allen's political pedigree was not a significant factor. The appointment was

a clear early message to the troops that the Fine Gael tribe was looking after its own warriors. Nothing had changed except the identity
of the dispensers of patronage. It was Fine Gael's turn. Allen would
never have been given this job by Fianna Fáil.

Two of Varadkar's nominees to the Road Safety Authority (RSA),
chaired by broadcaster Gay Byrne, raised Opposition eyebrows.
Ronan Melvin, a constituent of Varadkar's who nominated a Fine
Gael candidate, Kieran Dennison, in the 2009 local elections, and
Sean Finan, a regional organizer for Fine Gael in Roscommon, both
found themselves designated to save lives on the roads. They were
enriched by €8,100 a year. Finan's CV on the RSA website is full of
his commitment to 'voluntary and community' organizations and
highlights his involvement with Macra na Feirme, but his loyalty to
another 'voluntary' organization, Fine Gael, is somehow omitted.

Opposition mumbling over such appointments was par for the
course, but, more worryingly for the Cabinet, the *Irish Times* took up
the cudgel. Paul Cullen, a senior member of the paper's political staff,
listed twenty-one party sympathizers, supporters or donors who had
already received rewards when the coalition was barely eight months
in office.

The new Minister for the Arts, Jimmy Deenihan, took the opportunity of his first taste of office to promote two long-standing party
loyalists to the board of the National Concert Hall. Deenihan found
room for Pat Heneghan, a Fine Gael 'national handler' from way
back in the eighties, on the board. Heneghan's musical expertise was
not initially apparent although, late in life, he had married Deirdre
O'Callaghan, one of Ireland's most talented harpists. Heneghan was
joined on the board of the concert hall by the theologian Gina
Menzies, a former Fine Gael councillor and Senate candidate.

Fine Gael was not the only party plundering the spoils. Cullen discovered that Labour's Minister for Communications and Energy, Pat
Rabbitte, had been filling a few slots with old party warhorses.
Labour Party Treasurer James Wrynn (no stranger to the joys of the
semi-states since his spell as deputy chair of the ESB) headed for
the board of An Post at a fee of €15,760 a year, while Bride Rosney,

one-time adviser to Labour presidential candidate Mary Robinson, was given a seat on the board of EirGrid at a fee of €12,600.

Even Minister for Justice Alan Shatter, a man who had loudly charged Fianna Fáil with cronyism, was not shy about using his patronage powers to reward those who had shown him generosity at elections. His decision to name Oliver Connolly as a liaison for whistle-blowers in An Garda Síochána in June 2011 when he was barely three months in office, at a fee of €12,500, caused uproar. Connolly – the founder of Friary Law, which had developed a family mediation model with Shatter – had donated €1,000 to Shatter's election campaign in 2007. Shatter protested that Connolly's donation had 'no connection' with his appointment. 'Nobody has ever suggested,' he thundered, 'that an individual who contributes to democratic politics in this country should be discriminated against, pilloried and excluded from ever being appointed to any body whatsoever.'

Shatter's words echoed the utterances of Fianna Fáil apologists for cronyism six months earlier. This time it was Fianna Fáil's turn to protest. Their outrage had a point, but it was a bit rich coming from them. Connolly belonged in a similar category to Bernard Allen. They were both well qualified. Both came through a public selection process but were eventually selected by the relevant minister. Quite apart from the question of why Connolly was chosen, the appointment – like many such appointments – raised the possibility of a real or perceived conflict of interest. Any Garda whistle-blower has the potential to cause difficulties for the Minister for Justice. Where would Connolly, with his political and professional links to the minister, stand if he was forced to adjudicate on the merits of such a case?

As a pre-Christmas gift Shatter gave Declan O'Neill, another of his donors, a peach of a present: the keenly sought-after position of Taxing Master, a €145,000-a-year appointment described by the Citizens Information Bureau as providing an 'independent and impartial assessment of legal costs' for individuals involved in litigation. O'Neill, who had done legal work for the minister's own law firm, Gallagher Shatter, had also donated €1,000 to Shatter's 2007 election campaign.

Fianna Fáil sat back, exulting in the new government's conversion to the bad old ways of dealing with ministerial appointments. There were few speeches of condemnation from the Soldiers of Destiny. The government was enjoying a relatively free run because the main Opposition party was paralysed by its own past.

Fine Gael had spelled out its proposals for the reform of state and semi-state bodies. Parliamentary questions would be addressed directly to the agencies and answered on their behalf in the Dáil; Oireachtas committees would be given the power to reject agencies' annual reports; ministers would be obliged to respond to such rejections; the committees would consider the ministerial response followed by further hearings. That promise was the last time even as much as a whisper was heard of such democratic interaction. Fine Gael promised that the minutes of board meetings of state agencies would be published within two months. A year into the new government, not a single minute had seen the light of day.

Appointments would become transparent; all ministerial appointments would be laid before Oireachtas committees. Candidates would be forced to outline their qualification for the posts. Chairpersons and CEOs were to be ratified (or rejected) in their new jobs by the Dáil, after facing the relevant committee for questioning. Oireachtas committees would even – at their discretion – scrutinize candidates for ordinary directorships. Everyone was going to be put through their paces in public. Those patently lacking the qualifications would not be able to face the challenge.

That was the theory. The reality turned out differently.

When Fine Gael and Labour took power, the committees were given no right to reject the appointees. A few token chairpersons were subjected to a cursory inspection. Ordinary board members escaped with automatic right of passage. Varadkar courageously decided not to extend the controversial reign of long-time semi-state survivor John Lynch as the chair of CIÉ and its subsidiaries. The replacements were called to appear before the Oireachtas Committee on Transport, in keeping with the government's commitment. None would ever complain that they had suffered stress in the encounter.

On Tuesday 12 July, when the coalition was four months in office, Vivienne Jupp, the successor to John Lynch as chairperson of CIÉ, was called before the transport committee. Her task could have been tricky in view of the controversies that had haunted CIÉ under Lynch. Jupp might have expected a grilling about how she was going to clean up Lynch's legacy at CIÉ. She need not have fretted for a second. A total of one hour forty minutes was allotted for the twenty-seven committee members to interview her. And not just her: the committee had also summoned the chairs of the three CIÉ subsidiaries: Dublin Bus, Bus Éireann and Iarnród Éireann. All four were to be questioned by the committee. Twenty-five minutes was being allowed by the government for each chairperson to make a presentation, offer a vision for their individual semi-state, and take questions from the twenty-seven committee members.

The exercise was predictably worthless.

Jupp made a three-minute presentation of her 'vision'. She out-lined her past career. Apart from having held a full-time position with Accenture she had extensive quango experience. Her seven-paragraph presentation was desperately short on vision. Indeed it was desper-ately short, full stop. Ditto Kevin Bonner (Dublin Bus), Phil Gaffney (Iarnród Éireann) and Paul Mallee (Bus Éireann). Their ambitions seemed to extend little further than 'working with Vivienne Jupp'.

The chairman of the committee, the Labour Party's Ciaran Lynch, instructed the committee members not to address their questions to individuals but to 'group' them in 'batches of five', an age-old method of allowing the interviewees to pick those ones they wanted to answer and duck any dangerous missiles. They had nothing to fear. The chairman called four TDs to ask five questions each, before any of the interviewees needed to reply.

Ms Jupp responded to the initial questions with the truly visionary news that she took the No 7 bus. And, in words reminiscent of US Republican vice-presidential candidate Sarah Palin's claim that she knew all about foreign affairs because she could see Russia from her house, Ms Jupp boasted that 'the Dart is also close to me'. You could have heard a pin drop as the TDs gasped at their specially selected visionary.

Kevin Bonner took less than two minutes to inform the questioners that he used the 'No 144 bus from Blackrock to Sandyford'. He reassured the members that despite his lack of experience of transport matters 'the principles of management are transferable across disciplines'. Paul Mallee was a 'user of public transport services' but failed to give the number of the bus he used. He called himself a 'strategy consultant'. Phil Gaffney was the only witness who had any obvious experience of managing public transport so he was not reduced to sharing the secret of the number of his local bus with the committee. His answers – alone of the four – showed more than a superficial understanding of Ireland's public transport system.

The assembled TDs lacked any sense of occasion. Paudie Coffey, the Fine Gael TD for Waterford, set the tone when he mentioned the word 'Waterford' seven times in his remarks, which ate up three minutes. Others merely used their time to make statements about local transport problems. Others supinely welcomed the 'opportunity to address' the visitors – which is exactly what they were not mandated to do. They were supposed to be asking them hard questions, not pleading for favours in their constituencies.

But who could blame them? The chairpersons were already in place. The TDs had had no input into their appointments, as had originally been promised. There was nothing at stake.

The committee chairman, Ciaran Lynch, started to fuss about the need to wrap things up at 4.15 p.m. In the space of twenty minutes he reminded members of the deadline six times. The proceedings descended into undignified exchanges between the chair and the TDs. Then members began to tumble in late with questions that had already been asked in their absence. Patrick O'Donovan of Fine Gael asked about bonuses.

> *Chairman:* That question has been asked already.
> *Deputy O'Donovan:* No, with respect, it has not.
> *Chairman:* With respect . . .
> *Deputy O'Donovan:* If the chairman interrupted less . . .
> *Chairman:* With respect, the meeting will end at 4.15 p.m.
> *Deputy O'Donovan:* That is fine, it is 4.10.

Chairman: I ask Deputy O'Donovan to ask his question briefly and
we will move on.

Deputy O'Donovan: I will, if the chairman lets me.

Chairman: Move on.

Deputy O'Donovan: How many more times will I be interrupted?

Various members expressed dissatisfaction at the format and
conduct of the meeting. Eventually, Deputy James Bannon asked
the killer question: 'What is the point of this committee?' No one
offered an answer.

Chairman: I will conclude. It was agreed at the start of the meeting
that it would conclude at 4.15 p.m. A select committee is meeting
at 4.30 p.m.

Deputy Bannon: The chairman should not hold two committee meetings on the same afternoon. It is discourteous to our guests. It is the
last time that the chairman gets cooperation in regard to holding two
meetings on the same afternoon.

The 'guests' looked on, grinning from ear to ear as though they
had won the Lotto. At best, the exchanges were light entertainment.
At worst they were a fiasco. Not a single TD laid a glove on the
chosen ones. The changes in the system to allow scrutiny of semi-
state chiefs were exposed as meaningless. Nobody was fooled.

Fianna Fáil must have nurtured a secret admiration for their
successors. The charade before the committee was a piece of window-dressing of which they would have been proud.

Elsewhere, the appearances of the new chairpersons at Oireachtas
committees were sporadic. Varadkar had been meticulous, but his
fellow ministers were not so enthusiastic about putting their nominees through the wringer. Some attended, some did not. It was, to all
appearances, pot luck.

The reform of the quangos was similarly lacking in substance. Fine
Gael had promised in its election manifesto to abolish 145 quangos.
At the press conference launching the plan, Varadkar had dramati-
cally promised a 'cull'. Labour had been less specific, merely pledging

an end to political patronage. It would ensure that appointments would be 'based on a demonstrable capacity to do the job'. Labour would publicly advertise all vacancies, not just the chairs, and ensure that Oireachtas committees considered the suitability of nominated candidates.

In November 2011, the government's long-awaited announcement on public service reform was finally released. Media interest focused on the section dealing with the state agencies. It was the dampest squib of a wet autumn. The policy statement was, once again, strong on rhetoric. The government would press ahead 'resolutely' with the rationalization and reduction of state bodies. It would introduce 'sunset clauses' when new bodies were created. It would hold annual reviews on the continuing business case for all significant state bodies. And, feebly, it would 'set a requirement for robust Service Level Agreements between Departments and State bodies'.

The number of bodies to be scrapped was pathetic. The government would proceed with the 'rationalization' of forty-eight. Another forty-six would be nominated for 'critical review'. The policy document listed obscure bodies for amalgamation, rationalization or abolition. Some were already on the previous government's hit list.

There was hardly high drama in the merging of the Local Government Management Service Board with the Local Government Computer Service Board. Nor with the news that the Limerick Northside Regeneration Agency would be merged with the Limerick Southside Regeneration Agency. The Library Council would be subsumed into another body. The Sustainable Development Council would be integrated into the National Economic and Social Council.

In answer to a question from Shane Ross in February 2012 about how many quangos had been abolished or merged since the government had taken office eleven months earlier, Minister for Public Expenditure and Reform Brendan Howlin issued a list. The grand total came to eleven. Only six, invisible minnows of the sector, were for the axe.

A week earlier Taoiseach Enda Kenny, under questioning from Deputy Joe Higgins about quango reform, had been forced to talk in vague terms about the 'success' of the new policies and of the appearances of chairpersons of state boards in front of committees. His statement was, characteristically, unsupported by any evidence – as was his weak assertion that 'quite a number' have been before committees.

Deputy Gerry Adams pursued him, asking why all positions on state boards had not been advertised as promised. Adams pointed out that in the Department of Justice none of the appointments to eight state boards had been advertised, that the chair of the Equality Authority was reappointed without interview by a committee and that appointments to the board of the IDA, the National Consumer Agency and An Post had ignored the new procedures. Kenny was forced to admit that in his own department some appointments were 'not advertised, as I was happy with the quality of the nominees'. He then conceded, 'It could be argued that these appointments might perhaps be advertised on the next occasion.' Kenny claimed that he was 'reasonably happy' with the way the committee process was working. Luckily for the Taoiseach, he had not attended the comedy at the Oireachtas Committee on Transport with the four CIÉ chairpersons.

Opposition spokesmen's protests that the Programme for Government proposed thirty new quangos fell on deaf ears. No one was prepared to give any credibility to Fianna Fáil outrage about patronage. The emergence of such bodies as NewERA or the Fiscal Advisory Council passed without much scrutiny. The prospect emerged that there might even be more quangos by the end of the Fine Gael–Labour regime's term than they had inherited from Fianna Fáil. The few profitable quangos like Bord Gáis and the ESB were placed on the block for privatization to satisfy Ireland's debtors. The many failures would continue to burden the state.

When it came to political patronage, Kenny and Gilmore were proving themselves the equals of Ahern and Cowen.

5.   Fingers in Every Pie
The Lawyers and the Auditors

Around 10 p.m. one Wednesday night in March 2012, the night before the report of the Mahon Tribunal was to be published, Nick Webb's mobile phone rang. It was a withheld number. The voice at the end of the line told him to look closely at the RTÉ news footage of property developer Paddy McKillen attending court in London.

The case to which the caller referred was a complicated one: McKillen was trying to stop the Barclay brothers from taking over his shares in the Claridge's hotel business, which he had bought in a consortium with Derek Quinlan, with much of the deal funded by Anglo Irish Bank. Many of these loans would be transferred to NAMA from Anglo, and the state agency sold €800 million worth of these loans to the billionaire Barclay brothers, who own the *Daily Telegraph* and the Littlewoods retail chain.

Nick Webb checked out the RTÉ footage. As McKillen walked into the London court, he was flanked by a solemn-looking middle-aged man in spectacles and an expensive-looking suit. It was Conor McDonnell, a partner in Arthur Cox.

McKillen was being advised by a London firm called Herbert Smith, so what was a lawyer from Arthur Cox doing at his side? The court heard that McKillen had been helped by Arthur Cox when he had been working on the proposed transaction with Qatari investors.

The fingerprints of Arthur Cox were everywhere in the case. The firm, based in Earlsfort Terrace in Dublin, had a close relationship with most of the central players. Apart from advising McKillen, it had also worked with Derek Quinlan on a number of property deals. Arthur Cox had also worked with Anglo Irish Bank, including in debt-recovery actions against its former chairman Sean FitzPatrick. And it had advised on the setting up of NAMA in 2009, and continued to work on NAMA's legal panel.

The law firm was not formally retained by any of the parties in the McKillen case, according to sources, and it declined to comment when Nick Webb inquired about Conor McDonnell's role in the London courtroom that day.

The McKillen case was by no means the only high-profile, high-stakes situation in which Arthur Cox seemed to have its finger in every pie. In November of 2008, weeks after the state had guaranteed the liabilities of the teetering Irish banks, a consortium called Mallabraca, fronted by Irish financiers Nick Corcoran and Nigel McDermott, expressed interest in taking a stake in Bank of Ireland. Mallabraca, which had brought together a number of global private-equity giants, including Carlyle and J. C. Flowers, was advised by Arthur Cox. So was Bank of Ireland. And so was the government, whose permission would be needed for a deal.

Arthur Cox claimed that it didn't face any conflict of interest by virtue of being involved on all three sides of a potential transaction. Finance Minister Brian Lenihan said that it was not unusual that one of the larger financial or legal advisers had to deal with potential conflicts of interest in Ireland. 'I have been assured by my external advisers on the bank-guarantee scheme that where potential conflicts arise they are dealt with through the application of well-established "Chinese wall" structures which are overseen by their compliance departments,' he said. Self-regulation via Chinese walls has evidently worked extremely well for the big law firms. The Law Society has never fined or censured any of its members for breaches regarding conflict of interest. Rather like insider dealing, conflicts of interest just don't happen in Ireland. What the McKillen case and the Mallabraca affair showed, and showed spectacularly, was that Arthur Cox was simply everywhere. As the adviser to many of the key property developers, banks, government departments and state agencies, it was running a real risk of bumping into itself on the other side of a table.

The firm has held an esteemed position in the eyes of governments and the private sector for almost a century. Its founder, Arthur Cox, set up in practice in Dublin in 1920. He was a highly ambitious and intelligent lawyer who made his mark quickly, and was involved in certain legal aspects of the Treaty in 1921. He helped design the Company Law

Act of 1963, the principal piece of legislation regulating corporate Ireland. Tiring of legal life, Cox left to join the priesthood. After being ordained, he set off to do missionary work in Africa but died in a traffic accident in what was then Northern Rhodesia in 1965.

Through a series of mergers with smaller companies, the practice grew larger and larger, employing 60 staff by 1985. The 1990s saw Arthur Cox mushroom as the practice expanded along with the broader economy. By 2000, the firm had 300 staff, of which 100 were partners. In May 2012, *The Lawyer*, a respected British trade magazine, pegged Arthur Cox as Ireland's biggest law firm with revenues of €109 million per year.

Although Arthur Cox the man was appointed to the Senate in 1954 by John A. Costello, a Fine Gael Taoiseach, the firm he founded has for some time been joined at the hip to Fianna Fáil. It was at the centre of much of what happened in the vicinity of the throne during the Bertie Ahern and Brian Cowen regimes. But having real influence means getting close to whichever political party is in power and adapting to new rulers, and Arthur Cox is now an indispensable friend of the new establishment. Photographs of 'Ireland Day' at the New York Stock Exchange in March 2012 show Enda Kenny ringing the bell to open trading, surrounded by the likes of telecoms and media tycoon Denis O'Brien and Elan's Kelly Martin. Arthur Cox partner Ailish Finnerty was also listed as one of the central participants on the day. While the photograph of Enda on the stage led to headlines back home, another photograph taken the same day, at the launch of the Global Green Asset Management Network – part of a plan to turn the IFSC into a centre of green investment trading – shows Enda grinning away beside another Arthur Cox partner, Gary McSharry.

The banking crisis that has convulsed Ireland since 2008 has been brilliant for Arthur Cox. In January 2012, Michael Noonan revealed that the firm had been paid a mind-boggling €26.6 million by the Department of Finance, the NTMA, NAMA and the National Pensions Reserve Fund since 2008. About half of the money, some €13.6 million, was paid by the Department of Finance for advice related to the bank-guarantee scheme and various other banking issues. The NTMA coughed up €7.74 million for 'legal advice' and the NPRF paid out €2.28 million in fees related to the recapitalization of AIB and Bank of Ireland. Arthur Cox also bagged €3.07 million from NAMA. The firm's overall earnings from state bodies since the beginning of the financial crisis could be even higher than the figure cited by Noonan, as the Central Bank has refused to divulge who has received the near €30 million in fees paid out to advisers in 2011 alone, bringing its total spend on advisers and consultants of various hues to €39 million since the crisis began in late 2008.

Finance Minister Brian Lenihan was close to Pádraig Ó Ríordáin, the bespectacled managing partner of Arthur Cox, and the law firm was brought in to advise the state as the crisis reached a crescendo in September 2008. The job was not put out for tender; the state was in a rush, so the brief was just handed to Arthur Cox. Lenihan told Joe Higgins in a written response to a parliamentary question in September 2010:

> Arthur Cox was chosen because of its acknowledged expertise in the field of commercial law and because its size allows it to dedicate sufficient resources to the project to ensure that advice is provided in a timely manner. A good working relationship had also been established through Arthur Cox involvement with the Advisory Forum on Financial Legislation.

The firm's role in helping to decide what should happen to the banking sector and whether or not banks should be allowed to go bust sat awkwardly with the fact that it was meanwhile advising Bank of Ireland on its survival and also had relationships with AIB, Ulster Bank, EBS and Bank of Scotland (Ireland). Arthur Cox rarely makes any comment related to its business, but it has denied that it has conflicts of interest. The firm has really, really good Chinese walls, apparently. Ó Ríordáin told *The Parchment*, the magazine of the Dublin Solicitors Bar Association, in May 2011:

> We have entirely separate teams acting for Bank of Ireland and the State and they represent the interests of their clients as fully and robustly as separate firms would – perhaps even more so at times.

Ó Ríordáin also denied that the firm benefited from political favouritism.

> Whilst there may be a theme in the press about our having more conflicts than anyone else, every piece of work we are undertaking for the State in the banking crisis we have now won at public tender, which has included a repeated assessment of our conflicts position.

Every bit of work had been won at tender – except for the legal advice during the crisis.

Arthur Cox certainly isn't the only firm whose client base opens it up to major potential conflicts of interest. McCann FitzGerald, the law firm set up by former Fine Gael TD Alexis FitzGerald, has acted for AIB, Bank of Ireland and Anglo Irish Bank 'in various development loan workouts and restructurings', according to its website. It has also worked for some of those banks' biggest borrowers, including Treasury Holdings, Kelland Homes and Sean Dunne. And it acts for NAMA, too.

Matheson Ormsby Prentice, which was Anglo Irish Bank's law firm, is also getting paid by NAMA. The practice was involved in the legal side of Sean Dunne's €370 million deal to buy Jurys Hotel in Ballsbridge in 2005 – one of the two or three transactions that most vividly highlighted the utter insanity of the property market at that time.

A&L Goodbody has worked for the Department of Finance, NAMA, Ulster Bank and Bank of Ireland. The other member of the so-called 'big five' Dublin law firms is William Fry, which was involved in the Fairfax/Wilbur Ross deal to buy a majority stake in Bank of Ireland. It has also advised AIB. Harry Crosbie's Point Village development and Joe O'Reilly's Chartered Land have also been fee payers – awkward bedfellows with another client, NAMA. William Fry represented NAMA in its case against Treasury Holdings in spring 2012. The legal community is a small place. Former William Fry partner Sonja Price, who'd headed up the law firm's Public Private Partnerships division, moved to Treasury Holdings in January 2006. She advises the firm on a range of issues including 'litigation', according to her biography on the website of the National Convention Centre, a Treasury development, where she serves as a board member.

Arthur Cox has managed to be on as many sides of the fence as humanly possible when it comes to health care. In 2010, it won a three-year contract, worth €58 million, to provide legal services to the HSE (on whose board its chairman sat). Meanwhile, Arthur Cox, along with A&L Goodbody and McCann FitzGerald, were retained by tobacco firms Gallaher, British American Tobacco, P. J. Carroll and Imperial Tobacco to defend against lawsuits from close to 400 smokers from 1997 onwards. While litigation continues sporadically more than fifteen years later, the bulk of the litigants have either dropped their cases or died. Then there are the drug companies – Arthur Cox's client roster includes the major Irish pharmaceutical distributor United Drug as well as pharma multinational Wyeth Medica Ireland. The nursing board – An Bord Altranais – is another client. Private hospitals such as the Blackrock Clinic and the Beacon Medical Group have also been advised by the Earlsfort Terrace law firm.

In December 2011, Pádraig Ó Ríordáin, whose term as managing partner of Arthur Cox had just ended but who remained a partner in the firm, was appointed chairman of Dublin Airport Authority. It was an extraordinarily arrogant appointment by Transport Minister Leo Varadkar. It didn't matter that Arthur Cox was one of the semi-state body's legal advisers, having acted for the DAA in judicial review proceedings against the Commission for Aviation Regulation, and on various Terminal 2 contracts and a €600 million bond issue for DAA Finance Ltd. It didn't matter that Arthur Cox had also acted for DAA in disputes against Ryanair – the airport's biggest customer. As well as that, Arthur Cox was the legal adviser for Aer Lingus, another of the airport's biggest customers. The firm had made huge sums of money helping Aer Lingus defend two takeover attempts by Ryanair. Needless to say, Michael O'Leary was livid at the appointment, accusing the Department of Transport of cronyism.

In early January 2012, Ó Ríordáin was called in front of a joint

Oireachtas committee to be rubber-stamped for the job. The potential conflict of interest was skirted over in his opening statement. 'In
truth, although my firm advises it legally, I was not overly familiar
with the detail of the company or its business prior to the beginning
of this process,' Ó Ríordáin told the committee. 'I had never worked
with it, and had never met its board nor knew its executives.'

One lawyer wondered what would happen if the Dublin Airport
Authority was sued – and what would happen if it was sued because
its legal advice had been flawed? Ó Ríordáin would be put in an
incredibly awkward situation. He'd certainly have to leave the room.

One of Ó Ríordáin's predecessors at Arthur Cox, James O'Dwyer,
was a close associate of packaging tycoon Michael Smurfit. He also
served on the board of Jefferson Smurfit plc. In 2002, US private equity
firm Madison Dearborn Partners (MDP) made a €3.7 billion bid to
take over the Smurfit company. It was, at the time, Ireland's biggest
ever corporate deal. MDP needed an Irish-based law firm for its bid.
Out of all the corporate law practices in the country, it chose Arthur
Cox – the firm O'Dwyer chaired for twelve years until stepping down
in 2005. O'Dwyer notified the Smurfit board when it became clear that
a conflict could arise, and it was agreed that he could play no further
part in the transaction as a director. Fellow Smurfit director Mary
Redmond was also a partner in Arthur Cox, and she had to exclude
herself from negotiations as well. Legal and advisory fees on the €3.7
billion transaction will have swelled Arthur Cox coffers considerably.

O'Dwyer and another Arthur Cox partner, Bryan Strahan, were
also board members of Goldman Sachs Bank (Europe), alongside
former Fine Gael Attorney General Peter Sutherland. In September
2011, the Central Bank fined Goldman Sachs Bank (Europe) €160,000
for exceptionally serious breaches in financial regulations. The fact
that two of Arthur Cox's best-known names were directors of the
reprimanded bank made no evident difference to the earning power
of Arthur Cox.

Like a verruca, auditors are very hard to get rid of. They lose clients
very, very rarely. Over the last decade, it has taken a truly cataclysmic
event for an auditor to be changed.

When rogue trader John Rusnak lost $691 million at AIB's US subsidiary Allfirst in 2001, the incumbent auditor Pricewaterhouse-Coopers was replaced by KPMG; PwC was told not to apply when the gig went out to tender. Ernst & Young, which proved so oblivious to the systematic malpractice at Anglo Irish Bank – which cost the taxpayer €29.3 billion – lost the contract when Deloitte was appointed auditor to the nationalized bank in September 2009. KPMG audited Michael Fingleton's Irish Nationwide but lost the job when it was merged into Anglo Irish Bank.

But these cases are exceptional, and the big four Irish accountancy firms have shrugged them off. Despite a long catalogue of disasters, their power to command massive fees to provide services to state agencies, banks and big business has not diminished. KPMG remains auditor to the state-owned AIB; in 2010, it earned €5.2 million in fees. The same year, AIB announced losses of €10.4 billion. In 2010, PwC picked up a cheque for €8.2 million from Bank of Ireland which the taxpayer had to rescue with a €3.5 billion bailout cheque. The same year, the bank announced losses of €950 million.

The banks showered auditors with money during the boom. From 2000 to 2010, PwC, KPMG and Ernst & Young earned a staggering €164 million in fees from AIB, Bank of Ireland, Anglo Irish Bank, EBS and Irish Nationwide. For this kind of money, one might have expected that they would have noticed something was amiss.

The work done by the big accountancy firms came under legitimate scrutiny long before the current banking crisis began. Following revelations of widespread tax evasion that came to light during Oireachtas hearings into the DIRT scandal in the 1990s, the Dáil Public Accounts Committee produced a report concluding that banks should be forced to change their auditors every five years. It also called for a probe into whether auditors should be barred from providing 'non-audit' or other consultancy services to the banks they were supposed to be overseeing.

Mary Harney, then the Minister for Enterprise, Trade and Employment, set up a 'review group' to examine the various issues facing the accountancy sector. The review group came back with eighty recommendations on how to reform the industry – with the establishment of a regulatory watchdog its prime finding. The Irish Auditing and Accounting Supervisory Authority was set up. While IAASA provided regulatory oversight of the industry in Ireland, it did little to address the potential conflicts of interest that threatened to undermine the independence of audit firms from their clients.

The lucrative consultancy nixers were spared the chop, as the review group stopped short of calling for a ban on the practice, suggesting that it would 'damage competitiveness'. While the big accountancy firms will no doubt argue that their audits were extremely robust, it must have taken a superhuman effort for them not to have one eye on the audit work and another on the extremely well-paid consultancy jobs for the same clients. Forcing banks to change auditors every five years was also ruled out as 'it could impact negatively on the quality of the audit as, for example, a new audit firm would be less familiar with the audit client'. A reform that would have made the relationship between bank and auditor less cosy might have acted as a brake on the worst excesses of the boom, but it was not to be. The reform of the industry was a joke.

The relationship between bank and auditor is much deeper than merely checking whether the bank's numbers actually add up. There's a bit of backscratching, too. The auditors have been known to give their clients prestigious awards. In May 2007, AIB was awarded the prize for 'retail banking excellence' at the KPMG Financial Services Excellence Awards. 'The support of KPMG helps highlight both the outstanding contribution of the financial services sector to the Irish economy and the key role that KPMG plays in this area,' noted Brian Daly, Chairman of KPMG's Financial Services Group after the 2007 gongs were handed out at a black-tie dinner in the Burlington Hotel. The judges on the panel that year included Anglo's Sean FitzPatrick, Dan O'Connor (who would become executive chairman of AIB), former financial regulator Liam O'Reilly, former AIB chief executive Michael Buckley, and John Cunningham of the short-lived Rossbank (an early casualty of the banking crisis). KPMG was AIB's auditor. In 2007, with lending at the bank spiralling dangerously out of control, the auditors should have been shouting 'stop'; instead, they gave their employers a prize.

For some reason, KPMG decided not to honour AIB, or any other bank, in 2009. The massive hole in the balance sheets of AIB and the other Irish banks, which had to be plugged with billions of euros in public money, may have had something to do with it.

We now know that KPMG was aware of a looming catastrophe at Irish Nationwide Building Society as early as 2006. Writing in the *Sunday Independent* in January 2012, Tom Lyons revealed the existence of a 2006 letter from KPMG to the bank's management which highlighted problems ranging from 'inconsistent grading' of loans to governance issues and lack of controls over lending. But the company accounts were all signed off year after year, and there was no mention of these concerns in any of the Irish Nationwide annual reports distributed to members of the building society during the boom years. KPMG was also the auditor at Bank of Scotland (Ireland), earning €1.285 million in fees in 2007 and 2008 as the bank went on a lending bender. Now, the bank's owner, Lloyds Banking Group, faces €7 billion in losses on its Irish loans.

Three banks. Over €20 billion in losses. One auditor.

Long before the recent crisis, KPMG had audited a major Irish bank and failed to blow the whistle on a scandal unfolding under its very nose. In 1998 two government inspectors were appointed to examine widespread tax evasion and customer gouging at National Irish Bank, following revelations by RTÉ's Charlie Bird and George Lee. The report, finally published in 2004, found that the external auditors, KPMG, were 'remiss' in not requesting that management of the bank tell the Revenue Commissioners about potential tax issues related to the widespread DIRT fiddle. The firm's reputation should have been shredded, but few took any notice.

Despite its involvement with NIB in the 1990s and three catastrophically flawed banks in the 2000s, KPMG's services were in demand by the state. In 2010, the Comptroller and Auditor General revealed that KPMG had received €2 million 'for its help in drafting bank stabilization measures'. KPMG is also retained by the state-owned Irish Life & Permanent and was tasked with offloading its Irish Life business and its €8.1 billion UK loan book.

KPMG's role in advising the state doesn't fit well with its other work in advising the super-rich on how to avoid paying tax. The firm's use of loopholes in the tax code is legal, but clearly not in the best interests of the rest of us. Gerry McCaughey was one of the super-rich who benefited from KPMG's tax advice. The Century Homes entrepreneur was advised by KPMG that he could reduce his tax bill from selling his company to Kingspan for nearly €100m by taking part in a complicated – but legal – tax scheme. His shares in Century were sold to his wife, who then moved to Italy to become resident there. When the shares were sold on to Kingspan, the McCaugheys were able to pay a much reduced capital gains tax bill by virtue of his wife's Italian residency. The savings ran into the millions. The details of McCaughey's convoluted tax scheme were leaked to RTÉ when Environment Minister John Gormley appointed him as chairman of the Dublin Docklands Development Authority. It was legal, but it wasn't the sort of thing that a chairman of a state agency was supposed to be doing. He resigned before even chairing a meeting.

The 'Italian Job' had been used by KPMG before. It put together a similar tax scheme for Shane Ryan, son of the late Ryanair founder Tony Ryan, whose wife took up residency in Italy ahead of the sale of €19 million worth of Ryanair shares in October 2003. The Revenue Commissioners were not amused and challenged the move, but were unsuccessful. The state ended up around €5 million poorer.

KPMG were also advising some of their closest clients what to do when the whole house of cards came tumbling down. In May 2012, during the lawsuit between Paddy McKillen and the billionaire Barclay brothers over the ownership of Claridge's, property investor Derek Quinlan told a London court that he moved to Switzerland in 2009 'on the advice of KPMG'. He denied NAMA's claims that he'd left the UK to escape creditors and avoid writs and summonses being served on him. While KPMG was advising Quinlan on his personal finances, another part of the accountancy firm was also making fees by acting as a receiver to a number of Quinlan properties, including the landmark Bank of Ireland headquarters on Dublin's Baggot Street, which had been bought by a Quinlan-led consortium for over €200m in 2006.

KPMG isn't the only big accountancy practice that advises the super-rich on how to avoid paying their full whack of tax; it's just the only one that has been 'outed'. Coming out of the shadows is not something that accountants or other advisers like doing. Especially if it puts them in the frame with Fianna Fáil.

PricewaterhouseCoopers (PwC) was particularly well got with the Soldiers of Destiny. One of its partners, Feargal O'Rourke, is former Fianna Fáil minister Mary O'Rourke's son, and a cousin to both the late Brian Lenihan and former minister of state Conor Lenihan. In 2001, Taoiseach Bertie Ahern gave the firm a big suitcase that was full of documents going back sixteen years. He asked the firm to produce an income and expenditure account for his St Luke's constituency office. PwC managing partner Ronan Murphy appeared at the Mahon Tribunal in May 2008, describing the work on what was known as 'Project Luke'.

In mid-September 2008, the Financial Regulator hired PwC to investigate the state of the banks. Having crunched the numbers, PwC told the government that Anglo, Irish Nationwide and IL&P faced a 'stressed case' possibility of €5 billion in bad loans. In other words, things were bad – but not that bad. The banks could be fixed for an affordable €5 billion. This was a pivotal call in the days before the catastrophic bank guarantee. The decision to guarantee the €440 billion in bank deposits and bonds was hugely influenced by the PwC findings. The bill for the state would top €50 billion, even leaving out the cost of NAMA. The PwC assessment was catastrophically wrong.

While PwC was running the rule over the Irish banks, its Belfast office was also auditing Sean Quinn's empire. Quinn was Anglo's biggest shareholder, and its largest borrower – his companies owed up to €2.8 billion to Anglo. The audit firm was also involved in setting up the convoluted scheme whereby a variety of offshore companies – including one in Belize – were used to secretly buy a stake in Anglo.

The state continues to award contracts to PwC. In June 2011, the firm was appointed by the Department of the Environment to conduct a review into the state's water policy and to look at the creation of a new water utility. In October 2011, Minister for Social Protection Joan Burton announced that PwC was to conduct a major review into the pensions sector for her department. But the really big gravy is at the state-owned AIB. A decade after the Rusnak scandal, PwC is back at AIB.

In February 2012, it emerged that AIB had refused to tell the Minister for Finance how much it has paid PricewaterhouseCoopers, citing commercial sensitivity. PwC was hired to guide the bank through what it described as 'a period of extraordinary change and restructuring'. AIB chairman David Hodgkinson was a member of the UK advisory board of PwC from February 2009 until he joined the bank in October 2010.

Ernst & Young has the dubious distinction of having been auditor to the two biggest banking blow-ups ever. The firm did the accounts for Lehman Brothers, whose collapse in September 2008 caused a near Armageddon on financial markets. Lehman had used some pretty racy techniques to make its balance sheet look better than it was, including 'Repo 105' accounting that reclassifies debts as sales. In December 2010, New York State Attorney General Andrew Cuomo filed a civil fraud case against Ernst & Young alleging that the accountancy firm 'substantially assisted' a 'massive accounting fraud'. The lawsuit sought the return of up to $150 million in fees that E&Y had received from Lehman from 2001 to 2008 plus other damages. Ernst & Young is also been sued by Alameda County Employees' Retirement Association, which alleges the firm made misleading statements about Lehman's finances before it went splat.

While Lehman's was a catastrophe, it didn't capsize a country. The near collapse and subsequent bailout of Anglo Irish Bank did. Ernst & Young served as the bank's auditor, earning €10.3 million in fees from 2000 to 2008. During this period Anglo manipulated its balance sheet to make it seem healthier than it really was through a complicated €7 billion back-to-back deposit transaction with Irish Life & Permanent. And its chief executive and later chairman Sean Fitz-Patrick was involved in an elaborate scheme to conceal well over €100 million in personal loans advanced to him by the bank.

Ernst & Young too had a chequered past that pre-dated the crises of 2008. Its performance as external auditor to ACCBank during the 1990s had been found badly wanting by the DIRT tax inquiry. Not only had the firm failed to challenge ACCBank over its lack of disclosure to the Revenue; it also buried a report in which, long before the DIRT scandal was exposed publicly, it calculated that ACCBank had a potential liability of around €21.6 million. It was an extraordinary case of a watchdog failing to bark. But perhaps failing to bark isn't such a bad thing for an audit firm, because various state and private entities continue to throw business at Ernst & Young. Poodles are much nicer than Rottweilers.

Paul Smith, a qualified barrister and tax expert, became managing partner of Ernst & Young in 2000 and was re-elected three times. Under his leadership, Ernst & Young grew at an impressive rate, doubling in size in just six years. To celebrate the start of his third term in 2006, Smith gave a wide-ranging interview to Chartered Accountants Ireland's in-house magazine. When he was asked about auditor liability, he told the interviewer:

> There are clients that are difficult to audit – not sectors. You have to be careful about who your clients are, about 'knowing your clients', and having the appropriate relationship with them. We have lots of processes around this. In the first place our job is to evaluate our engagement with clients to make sure that they are people that we are happy to do business with.

Sean FitzPatrick turned out to be dodgier than a six-euro note, but Ernst & Young was evidently 'happy to do business' with Anglo and signed off its accounts every year. When the scale of the Anglo debacle started to become clear in September 2008, the obvious question was how this had been allowed to happen. While the bank's executives and directors rightly got spanked, it took time for the role of Ernst & Young to come into focus.

In February 2009, just after Anglo had been taken over by the state, the Oireachtas Joint Committee on Economic Regulatory Affairs, which had been tasked with finding out what the hell had just happened, requested Ernst & Young explain its role in front of TDs. The taxpayer, it reasoned, had a right to find out why it was being asked to rescue a bank. The firm refused point-blank. It released an astonishingly arrogant statement in which it 'thanked' the joint committee for its invitation to appear at the hearing but said it 'respectfully declined'. An appearance before the committee would 'not be appropriate' it added. The Ernst & Young statement added that it understood that Anglo shareholders were 'upset' at events in the bank. 'However, as we have already said, we are confident that our audit work at Anglo Irish met the appropriate standards,' it noted. The controversial €7 billion balance-sheet-boosting deal between Anglo and Irish Life & Permanent was also brushed off. 'No information concerning the re-financing transactions that have been at the centre of the current controversy was made available to us until late 2008,' the company said. Sean FitzPatrick's loans were also covered:

> As part of the normal audit process, we received written representations from management confirming the completeness of directors' loan disclosures and confirmation in respect of each of the directors' loan balances outstanding at the financial year end.

In other words, it hadn't come across any of these controversial transactions because it hadn't been told about them. What exactly had it been paid €10.3 million to do? Was it just to take the bank's word about everything?

Paul Smith retired in 2009; he was replaced by Mike McKerr of Ernst & Young's Belfast office. McKerr gave an interview to *Business & Finance* magazine in October of that year. Referring to the work his new colleagues had done at Anglo, he said:

> They did a fantastic job. Anglo may have been at the centre of a storm but a lot of work remained to sign off accounts and make full disclosures. Our team worked tirelessly to make sure that happened under an awful lot of pressure with speculation in the press every day. We are very proud of the job they did as individuals.

McKerr argued that part of the problem was 'a perception gap between what the public expect an auditor to do and what its role and responsibilities actually are'. He suggested that the role is to audit the accounts as presented by the board of the company in accordance with the guidelines, the regulations and the law. That, according to McKerr, is exactly what Ernst & Young did.

But Ernst & Young even came under a bit of pressure from its own trade body. The Chartered Accountants' Regulatory Board, the supervisory arm of the Institute of Chartered Accountants in Ireland, had hired former Comptroller and Auditor General John Purcell to investigate Ernst & Young's role in the Anglo debacle in 2009. Ernst & Young tried to block the investigation, but in May 2011 the High Court threw out its objections to the investigation. In September 2011, Purcell reported back. The report found that Ernst & Young had cases to answer in relation to Sean Fitzpatrick's loans, loans to Anglo finance chief Willie McAteer and the back-to-back deposits of €7 billion between Anglo and Irish Life & Permanent. The penalty for any firm found guilty of these crimes was a potential fine of up to €30,000 for partners and a ban on doing audit work for a prescribed period. The latter sanction, if applied, was a potential game changer.

In a statement, Ernst & Young said it 'fundamentally disagrees' with Purcell's view that there was a prima facie case to answer on three points under investigation. 'This is a preliminary stage of the process and, for the avoidance of doubt, there has been no adverse finding made against Ernst & Young in respect of the audit of Anglo Irish Bank,' the company said, adding that it would 'vigorously defend' its work before a hearing of the disciplinary panel.

Despite the obvious problems with the various accountancy firms' performance in auditing the banks, the industry stonewalled plans to tighten up oversight. In October 2011, it emerged that financial regulator Matthew Elderfield had been rebuffed in attempts to get auditors to meet with the Central Bank twice a year to discuss what was going on inside the banks. Ernst & Young claimed that there was no proper legal framework for these discussions to take place. The firm also took issue with the proposal that an auditor's role should be extended to look at future risks facing a company.

Since 1999, Ernst & Young has sponsored the Entrepreneur of the Year competition. Previous winners of various gongs have included John McColgan and Moya Doherty, as well as Taxback.com's Terry Clune and Randox chief Peter FitzGerald. But the Ernst & Young endorsement has also proved the kiss of death for some award winners and nominees. Treasury Holdings duo Johnny Ronan and Richard Barrett won the 2006 Industry Award – one of the chief categories. Their great business idea had been to borrow a ridiculous amount of money from banks and spend it buying overpriced property. A splendid wheeze and one well worth applauding, thought the Ernst & Young judges. NAMA has appointed receivers to a bundle of Treasury's companies, and bankers have taken control of its landmark Battersea Power Station project.

Developer Ray Grehan was one of the finalists for the award in 2006; in 2011 he declared himself bankrupt after his debt-laden firm collapsed. Michael Taggart's Taggart Holdings won the Industry Award in 2007, months before the property company went wallop. Aer Arann's Padraig O'Ceidigh, a winner in 2002, later hit turbulence, and examiners were appointed to dig the business out of a hole in 2010. Mark Elliot of civil engineering group P. Elliott was nominated in 2006, five years before the firm went into receivership. Gerry McCaughey, the 2003 Industry Award winner, stepped down as the chairman of the Dublin Docklands Development Authority in March 2009 after details of his tax affairs were leaked. Word Perfect Translations, set up by former Ernst & Young 'emerging ethnic entrepreneur' Olga Gashi, made a €1.67 million settlement with the Revenue Commissioners in 2010 over under-declaration of tax.

While the firm's reputation may have been dragged through the mud, its coffers didn't seem to be affected. The state continued to hurl money at Ernst & Young. The audit firm refused to answer questions to the country's elected representatives, but it was happy to take the taxpayers' money. You'd have to wonder what somebody has to do to get blacklisted in this town?

Ernst & Young was hired by the state-owned Irish Nationwide in April 2009 to conduct a 'forensic' review of the lending practices at Michael Fingleton's toxic building society. The report has not been published. Ernst & Young was also retained to advise the Financial Regulator in February 2009 – after Anglo was nationalized. Several of Ernst & Young's staff were seconded to the regulator. The firm received €120,000 in fees in 2009 and over €121,000 in 2010. Ernst & Young was also appointed by the Financial Regulator to examine developer loans being transferred to NAMA in March 2010. And in January 2012, the firm was hired by the Central Bank to perform a special probe into more than a dozen debt-management companies.

At the same time, Ernst & Young's restructuring and insolvency practice was also making huge fees through acting as a receiver for Irish Nationwide, other state-owned banks and NAMA. Anglo appointed Ernst & Young as receiver to some of Johnny Moran's hotel businesses in January 2011. Moran's hotels, which included the Holiday Inn on Dublin's Pearse Street, owed Anglo €18 million. The audit firm has landed lucrative NAMA receiverships at Treasury Holdings and at the former Dublin Sports Hotel in Kilternan, where Hugh O'Regan borrowed €170 million to develop a luxury hotel and business campus. The Central Bank moved to put in Ernst & Young to run one of the country's largest credit unions, in Newbridge, Co. Kildare, in January 2012 – with partner Luke Charleton earning €423 per hour.

Ernst & Young isn't the only major accountancy practice making a fortune as its banking clients send receivers into indebted firms. AIB auditor KPMG landed the Superquinn receivership, after a syndicate of banks including AIB pulled the plug on the retailer. PwC, which audited Bank of Ireland, was appointed as examiner to McInerney – a Bank of Ireland borrower. It also acted as a receiver to part of Michael Taggart's property empire, when Bank of Ireland called stop. It's an absolutely brilliant business plan. Auditors get money from the banks, which lend to private companies. They also get money from the companies being lent the money by banks. When the companies go under, the auditors crawl over the carcass getting fees as liquidators, examiners or receivers.

The 'Big Four' – KPMG, PwC, Ernst & Young and Deloitte – have woven themselves into the fabric of Irish business. The top companies have recruited incestuously from the auditing firms which used to do their books. DCC's finance chief Fergal O'Dwyer is an ex-PwC bean counter; PwC picked up €2.55 million from DCC in 2011. Ryanair's Michael O'Leary started off at KPMG; the firm audits the airline's books. Kerry Group's finance chief Brian Mehigan kicked off his career with Deloitte, which is now the food group's auditor. KPMG counted Patrick Kennedy among its alumni; it now audits his firm Paddy Power.

As well as crunching numbers and making sure company ledgers all add up correctly, the big accountancy outfits have also evolved into consultancy firms, providing advice on all manner of other things. Auditors are supposed to have an extremely robust relationship with their clients, and slap them around a bit if necessary to make sure that the books are squeaky clean. They are supposed to be independent. This can become something of a sham when the same set of accountants is picking up large fees for advising the company on other matters. PIRC, the British corporate-governance consultancy, has consistently urged a ban on non-audit activity by auditors over fears that it compromises auditors' independence and discourages them from confronting directors on really difficult issues.

Banana company Fyffes paid €493,000 to KPMG to audit its books between 2009 and the end of 2010; over the same period KPMG earned €547,000 from Fyffes for various taxation or non-audit services. Ernst & Young picked up €1 million in 2010 and another €1 million in 2009 in 'tax fees' – essentially for advice on how to reduce the corporate tax bill – from CRH, while also carrying out the building-materials giant's audit. KPMG received €1.55 million from Grafton Group in 2011 for 'tax advisory services'; this was on top of the €759,000 it earned for auditing the firm's books. PwC is Glanbia's auditor. It bagged €546,000 for audit services and another €1.3 million in fees for other consultancy work in 2010.

A big chunk of the accountants' earnings come from non-audit fees. Bank of Ireland paid €56.6 million to PwC for services including 'reporting to regulators' and providing 'letters of comfort'. A letter of comfort does what it says on the tin. It's a proclamation from the auditor that everything is hunky-dory at a client firm. No nasty surprises. No giant big black holes. AIB paid KPMG €11 million for services outside its audit, including tax advice and providing 'assurance to third parties'. Anglo coughed up around €1.9 million for various fancy non-audit fees to Ernst & Young. It was equivalent to a quarter of the entire amount earned by Ernst & Young in audit fees from 2000 to 2010. It showed how important a revenue stream advisory and consultancy services had become to the big audit firms. Sticking to the knitting didn't bring in the big bucks.

Accountancy firms tend to argue – in the words of Lord Justice Lopes in the Kingston Cotton Mills case in 1876 – that the auditor is 'a watchdog, not a bloodhound'. In other words, it is not the role of the auditor to look for trouble or to doubt the honesty of his employers. But there is a growing understanding that Irish accountancy firms have been far too passive. In his April 2011 report on the banking crisis, former IMF official Peter Nyberg described the auditors of big banks as 'silent observers', saying they interpreted their role too narrowly.

In June 2011, Frank Daly, the chairman of NAMA, gave an uncharacteristically lively speech at the National Conference of Accountants and Auditors at Carton House in Co. Kildare, in which he told his audience that they needed to look in the mirror before 'absolving themselves of responsibility' for the banking disaster. He added:

> After all that has happened, can the auditing profession continue to suggest that it is not its responsibility to draw attention to significant risks, such as the extraordinary concentration of risk? We cannot go back to a situation whereby an audit firm can complete its audit and then claim either that it did not spot the elephant in the room or that it was not its job to point out that four-legged hunk with the trunk in the corner. It is now time for the profession to have a serious review of what its role and responsibilities should be.

In another speech three months later, Daly, a former head of the Revenue Commissioners, also called for auditors to review their role in the aftermath of the banking crisis and scrutinize the long-term sustainability of businesses and the risks they take. In a speech to the

Corporate Governance Association of Ireland, Daly said the auditing profession needed to reinterpret its role to be more forward-looking and to assess long-term strategies underlying business risks and ethical behaviour. 'The profession is excessively focused on historic accounts, which forces them to look backwards, not forwards,' Daly argued. The NAMA chairman warned that there was an 'expectations gap' between the statutory role of an audit and the public expectation of the assurance that an audit should offer: 'The prudent strategic response for the profession would be to move in the direction of fulfilling the public expectation of its role.'

Corporate watchdog Paul Appleby, who headed the Office of the Director of Corporate Enforcement, was also critical of auditors. In February 2011, Appleby said that auditors 'report surprisingly few types of company law offences to us', and that the so-called 'Big Four' firms account for just 5 per cent of all reports.

Ireland may be just a pimple on the bottom of the rest of the world, but it hasn't stopped the giant Wall Street investment banks and other serious international players from milking enormous fees and profits out of us.

Daniel Tully was a proper master of the universe on Wall Street. During his period as chief executive and chairman of investment bank Merrill Lynch in the mid-1990s, the company's share price trebled. The Irish American was tapped up to become a board member of the fledgling National Pensions Reserve Fund by the then Minister for Finance, Charlie McCreevy, in 2001 after leaving Merrill Lynch. Tully had also been appointed as a board member of Irish drug company Elan in 1999. Elan's then boss – the late Donal Geaney – was the first chairman of the National Pensions Reserve Fund. Tully's Irish links were strengthened by his involvement with the Ireland–US Council. In 2003, Tully helped arrange a visit by Bertie Ahern to the US, where the Taoiseach picked up an honorary degree from Fairfield University in Connecticut.

Tully and Merrill Lynch would become the favoured international adviser of Fianna Fáil-led governments. In 1999, Merrill Lynch bagged one of the crucial joint jobs as global coordinator of the

€5 billion Eircom flotation, the biggest ever disposal of an Irish state asset. The investment bank would split over €74 million in fees with fellow coordinator AIB. Financier Russell Chambers was a key figure on the Merrill Lynch team. He would later move to rival investment bank UBS, which would subsequently handle the flotation of the then state-owned Aer Lingus. Merrill Lynch was also appointed by the Department of Communications, Energy and Natural Resources to examine strategic options for Coillte. But it was in the banking sector that the company would have most impact.

Merrill Lynch was one of the first to see the vast iceberg approaching the Irish banking sector. In March 2008, analyst Phil Ingram produced an explosive report into commercial property lending in the UK. The key finding was that Anglo Irish Bank and the other banks heavily exposed to the market were in trouble, as the bubble was popping. Merrill came under major pressure from Anglo, and Ingram's superiors pulled the report.

As the financial and banking crisis intensified in mid-2008, Finance Minister Brian Lenihan turned to Merrill Lynch for advice. Merrill was fighting for its own existence at the time, as it had racked up massive losses in the US sub-prime market. So the state had turned to a bank that was on the brink of going under because of stupid bets on risky assets to advise it on how to rescue Irish banks that were on the brink of going under because of stupid bets on risky assets.

The UK-based Merrill Lynch team hired to advise the government included high-flying executive Henrietta Baldock and other members of the team that had helped put together Royal Bank of Scotland's disastrous €71 billion buyout of ABN Amro earlier that year. The deal, which was done right at the top of the market, was seen as a key reason for the meltdown at RBS, which needed to be rescued by the British government. Now Merrill Lynch had been handed the task of saving the Irish banks from going wallop. The slick-suited Wall Street bankers were barely able to keep their own firm afloat, but they came up with a range of possibilities including a special €20 billion liquidity scheme for the banks and a hotchpotch of other wheezes including nationalizations, deposit guarantees and even a form of 'bad bank' to house bum loans.

In a sign of the desperation unfolding in the Department of Finance on the eve of the infamous bank guarantee night, Kevin Cardiff – who was Lenihan's departmental go-to guy for the banking crisis – emailed Henrietta Baldock at Merrill Lynch seeking a crib sheet on the pros and cons of guaranteeing the banks. Why the department didn't have all the details already isn't clear. Baldock fired him over a seven-page document. It was constructed completely out of fudge. It noted 'there is no right or wrong answer' to the banking crisis. And this is what Merrill was getting paid millions for? The email claimed that 'all of the Irish banks are profitable and well capitalized', but warned that liquidity for some could simply dry up in a matter of days. Baldock floated the introduction of a secured lending scheme for the banks, under which commercial property could be exchanged for government bonds or hard currency, which would have kept the banks from running out of cash. She suggested that the alternative was a blanket guarantee covering all depositors and senior creditors. Merrill's expensive advice to the government consisted of a bunch of potential options with precious little in the way of a recommendation.

In June 2009, Merrill Lynch's contract with the state expired. L. M. Rothschild replaced Merrill Lynch as the key adviser to the government on trying to fix the banking sector. Since taking over the role, L. M. Rothschild has earned over €6.96 million. Goldman Sachs, meanwhile, was paid €6.29 million on the capital-raising exercise specified by the Central Bank for AIB, Bank of Ireland, EBS and Irish Life & Permanent.

Now there's a new kid on the block. And it's a big one. Blackstone is a US private equity company valued at €130 billion. It's listed on the New York Stock Exchange and has made its partners extraordinarily rich by being a little bit smarter than some of its rivals. Blackstone is all over Ireland like a rash. On 8 November 2011, Enda Kenny and Minister for Finance Michael Noonan met with the chairman of the Blackstone Group, Stephen Schwarzman, in Dublin. Gerry Murphy, the former chief executive of food group Greencore, is its go-to guy for Ireland.

Blackstone is interested in Irish banks. It was linked with a move to buy part of Anglo's €8 billion US loan book in mid 2011; it has also tried to buy large swathes of distressed loans from NAMA – in the billions rather than mere tens or hundreds of millions. The private equity firm bought IFSC-based asset manager Harbourmaster Capital in October 2011. Blackstone emerged as one of the biggest holders of Eircom debt and became one of the telecoms firm's principal owners after a complex restructuring in May 2012. Blackstone has left big footprints all over corporate Ireland. But Blackstone is also getting close to the state. In January 2012, Tom Lyons revealed in the *Sunday Independent* that Gerry Murphy was being lined up to become one of the members of a new group which was to advise the board of NAMA. Given that Blackstone had been sniffing around bank assets and loans for the best part of two years, it seemed a bizarre approach by the government. Murphy didn't bite.

Irish Bank Resolution Corporation – comprising the carcasses of Anglo and Irish Nationwide – hired Blackstone to advise on the sale of up to €30 billion worth of US and UK assets. There was a clear potential for a major conflict of interests, especially as Blackstone had already been on the other side of the table. Anglo hired FTI Consulting to advise it on this potential conflict of interest. But FTI, which had been run by Declan Kelly – the brother of Labour minister of state Alan Kelly – had its own issues. It had hired a former vice-president of Anglo, Brett Witherell. The Department of Finance sought clarity on this appointment and subsequently Michael Noonan told the Dáil that Witherell had been hired on 19 December 2011 as a director in its corporate financing restructuring practice. This, Noonan had been told by FTI, was after FTI's work on Anglo's US loan portfolio was completed and without the knowledge of the bank. So what we had was a potential conflict of interest being investigated by a firm that was itself facing a potential conflict of interest.

You couldn't make this stuff up.

While they advise the state about banking, the banks about the state, and private equity firms about banking and the state, some partners at the top legal and accountancy practices have a painful personal awareness of the sharp falls in the property market since 2007. Some of the most powerful and influential individuals at the top of firms advising the state put their own money into property investments. We don't know how all of these investments have fared, but given the general movement of the market in recent years we can only assume that a great number of them are underwater. We can only assume, too, that there is full transparency between clients and advisers over these personal exposures.

Former Arthur Cox partner and property lawyer Dan O'Connor 'acted in many property acquisitions for Quinlan Private Asset Management', according to the Arthur Cox website. He was also a member of a Quinlan consortium called the Airpair partnership, along with RTÉ legend Gay Byrne, former AIB chairman Dermot Gleeson and a smattering of other professionals. O'Connor is also listed – in Companies Office filings – as a member of The Main Partnership with Irish Ferries boss Eamonn Rothwell, former Guinness & Mahon banker Peter Ledbetter and Liam Reidy SC.

Luxembourg corporate documents for the Quinlan-led Carraig Beag consortium, which was involved in major property dealing in the centre of London, reveals the presence of many of the great and the good of corporate life, ranging from Trinity Biotech's Ronan O'Caoimh to Riverdeep's Barry O'Callaghan, Davy Stockbrokers' Kyran McLaughlin and developer Paddy McKillen. But also on the list are Arthur Cox partners Sarah Cunniff and Caroline Devlin, and William Fry partner Dan Morrissey, who had been involved with other Derek Quinlan deals. He was part of the original consortium behind the Four Seasons Hotel deal in Ballsbridge, where Quinlan made his name, as well as being a member of Quinlan's Airpar, O'Shea and Conduit Partnerships. Morrissey's associates in William Fry were involved in the €1.16 billion sale of the Jurys Inns business to a Quinlan-led consortium in 2006.

McCann FitzGerald partner Julian Conlon is listed in Companies Office filings as being part of the Maple Partnership, a syndicate set up by Derek Quinlan. He's hooked in with former Arnotts head Richard Nesbitt, barrister Stephen Hamilton, logistics tycoon Finn O'Sullivan and former A&L Goodbody chief Frank O'Riordan. Another Quinlan grouping of investors is the Direct Partnership, which also numbers O'Riordan among its members. Arthur Cox partner William Johnston is also involved. Another Quinlan vehicle called the College Partnership includes Arthur Cox partner Carl O'Sullivan among its number; he's also involved with other Quinlan projects including the Timer Partnership, the Dew Partnership and the Conduit partnership, which includes Gay Byrne and Pat Kenny among its members, according to filings. A&L Goodbody partner Eric Brunker is listed as a member of Quinlan's Firstwood Partnership along with Patrick Mooney, the Kildare developer who was part of the consortium that bought the €180 million Bank of Ireland headquarters during the boom.

KPMG partners have also dipped their toes into personal property investments. KPMG partners Jon D'Arcy, Eamonn Donaghy, Arthur O'Brien and Paul Hollway set up a property investment firm called JEAP. It backed a number of property development companies including one building homes in Killea in Donegal. Some thirty-four homes were to have been built, but the crash of the market has left the site mothballed. JEAP also wrote off close to €1 million invested in Belfast firm Laemont Developments and almost €500,000 in Duleek Limited Partnership. The most recent figures show that from 2008 to 2010 the company lost around €3.1 million.

It's not just the well-known names at major legal or accountancy practices who got bitten by the property bug. Two partners in Limerick solicitors firm Dermot G. O'Donovan served as directors of the Fordmount Group, which went into receivership in December 2009 owing up to €200 million to Anglo Irish Bank. Adrian Frawley and Michael Sherry are partners in the law firm and shareholders in Fordmount. The company was behind €300 million worth of development in Limerick, including the landmark Riverpoint Development, the Savoy Hotel and the Park Nursing Home. In February 2010, two months after Fordmount went into receivership, the firm Dermot G. O'Donovan was appointed as a legal advisor to NAMA.

Limerick builder Seoirse Clancy, whose company is owed up to €1 million by Fordmount, told Joe Duffy's *Liveline* programme of his annoyance over the appointment. Clancy said he believed a conflict of interest existed between the solicitors and NAMA: 'The legal firm now has been appointed to the NAMA panel and its duty will be to collect and chase money from companies like Fordmount. That is where the conflict of interest comes in.'

The Limerick law firm issued a statement which said that there would be no conflict of interest.

> Dermot G. O'Donovan solicitors tendered for and was appointed to the NAMA panel. All relevant information was given in the tender process, with due emphasis on the potential conflict of interests section. And we are satisfied there will be absolutely no conflict of interest in any work undertaken on behalf of NAMA.

It's the same line being peddled over and over again. The big legal firms and accountancy practices know what they are doing. They have 'systems' in place to prevent clients – including the taxpayer – from getting shafted. Chinese walls are in place to protect our best interests. A pinstriped suit, well-spoken accent and an old school tie will do the rest.

6. Your Future Is in Their Hands

The Pensions Disaster

In 2005, Anglo Irish Bank boss Sean FitzPatrick made his controversial leap from chief executive to chairman. Tiarnan O'Mahoney,
head of the rogue bank's treasury arm, was the hot favourite to
succeed him. When the chief executive's job surprisingly went to the
relatively obscure David Drumm, O'Mahoney left Anglo in a bit of
a huff, as did Tom Browne (head of lending in Ireland) and John
Rowan (chief executive of the UK operation), who had been the
second and third favourites for the succession. O'Mahoney's parting
gift was a stunning €3.65 million, plus a €250,000 top-up to his
pension fund. Over the previous three years he'd been paid a combined €4.4 million.

O'Mahoney was only forty-five when he exited from Anglo. He
left a spectacularly successful bank with hidden, but fatal, flaws to
start a new business with huge potential – and equally huge risks. It
was a specialist lending outfit called International Securities Trading
Corporation (ISTC). He had no problem finding investors for his
project. They came flooding in. After he had invested €5 million personally, high-fliers from his old workplace at Anglo – including Sean
FitzPatrick himself, who sank €1 million into the venture – gave him
a dream lift-off. According to the *Sunday Times*, property developer
Seamus Ross invested €10 million. Denis O'Brien, Sean Quinn, Gary
McGann of Smurfit and developer Paddy Kelly also jumped on the
O'Mahoney express train.

ISTC's business model drew on O'Mahoney's twenty years of
expertise in banking and treasury. The firm borrowed money in the
global debt markets, invested it in complex instruments and lent it on
to the banks. It also brokered debt deals for financial institutions.
O'Mahoney confidently told the *Sunday Business Post*:

The real attraction of this business is that you are lending to the highest quality borrower that there is. Banks are highly regulated, with the regulator ensuring they are in a position to meet their obligations. That's why I think it's such a safe form of business. You can't say that banks don't fail, but everybody agrees banks are a fairly safe bet.

He added that, 'There is only one objective of International Securities Trading, and that is to make money. This is unashamed capitalism.' The adventurous characters who had entrusted him with their money were hardly the types to lose sleep because O'Mahoney's vehicle was not subject to state regulation. Although ISTC handled money, it took no deposits. Consequently it did not need a banking licence. It operated in a regulatory vacuum.

O'Mahoney's bold enterprise had an encouraging first two years. In May 2007 it reported profits of €6.8 million. The original ISTC shares, issued at €100 each in July 2005, had by this time risen to €325. It became a badge of honour among the movers and shakers of the Irish financial world to be on board with O'Mahoney. Disaster struck later in 2007, when the US sub-prime crisis sparked a global credit crunch. ISTC had invested $305 million in complex debt instruments known as Structured Investment Vehicles (SIVs), which were managed by global banks.

SIVs attempted to profit from the difference between short-term borrowing rates and returns on longer-term securities. The business model meant that SIVs were constantly refinancing – and this proved a problem when the credit crunch hit. In addition, in the middle of the sell-off of all investments with even a whiff of sub-prime debt, the credit ratings of SIVs were downgraded by Moody's Investor Services. ISTC's SIV investments were consequently slashed in value. The banking clients of ISTC made margin calls. ISTC could not meet the calls. It was forced to take a €70 million hit on the valuation of its chosen SIV capital notes. Trading in its own shares, which had enjoyed a meteoric rise, was suspended. ISTC sought the protection of the High Court.

O'Mahoney made frantic efforts to find a white knight, including Dermot Desmond – a man with deep pockets but no appetite for rescuing drowning corpses. Within three months O'Mahoney was forced to write off €820 million, up to that date the largest sum ever written off by an Irish company. Eventually, ISTC was sold by examiner John McStay to UK brokers Collins Stewart for a token €5 million.

If O'Mahoney and a few big bankers had been lone losers in the venture, few would have shed tears for the losses of such hardened market dealers. Unfortunately, there were also smaller punters, some of whom were ignorant of the dangers of high-risk investments, who got badly burned. Some had invested their life savings or their pensions in ISTC through Friends First bonds. Banks were paid 12 cents for every euro owed to them by ISTC as part of the final settlement; less privileged private punters received nothing.

Financial Services Ombudsman Joe Meade expressed his concern about the sales of ISTC bonds to the elderly via banks, investment intermediaries and stockbrokers. Many investors were over seventy, some over eighty and one a nonagenarian. The bonds were marketed to smaller investors by Friends First, who wrapped them in a life insurance policy. Meade voiced his worry about whether small investors realized that their investment was a high-risk ISTC product, or mistakenly believed that it was a safer insurance purchase. The chaotic losses from O'Mahoney's shenanigans at ISTC would have left a sour taste in the mouth of any ordinary decent regulator.

One ordinary decent regulator who was deeply embroiled in the unregulated chaos in ISTC was the nation's top pensions regulator. His name was Tiarnan O'Mahoney.

The story is staggering: the man who had run treasury operations at Ireland's most buccaneering bank, and had then managed to lose the guts of a billion euro in three years with ISTC, doubled up as chairman of the Irish Pensions Board – the regulator, protector and guardian of the nation's retirement funds.

The Pensions Act 1990 gave O'Mahoney's Pensions Board a wide remit. Its functions include an all-embracing requirement 'to advise the Minister . . . on all matters relating to pensions generally'. It is entrusted 'to monitor and supervise the operation of the Pensions Act and pensions development generally'.

In its mission statement, the Pensions Board claims lofty ambitions and a broad brief. It professes itself to be the promoter of 'the security and protection of members of occupational schemes and contributors to Personal Retirement Savings Accounts'. It aims:

> ... to promote the development of efficient national pension structures, to promote a level of participation in the national pension system which enables all citizens to acquire an adequate retirement income and to provide information and authoritative guidance to relevant parties in support of pension security, structures and participation.

It was Tiarnan O'Mahoney's task, as chairman of the Pensions Board, to fulfil these ambitions: above all to provide security to those saving for their old age.

O'Mahoney was appointed to the chair of the Pensions Board in late 2005 by the late Seamus Brennan, Fianna Fáil's Minister for Social and Family Affairs. O'Mahoney had recently left Anglo, which was still viewed as a wonderbank. Brennan could have justified this appointment by suggesting that he was putting an acknowledged financial wizard in charge. Less charitable observers point out that Anglo Irish Bank had close associations with the minister, whose son, Shay Brennan, worked in the bank's treasury risk department. After Seamus Brennan's death in 2008, young Shay was selected as the Fianna Fáil by-election candidate in the constituency of Dublin South.

O'Mahoney had no known pensions acumen. His elevation to such a sensitive position as pensions regulator underlines the reality that it was not seen in political circles as necessary for the chair of the Pensions Board to be filled by a person with expertise in the field. The shock feature of this affair was not O'Mahoney's appointment in the first place, but that he did not resign the chair of the Pensions Board on the spot when ISTC went into examinership. As the horror of the losses under O'Mahoney's stewardship at ISTC became apparent, the pensioners of Ireland must have shuddered.

How confident could they feel about the safety of their nest eggs given that the chairman of the Pensions Board was a man who had lost over €800 million of other people's money?

O'Mahoney decided to tough it out. His political patrons allowed him to stay put. The Pensions Board went about its business as though O'Mahoney's stature was undiminished. He dug himself in, even as the full horrors of Anglo Irish Bank started to become known. O'Mahoney was not in the front line of the Anglo controversies, but he had been one of the top executives in the rogue bank, a full board member, a member of the risk committee, and very much part of the inner circle. He had been greatly enriched by Anglo, leaving only because he had been passed over for the top job. His position as chairman of the Pensions Board should have been untenable.

At a tense meeting of the Dáil's Public Accounts Committee in November 2011, the chief executive of the Pensions Board, Brendan Kennedy, answered a series of questions about the reaction of the other directors to the news that their chairman had lost over €800 million of other people's money. According to Kennedy, no one had ever mentioned the war. If you listened to the Pensions Board's chief executive you would believe that their chairman's financial acrobatics elsewhere never entered their heads.

Shane Ross: What did Mr O'Mahoney bring to the party?

Brendan Kennedy: The appointment of Mr O'Mahoney was a matter for the minister.

Shane Ross: That is correct, but what did he contribute to the board? Mr Kennedy was there when he was appointed to the board. He was appointed in 2005. Is that correct?

Brendan Kennedy: Yes.

Shane Ross: He served until 2010. What did he contribute to the Pensions Board?

Brendan Kennedy: Mr O'Mahoney was the chair of the board and actively participated in and chaired all board meetings during his time.

Shane Ross: The point that I am making is that, as everybody knows, Mr O'Mahoney was a senior person in Anglo Irish Bank at the time.

Chairman [John McGuinness]: I must caution the Deputy in regard to . . .

Shane Ross: I want to know what the reaction of the board was to him. He then proceeded as chairman of the board to run a company called ISTC, which proceeded to lose €865 million . . . Did the board at any time question his credentials to be chairman with his particular record, particularly having been in charge of an organization that lost €865 million?

Brendan Kennedy: The issue never came up at any board meeting that I attended. I would have attended all board meetings subsequent to the events the Deputy describes and the issue was never raised at a board meeting.

Chairman: Deputy Ross should move on from that issue.

Ultimately it was for the government to unseat O'Mahoney, but it was not prepared to admit that his appointment had been an error. The only conclusion that can reasonably be drawn from its nonchalance is that the government did not consider the Pensions Board important enough.

In 2010, when O'Mahoney retired from the Pensions Board shortly before the end of his five-year term, the late Seamus Brennan's successor as minister, Éamon Ó Cuív, paid him a handsome tribute as he went out the door. Ó Cuív effusively thanked O'Mahoney 'for steering the Pensions Board through a difficult economic environment'. Then he spoke of O'Mahoney's commitment to 'the highest standard of regulation' and of his 'significant public service contribution'.

O'Mahoney's more significant legacies in the area of regulation were surely the spectacular failures at ISTC and Anglo. He could write a book on the pitfalls of poor regulation.

There was nothing anomalous about the presence of Tiarnan O'Mahoney in the Pensions Board's chair. The board was there for political patronage; the needs of pensioners were secondary.

O'Mahoney's predecessor, Michael McNulty, had enough letters after his name to justify a claim to being a competent number cruncher, but his suitability to chair the pensions regulator was less obvious. He had been a senior audit partner in top accountancy firm Ernst & Young. More interestingly, he had been appointed a director of both An Post and Temple Bar Properties by Fianna Fáil ministers. After Fianna Fáil's Máire Geoghegan Quinn had put him on An Post's board in 1992, he was favoured with a second term in 1997. His position on Temple Bar Properties was thanks to Taoiseach Charlie Haughey. He was later reported by the *Longford Leader* to have attended a €100-a-head Fianna Fáil fund-raiser in 2006. The dinner was addressed by Finance Minister Brian Cowen.

McNulty's predecessor, Grainne Clohessy, was a less obvious, but more interesting, choice than McNulty back in 2000. She was in the middle of a promising legal career that would hardly have marked her out as a natural for the position. Grainne Clohessy was a successful junior counsel. She had been educated at University College Dublin, had worked as a tax consultant with Ernst & Young and later in insolvency for Price Waterhouse. She had been a member of the pensions committee of the Bar Council. She had co-authored *Butterworths Tax Guide 1996–97*. More interestingly, perhaps, from the perspective of the government, in 1997 she acted for Fianna Fáil in the McCracken Tribunal inquiring into payments to politicians. She was in attendance when Bertie Ahern was being examined.

Later, in 2000, the Minister for Social and Family Affairs, Fianna Fáil's Dermot Ahern, parachuted her into the calmer waters of the Pensions Board. During Clohessy's tenure, dark clouds were gathering on the pensions horizon. A slow awareness of a pensions time bomb was dawning over Europe. An ageing population and increasing life expectancy meant that the ratio of workers to retirees was growing ever smaller. In 2001, Ireland had five workers for every pensioner. Actuarial forecasts suggested that by 2050 the ratio would fall to 2:1. The strain on pension funds could become unsustainable. The National Pensions Reserve Fund was created in 2001 specifically to address this looming problem, but within less than a decade it was to be virtually cleaned out to rescue the banks.

It was unfortunate that one of the few events that drew attention to Clohessy's Pensions Board was a junket. In June 2003, Jody Corcoran revealed in the *Sunday Independent* that virtually the entire board had enjoyed the luxuries of an overnight stay in Tinakilly House in Wicklow – golf, dinner and free bar – at a cost to the taxpayer of €30,000. Meanwhile, pensions were heading for a crisis. There was a political rumpus, but Fianna Fáil minister Mary Coughlan waded in to the rescue, describing the junket as a 'useful and worthwhile exercise' and declaring 'I support the work of the board'.

In December 2003, Clohessy surprised observers by suddenly resigning as chairperson of the board. The move was presumed to be because of lack of time at a period when her legal career was beginning to blossom. Apart from her lucrative work in the McCracken Tribunal, between May 2000 and November 2001 she had picked up €652,000 working for another state inquiry, the Lindsay Tribunal investigating HIV and hepatitis C infections of persons with haemophilia. She was obviously ultra busy.

Clohessy's legal career continued to blossom after she left the Pensions Board. Since 2006 her earnings from the state have mushroomed. The Revenue Commissioners have been among her biggest fans, sending her briefs worth €1.23 million in the six years between 2006 and 2011.

Apart from the chairperson, there are sixteen ordinary board members. All are appointed by the government, but the Pensions Act specifies that the board must include representatives of trade unions, employers, the government, the pensions industry, member trustees, and professional groups involved in pensions.

In 2005, when O'Mahoney took over, a quarter of the membership of the board was drawn from the social partners: two from the Irish Congress of Trade Unions and two from IBEC. The heavy presence of the social partners is difficult to explain on any level bar the normal political imperative to keep them happy with soft seats on state boards. Other nominees came from the Irish Insurance Federation, the Society of Actuaries, the Irish Association of Pension Funds, Ireland's accountancy bodies and the Pension Lawyers in Ireland. The finance minister nominated a single member while the social welfare minister nominated six ordinary directors. Then the social welfare minister appointed two others: one to represent the pensioners and another to be the voice of consumer interests. In other words, the pensioners held just one seat out of seventeen. The social partners outnumbered him by 4:1. The rest of the board had varied agendas, many nominated to protect their comfortable patches in an industry bulging with cash.

This was the structure of the board that failed to challenge Tiarnan O'Mahoney's continuation in the chair after the ISTC meltdown. Not even Fergus Whelan, one of the two nominees of the supposedly conscientious ICTU, raised his voice to query O'Mahoney's future after the ISTC debacle. Perhaps it was because he wasn't present at board meetings: attendance records are not available before 2009, but in that year he missed three out of nine meetings, and in 2010 he missed six of nine.

In 1990, when the Pensions Board was established, there was no pensions crisis on today's scale. The industry was small, cosy and regarded by most as a specialist no-go area run by experts. It benefited from the NTMA syndrome of being seen as a forbidden planet peopled with pointy-headed actuaries. It benefited, too, from being perceived as unbearably boring – this probably made it less vulnerable to demands for transparency and accountability. The media regarded pensions as a turn-off. Business editors were known to ban the word 'pension' from the headlines in their pages for fear of losing younger readers. These were ideal conditions for an industry that had plenty to hide.

It could not last for ever. And it didn't.

All ran relatively smoothly until the turn of the millennium. Globally, most pensions had traditionally been run on the basis that the bulk of members' savings should be sunk into equities. It had worked. Shares had outperformed bonds and cash over the long term. Bonds were a specialist area offering less attractive potential returns, while the derivatives markets were less developed than they are today. Options, futures and hedge funds were far smaller elements of the investment manager's life. The equity was king. Irish pension funds bought into the doctrine. Irish banks, which had begun to build up – or acquire – pension fund management arms, loved the market muscle it gave them. Stockbrokers, often owned by the same banks, saw equities as a lucrative source of commission. All the financial

pressures and conventions pushed pension funds in the direction of
the equity merry-go-round. No one cried 'stop'.

The attacks of 11 September 2001 and the bursting of the dot.com
bubble marked a turning of the tide. The two events ushered in a
dark decade for Ireland's pension funds.

Ireland's pension funds can make a case for a respectable performance if they are reviewed over a twenty-year period. Figures covering
Group Managed Pension Funds performance provided by Rubicon
Investment Consultants show that the average pension fund has given
an average 7 per cent yield since 1992. But the credit for that positive
performance is nearly all provided by figures for the 1990s, when
stock markets boomed. The average yield for pension funds since the
year 2000 is a miserable 1.1 per cent, well below the rate of inflation.
Over the five years up to the end of 2011, the funds show average
annual losses of 3.7 per cent.

The pitiful performance was partly due to Irish fund managers'
devotion to equities, in particular Irish equities. According to the
chairman of the Irish Association of Pension Funds (IAPF), Brian
Aylward, back in 1997, around 67 per cent of the funds were invested
in the Irish market, including about 30 per cent in Irish equities.
Another 20 per cent was held in Irish gilts, and about 17 per cent was
in Irish property.

Unfortunately, Irish pension fund managers never diversified
prudently. According to figures from the IAPF in 2000, equities
remained an extraordinarily high proportion of their funds, making
up 64.4 per cent of their investments; in 2005 the figure was 65 per
cent. The proportion of equities peaked at 66.3 per cent in 2007,
before the market crash in 2008 slashed the figure to 52.3 per cent.
This drop was caused not by a sell-off of shares by the Irish pension
funds, but by the dramatic reduction in the value of the funds' share
portfolios, driven in large part by the plummeting prices of Irish
bank shares to near zero. After the crash, the equity content in
Ireland's pension funds was topped up to bring it back to levels in the
middle sixties.

Even as the prices of shares rose beyond levels at which they could
realistically be viewed as good value, the so-called professionals made

no meaningful reduction in the level of their weightings in equities. Even if the fund management outfits, some of which are owned by Irish banks, had seen the banking crash coming, it is questionable whether – due to domestic pressures and loyalty to their employers – they would have felt able to sell bank shares.

The Irish fund managers had reduced the weighting of Irish equities in their portfolios from the extraordinary 30 per cent of 1997, but by 2009 they still held 5.06 per cent of their investments in the battered Irish market. The Irish stock market represented between 0.12 per cent and 0.16 per cent of the world's equities over the past ten years. Irish pension funds were thirty times overweight in their native shares.

The IAPF admitted that the 2009 proportion was higher than might have been expected, 'which may indicate new cash flow into this market during the year'. More remarkable still was its observation after the 2008 crash that the '€3.2 billion that is invested in Irish equities on behalf of Irish pension schemes represents 10.0% of the total Irish equity market, compared with 7.6% at the end of 2007'. In other words, pension funds' share of the Irish market was rising. They had dug themselves into a big hole. And they were still digging.

Irish pension funds were doubly exposed to property. Firstly by their investment in banking and construction shares, but also by their misplaced confidence in Irish property itself. They held a steady 8 to 9 per cent of their portfolios in property during the years leading up to 2008. After the collapse in 2009, this sank to 3 per cent – again due mainly to the assets' loss of value.

In the aftermath of the depressed equity markets of 2002, many of Ireland's occupational defined-benefit pension funds were technically insolvent, incapable of paying off their liabilities if they had been called on to do so. In 2003, the Pensions Board's solution was to perform an act that would embarrass an ostrich. They simply redefined insolvency. They extended the recovery time granted to pension funds to correct their deficits from three and a half years to ten.

Pension funds were required to produce a backup funding plan to win an extension. Occupational pension funds produced the required revised plans. In their hundreds they flocked towards this lifeline. Insolvency had been successfully redefined, but the problem remained: in 2010 the Pensions Board's annual report revealed that 75 per cent of defined-benefit pension schemes were in deficit. The board had already approved the revised funding plans of over 90 per cent of those troubled pension funds which had applied to be placed on life support.

An indication of the depth to which the industry had sunk was flagged by an RTÉ programme, *Pension Shock*, presented in October 2011 by George Lee. The programme pulled the players in the pensions shambles to shreds, highlighting the deficits, high charges, low performance and lax regulation. Lee interviewed many representatives of the galaxy of vested interests drawing out of the pensions pot. The Pensions Board, which habitually proclaimed one of its primary roles as communicating with the public through the media, declined to defend its patch. The board later pleaded that the interviews were filmed six weeks before their release and would have been out of date by the time of the broadcast. From a body that had been procrastinating for a living, this was a rich excuse.

Lee explained how seemingly modest fee percentages could eat up huge chunks of the value of a pensioner's fund. As Lee put it, 'the fees are enormous and there's no link between the fees and the performance and the performance has been quite bad'.

Lee was being charitable. The investment performance of Ireland's pension fund managers has not been bad. It has been woeful. An OECD report in 2009 delivered a devastating indictment of Ireland's pension fund managers during the crash of 2008. It surveyed twenty-three countries. Ireland came in with the wooden spoon. Irish equities fell by 66 per cent in 2008, underperforming other markets – awful news for Irish pension funds, which remained overinvested in home-grown stocks. Not only were our native funds bottom of the league, losing 37.5 per cent in a single year, they were bottom by a country mile. Second from the bottom came Australia with losses of 26.7 per cent. The chickens came home to roost in a twelve-month period. The price of investing too heavily in a single asset class (equities –

and, worse still, Irish equities) exposed the folly of the Irish managers' refusal to diversify adequately.

All was not lost. Within two years the OECD brought a more cheerful message to the world's pensioners. Pension fund assets were returning to pre-crisis levels. Unfortunately, there were a few notable exceptions. Once again the worst performer was Ireland (still down 13 per cent from its 2007 levels) followed by Portugal (12 per cent), Belgium (10 per cent), Japan (8 per cent), Spain (3 per cent) and the United States (3 per cent).

Other countries' fund managers had discovered bonds. According to the OECD Global Statistics survey of selected countries (not including Ireland) in 2010, an average of 50 per cent of their pension fund assets were now in the relative safety of government stocks and other bonds. The United States was the biggest believer in equities of the twenty-seven countries studied. Its pension funds held 49.3 per cent of their investments in equities, followed by Finland at 47.6 per cent, Australia 46.5 per cent and Chile at 43.9 per cent. No other nation's pension funds surveyed held above 40 per cent in equities. The average investment in equities of all twenty-seven nations surveyed was 14.5 per cent.

What about Ireland, which was not included in the OECD survey? In 2010, according to the IAPF, Ireland's pension fund managers were still holding 59 per cent of their investments in equities. They were still out on the same limb that had caused them to be the world's worst performers. Pensioners paid the price.

The overall performance of Irish pension managers was consistent. It was consistently deplorable. Over a ten-year period, the ten pension providers surveyed by Rubicon all finished within 3.5 percentage points of each other. There was no room for outriders in this club. They shadowed each other, holding similar weightings in various assets. They were bunched together like horses in a perfectly handicapped race, only separating as they approached the line.

Fund managers shun personal publicity, preferring the protection of the anonymous herd. They rarely give media interviews. None are household names. They all aspire to marginally beat the chosen index or to come in the top half of a closely bunched field. Today's winner could be tomorrow's back marker, and vice versa. They rarely make any attempt to publicize any yawning difference in their perform-ances. Groupthink rules. There is no point in dog eating dog in the fund managers' racket. There is plenty of fat to be shared around if no one spoils the party. They are all creaming it from the same pension pot.

Irish fund managers, like fund managers in most of the world, are paid a percentage of the value of funds under management. The theory is that although this fee structure does not directly reward good performance or punish poor performance, it does so indirectly because bad managers will lose funds to competitors. But it doesn't really work this way in Ireland, because the competition tends to be made up of copycats. Their performances have been so similarly bad that the incentive for trustees to go to the trouble of switching managers is limited.

One basic problem facing researchers into pension funds has been a lack of transparency: it can be very hard to find out how much the pen-sion providers charge their clients. It is usually impossible to pin down what proportion of the fees goes to fund managers, administrators, lawyers, intermediaries, custodians, consultants and to other hangers-on, all with their paws in the till. Such a lack of transparency suits the entire industry. It serves to protect the already sheltered players.

Thanks to Aidan Mahon, a postgraduate student at the Waterford Institute of Technology (WIT), we know a bit more about fees than the industry would like. In a 2006 paper, Mahon discovered that in Ireland the average slice of the assets absorbed by fees ranged from 0.32 per cent to 3.64 per cent – compared with between 0.2 per cent and 0.9 per cent in the United States. Furthermore, Mahon dis-covered that charges in Ireland ate up 26 per cent of the total pot of retirement income over the lifetime of a pension.

Costs of between 0.32 per cent and 3.64 per cent may not sound like that big a deal, but in a paper on pensions delivered to the Dublin Economics Workshop at a conference in Kenmare in October 2011, Donal de Buitlear and Don Thornhill illustrated how such costs can crucify a fund over time. They illustrated the point with a simple example where €1 million is invested at a gross market rate of 10 per cent per annum. Without costs, this would increase to €10.8 million over twenty-five years. But if annual costs are 2 per cent, the net return is €6.8 million – a penalty of €4 million, or 37 per cent.

A feeble government drive to increase the worryingly low percentage of the population covered by pensions was led by the launch of personal retirement savings accounts (PRSAs) in 2003. The government allowed PRSAs to become yet another honeypot for insiders. Standard PRSAs could charge up to 5 per cent on entry, plus a 1 per cent annual management fee. A similar product launched in the UK had an entry charge of 2 per cent and an annual fee of 0.3 per cent.

The entire pensions maze – the high fees, the poor performance, the pretence that funds in deficit have hopes of future solvency, the government's acquiescence in it all – begins to look like a conspiracy by insiders against the nation's future pensioners, the source of the biggest cash hoard in the state.

The apparatus for defending individual pensioners from abuse by the powerful pension forces is theoretically in place, in the figure of the Pensions Ombudsman, an office that was established in 2003. Paul Kenny, who has served in the position since its inception, dealt with more than 6,000 complaints in the eight years to 2010. The numbers had risen steadily from just 452 in the first year, peaking at 1,766 in 2009 before levelling off at 1,312 in 2010. The hits on his website rocketed to over 900,000 in 2010, up from 628,000 in 2009. There is plenty of disquiet out there. The real question is whether Kenny, as the ombudsman, tackles the symptoms or the disease.

According to Kenny, investment complaints were at the core of many of the cases referred to him:

> . . . a great many members have no clear idea of how or where their pension fund money is invested or of their responsibilities in relation to the investment of that money. It is essential that members understand what sort of assets their pension fund is invested in, and duly instruct their trustees if they wish to change the basis or nature of this.

If members go digging they can theoretically find out what their trustees and investment managers are doing, but questions are met by a wall of jargon, delays and deliberate references from one layer of insiders on to another. Members often give up. Most do not even know the name of their initial point of contact, the trustee of the pension scheme. They are house-trained to accept that pensions are far too complicated for ordinary mortals. Which, as operated in Ireland, they are.

Such inaccessibility suits the big guns. They have positioned themselves out of reach of their clients. Kenny himself deals with individual complaints, but he has no power to sort out the industry itself.

While Paul Kenny was in his eighth year of doggedly tackling the escalating number of grievances from individuals, Ireland's pensioners were delivered a body blow. Minister for Finance Michael Noonan announced that private pension funds were to be hit by an annual levy of 0.6 per cent.

It was a dawn raid. Pensioners were being plucked for the second time since the banking and fiscal crisis had broken. First the National Pensions Reserve Fund (NPRF) had been virtually cleaned out by Fianna Fáil to save the banks; now it was the turn of private schemes to rescue Fine Gael and Labour. A cash-strapped administration, flailing around in search of funds, had decided to raid a cash cow. Economist Colm McCarthy estimated that the levy would cost pension savers €920 per annum on average. It was an attack on the capital assets of €80 billion held in the nation's private occupational pension schemes. It was projected to raise €470 million a year over its four-year life.

When the government came under attack over the measure, they pledged – without conviction – to examine the pensions industry's fees and charges to see if savings could be made in this area. It had apparently never occurred to them to start the savings by cutting the fat in the industry itself. When questions were asked about why they had not forced a reduction in management fees and taxed the bloated industry, they answered as always, by promising a review.

Pleadings by cabinet ministers that the levy was temporary

rang hollow for the victims. Taoiseach Enda Kenny pointed out that pension savers had benefited from generous tax reliefs on their contributions for years. He conspicuously made no promises that commitments to phase out these benefits, made to the lenders of the EU/IMF/ECB troika as part of Ireland's bailout deal, would now be shelved. But the government will not be anxious to tinker with the tax relief. They fear that any dramatic change in the tax relief could mean that thousands of salary earners, large and small, would stop paying more than the minimum required by law in contributions towards their pensions. Some would pay nothing. Many punters are well aware that their pension funds are a rip-off, but the tax incentive makes pension contributions a no-brainer for many, particularly those paying tax at the top marginal rate. The removal or weakening of the tax break could change that, with the result that an even bigger swathe of the population might find their pensions far too small for their needs.

Where was the Pensions Board in all of this? The Minister for Finance, Michael Noonan, admitted that he had not even bothered to consult with the Pensions Board on the levy. At the November 2011 meeting of the Dáil's Public Accounts Committee, the chairman, John McGuinness, cast doubt on the board's value.

The introduction of the pension levy coincided with a sudden crack in the united edifice of the interdependent godfathers of the industry. In June 2011, the Pensions Board's chief executive, Brendan Kennedy, broke cover and warned pension trustees about exposing members to significant risk. In a surprise outburst in the board's annual report, he claimed that it was now over three years since stock markets had crashed but that there had been no noticeable reduction by Irish pension funds in their exposure to equities. He went to war on investment risk, and blamed the failure of others to manage it as the main reason why some pensions would now fall short of expectations.

The warning was about ten years too late. If the Irish Pensions Board had shone the amber light on risk and forced the trustees of the schemes to take notice in 2001, it would have emerged with kudos. By 2011 the damage was irreparable. The horse had bolted.

Kennedy pointed a finger at the pension fund trustees. But as the only unpaid players in the pension game, they had good cause to feel aggrieved about such criticism. Trustees are volunteers drawn from the ranks of employers and employees. They are not involved in day-to-day investment decisions. Their duties are arduous and tiresome. They have to spend endless hours ensuring that regulations are adhered to, that minimum funding standards are complied with, that records and administration are in order. They appoint the investment managers, give them their brief and send them on their bikes to use their skills in picking the portfolio. They carry legal liability for mistakes made by them in the performance of their duties and can be fined, or even imprisoned, for failure to fulfil them. Unlike fund managers, they are not normally indemnified against possible mistakes. Theirs is a thankless and unrewarded task. God only knows why anyone serves as a trustee.

Employee trustees are usually outnumbered on the board of trustees by the employer representatives. The priority of the employer trustees is frequently to safeguard the company's cash and consequently to restrict the benefits for the pensioners. The two sides often see themselves as representing different constituencies. If there is a conflict on the board of trustees, the employer, which usually holds the chair and the casting vote, tends to prevail. The interests of the employers have a nasty habit of coinciding with the agenda set by the big beasts of the pensions jungle.

Will no one ever take responsibility for the peril that has engulfed Irish pensioners?

It will be difficult, because all the darkest forces in the financial world are lined up against the battered pension fund members. The plundering is destined to continue, enriching a very few, impoverishing a great many and connived at by official Ireland.

7. The Property-Pushers' Bailout

August 2009 was a grim month for those in the property and construction business. House prices suffered their biggest monthly drop of the year. Ulster Bank was closing its First Active mortgage division and Anglo Irish Bank was in the process of getting one of its bailouts from the state. The big property developers and their sharp-suited banking partners were up to their knees in doo-doo. They'd be swimming in it soon.

That month saw developer Liam Carroll – who had built thousands of shoebox apartments around Dublin – head to the Four Courts in a desperate bid to save his empire. Carroll had borrowed hundreds of millions, property values were falling fast and nobody was buying his tiny apartments any more. The banks wanted their money back. But Carroll had a plan. If he could persuade the courts to let his companies go into examinership, there was a chance that he'd be able to keep control of at least part of his business.

The tycoon had hired some of the most respected names on the Irish corporate landscape to back his claims that, despite the property crash and the general economic misery, his companies would be able to trade their way out of difficulty. The High Court heard how David Cantwell of estate agency Hooke & MacDonald had predicted that over the next thirty months, 150 of Carroll's residential properties could be sold each year at or within 10 per cent of the forecasted asking price. An affidavit from property consultancy CBRE's deputy managing director Enda Luddy claimed to detect an upturn in the commercial property market, suggesting that international investors had expressed interest in snapping up close to €400 million worth of property assets on the Irish market. (Most of that €400 million related to an approach to buy a 50 per cent stake in Liffey Valley shopping centre – a deal that never got off the ground.) Luddy's affidavit contained the remarkable forecast that 'the sector is not on its last legs'. In fact, it was abundantly clear to most observers that it wasn't even able to stand up.

Fergal McGrath of accountancy firm LHM Casey McGrath – auditor to a number of Carroll's companies – produced a report which claimed that a number of the developer's firms could survive and trade out of difficulty. The accountancy firm KPMG projected that within fifteen months the assets of Carroll's Zoe group of companies would be worth more than its debts – in other words, the company would actually grow. KPMG's David Wilkinson believed that there was a reasonable prospect of survival for the companies if a court-approved restructuring of Carroll's debts, including interest-only payments on his bank loans, was put in place.

Carroll was more likely to be rescued by a heavenly choir bearing bank drafts. Judge Peter Kelly described the survival plan submitted by Carroll's lawyers as 'lacking in reality'. McGrath's projection, which had the Carroll group moving from insolvency and a deficit of more than €1 billion to a surplus of €290 million within three years, was also sarcastically described by Kelly as 'a remarkable turnaround'.

The country's biggest accountancy firm, the largest property consultancy, a major estate agency and a respected corporate audit practice had all come together to bat for their client Liam Carroll. The tycoon's bid failed because the judge didn't buy any of the baloney offered by the phalanx of so-called experts for hire. They had gone before the courts and made complete fools out of themselves with ridiculous projections. In any normal jurisdiction they would have been laughed out of town. Instead, before long most of them had landed plum contracts to provide advice and property services to the agency established by the state to clean up the property mess: NAMA.

Jim McConnon is a shopkeeper in Castleblayney, Co. Monaghan. He owns the local Supervalu store on the main street. Like many other people in the country, he caught a bad case of the property bug. Starting in 2003, he bought a number of sites close to his store with the intention of developing a giant shopping centre in the middle of the small rural town.

AIB financed the early stages of the project, but in November 2006 the bank decided that it did not want to go ahead with the funding of a major shopping centre on McConnon's sites. In April 2007, Zurich Bank – not widely known for property finance in Ireland – stepped in with an offer to fund McConnon's plan. The bank lent him €32 million for his development. CBRE had valued the project at €30 million.

Think about this for a moment.

Castleblayney has a population of 3,000 people. That meant that the development costs for the shopping centre were about €10,000 for every single inhabitant of the town. The surrounding area is sparsely populated. How on earth did anyone think that a shopping centre there could be worth €30 million? And how could anyone think that it was a good idea to lend that kind of money to someone with zero experience of the property market?

Unsurprisingly, McConnon couldn't get tenants for his newly built shopping centre, because the economy had fallen off a cliff. Receivers were appointed in October 2010. In early 2011, Zurich sought a summary judgement against McConnon to the tune of €32 million. The shopkeeper claimed that he shouldn't have to pay back the money for a number of reasons, including the fact that Zurich had allegedly failed to properly scrutinize 'nonsensical' site valuations provided by CBRE in 2007.

In March 2011, Zurich won the case – but it's unlikely to get its money back after the receivership process, as the shopping centre is now valued at less than €2 million. McConnon lost a subsequent appeal in June 2012. He faces financial ruin and Zurich has a big fat hole in its balance sheet.

CBRE, which valued a Castleblayney shopping centre at €30 million five years ago, is now one of NAMA's principal valuers.

The big estate agencies and accountancy, finance and legal firms in Ireland did spectacularly well out of the property boom. The big, complicated deals undertaken by the leading developers involved plenty of lucrative action for valuers, bean counters, financiers and solicitors. But when the bubble burst, all that was left was a stale smell and a deathly quiet. Banks weren't lending, punters weren't buying and the developers were actually being asked to pay some of their loans back. No transactions meant no fees. Savage redundancies and the closure of some of the best-known names in the industry were on the cards.

And then, out of nowhere at the end of 2009, came salvation – a new agency with a ridiculously large pot of money to spend on advisers and property professionals.

In late 2008, Finance Minister Brian Lenihan had asked economist Peter Bacon to examine the possibility of setting up a so-called 'bad bank' to cleanse the Irish banks of toxic loans, fixing their balance sheets and enabling them to start lending again. Bacon had authored a number of reports on the Irish property market; he had also been a director of Sean Mulryan's Ballymore Properties – which would become one of the top ten borrowers whose loans were taken over by NAMA.

Bacon's report, 'Proposal for a National Asset Management Agency', was delivered to Lenihan in April 2009. It would provide the blueprint for the creation of the new agency. (Three years later, Bacon would turn on his own creation. In June 2012, the economist produced a report on NAMA which claimed that the state agency wasn't 'achieving its potential' and should be sold off. The report was paid for by property company Treasury Holdings, which was locked in a savage legal battle with NAMA.) An interim team of NTMA staffers, including Brendan McDonagh, was tasked with getting the new body ready for launch.

The National Asset Management Agency's job was to acquire bad loans from the broken Irish banks and to work with developers to achieve maximum value for the underlying properties and hence maximum payback on the loans. NAMA became arguably the biggest property company on the planet. It controls €72 billion worth of loans secured on 35,000 individual properties or bits of land from Manhattan to Finglas.

Just like the developers during the boom, NAMA would need advice from estate agents, accountants and lawyers in trying to squeeze value out of its assets, and it had a €2.5 billion budget to spread about over the next decade. It's not as if Irish property professionals were in great demand from rival industries; many of the people employed in the business would have been lucky to work in the property sector ever again after the crash. Yet NAMA paid hefty salaries to people who had been at the coalface of the crash. You could have advised a developer to pay tens of millions for a field in the middle of nowhere based on valuations that turned out to be nonsensical, but it didn't damage your career. Not a jot. NAMA was there to take up the slack, and all previous errors were forgotten.

It was a bailout for the professional classes. In March 2012, Michael Noonan told the Dáil that from January 2010 to the end of January 2012, NAMA had spent an astounding €114.7 million in fees for professional advisers.

The country's largest accountancy firm, KPMG, had been paid €18.1 million, or close to €23,000 per day. Around €16.7 million of the fee was due to its role as NAMA's audit 'coordinator'. The sheer level of the fee paid to KPMG was extraordinary given the incestuous relationship KPMG had with both the bankers and the developers that had led the country to bankruptcy. KPMG had been AIB's auditor during its lending binge from 2002 to 2009, earning €49.9 million in fees. The bank's shambolic property lending practices ultimately saw it nationalized, and billions of euros worth of loans were transferred to NAMA. KPMG was also hand in glove with the country's most powerful property tycoons. These included Sean Mulryan's sprawling Ballymore Group. Liam Carroll, as we have seen, was a client, as were Cosgrave Developments, Paddy McKillen, Noel Smyth, Johnny Ronan and Richard Barrett's Treasury Holdings, Bernard McNamara's company Donatex, and the Dublin Docklands Development Authority.

While KPMG was the auditor of choice among the powerful property developers, it wasn't the only firm that had filing cabinets full of builders and land speculators. Anglo Irish bank auditor Ernst & Young was Galway developer Gerry Barrett's number cruncher. Despite having failed to spot the calamity unfolding at Anglo and the overloading of debt at Gerry Barrett's Edward Holdings, Ernst &

Young was hired by NAMA. It was a slap in the face for the taxpayer, who had to fork out for the near €30 billion bailout of Anglo and then cover Ernst & Young's fees at NAMA. The accountancy and consultancy firm earned €8.4 million from the state agency from January 2010 to the end of January 2012. Most of this fee related to 'loan valuation and related due diligence'. Ernst & Young was also appointed to a number of NAMA advisory panels and provides 'tax advisory' services to the agency.

You couldn't make it up.

BDO Simpson Xavier was Dundrum Shopping Centre developer Joe O'Reilly's principal auditor; it was paid €4.8 million for providing advice to NAMA in the two years up to January 2012.

PwC had less of a presence among the ranks of the developers than some of its competitors, but it was the biggest earner from the banks. PwC had earned a staggering €100.6 million from auditing Bank of Ireland's books during the property lending splurge. That certainly didn't exclude it from suckling at the NAMA teat: it earned €13.3 million in fees from NAMA from January 2010 to January 2012, while also picking up what is thought to be an eight-figure sum for helping to run state-owned AIB.

In March 2012, it emerged that NAMA had spent €27.55 million on legal expenses since it was established in December 2009. There was little surprise to find out that the consummate insiders Arthur Cox had trousered the biggest slice of pie, earning a total of €3.07 million in fees. This is the same Arthur Cox that advised the state. The legal firm also advised Bank of Ireland, as well as developers Treasury Holdings, Derek Quinlan's Quinlan Private, Paddy McKillen, Sean Mulryan's Ballymore Properties and Michael Cotter's Park Developments.

The international law firm Hogan Lovells picked up €2.93 million and London practice Allen & Overy received €2.47 million. The remaining firms in the top ten were Maples and Calder, which earned €2.05 million, Matheson Ormsby Prentice with €1.58 million, ByrneWallace with €1.51 million, William Fry with €1.45 million, A&L Goodbody with €1.37 million, Dillon Eustace with €1.19

million and Beauchamps with €1.17 million. (ByrneWallace was on the wrong end of a €17.7 million High Court judgement in July 2012. The court found that ByrneWallace had presided over 'most serious' failures when supposedly ensuring that KBC Bank had proper security over massive loans made to a large property developer.) Finance Minister Michael Noonan told the Dáil that NAMA would spend around €25 million on legal fees for the entirety of 2012.

The relationship between some of the powerful legal and accountancy firms and their builder clients was a giant circle jerk. Apart from auditing and providing consultancy work for their principal clients, some of the major players took it a step further: the clients became landlords. Treasury Holdings owns the Russell Court headquarters of KPMG. Sean Mulryan's Ballymore Properties built an enormous €160 million mixed-use development in Birmingham called the Snow Hill; the British wing of Ballymore's auditor KPMG moved into the building in 2006. It was the biggest pre-let outside of London since 2003.

Joe O'Reilly's company Chartered Land developed a swanky office block down at Grand Canal Quay; Chartered Land's lawyers BCM Hanby Wallace (later renamed ByrneWallace) became one of the key tenants, taking a massive 150,000 square foot block of the development. Liam Carroll's lawyers O'Donnell Sweeney were also set to move into the tycoon's planned 'mini Manhattan' office block scheme on the North Quays before the market slumped. Paddy Kelly's Redquartz Developments lists Beauchamps solicitors as one of its advisers; the law firm became the anchor tenant of Riverside Two, the landmark office block overlooking the Liffey, which was built by Kelly and his partners.

The mere fact that the lawyers and auditors would have to negotiate rents – which ran into the hundreds of thousands of euros each year – with their clients, had the potential to undermine their independence completely.

In October 2011, NAMA announced that only companies with a turnover of more than €25 million could tender to provide it with services. 'A minimum turnover is one of the indicators that helps

NAMA assess the capacity of a tenderer to meet its obligations and potential liabilities under that given contract,' a spokesman for the agency said.

The big firms, most of which had been in bed with the banks and developers, knew that their fee income would be safe – not that they'd ever had much reason to worry.

NAMA was set up in the white heat of the biggest economic crisis ever to hit Ireland. In the haste to get it up and running, some extraordinary compromises were made. In its bid to bulk up rapidly, NAMA went on a recruitment spree. While estate agents and commercial property players were gasping for breath as business slumped, NAMA started to wave massive salaries in front of certain property professionals. Some of the people who had been involved in the highest-profile land deals of the bubble period, and who were wondering how much longer they'd have a job, were now being offered a chance to bag healthy wages to assist in clearing up the mess they'd helped create. NAMA was going to be around for ten years at least, making it a far better long-term bet for employment than any of the struggling property consultancies around the town.

Brendan McDonagh, a chartered management accountant from Kerry who had been in charge of finance, technology and risk at the NTMA, became NAMA's chief executive in May 2009. Former school teacher turned taxman Frank Daly joined him as chairman in the autumn. Daly, a Dungarvan native, had joined the Revenue in 1963, and eventually rose to become the chairman of the Revenue Commissioners. On his retirement he was appointed as a public-interest director at Anglo Irish Bank. It was fairly clear that he couldn't work for both NAMA and Anglo, so he stepped down from the board of the bank to take the reins at the toxic-loan agency.

While McDonagh would have been used to the monster wages at the NTMA – by far the highest in the public sector – Daly's jaw must have dropped when he saw the riches on offer. McDonagh initially had a package of €500,000, with Daly earning around €250,000. McDonagh agreed a pay cut in line with other members of the public sector and is now paid €365,000 – almost twice as much as the

Taoiseach. In June 2011, it would emerge that sixteen members of McDonagh's team were earning €200,000 per year or more. That means that the faceless property executives working in the bowels of NAMA are getting paid more than departmental secretaries general, government ministers and some of the chief executives of semi-state companies. Another twenty-two staff members were being paid between €150,000 and €200,000, and a further sixty-five were taking home between €100,000 and €150,000 per year. These were quite obscene wages for a state agency that was trying to clean up a private-sector failure.

In February 2010, John Mulcahy, formerly of commercial property firm Jones Lang LaSalle, was brought in as NAMA's head of portfolio management, having served as an external adviser since the agency's establishment the previous year. Bertie Ahern had appointed Mulcahy to the board of the 'Bertie Bowl' steering group Campus and Stadium Ireland Development in March 2000; the project, which always looked like being a white elephant, was killed off in 2001.

Jones Lang LaSalle was one of the busiest commercial property advisory firms during the boom. It advised Dublin Port and South Wharf on the €412 million sale of the Irish Glass Bottle site in Ringsend to developers in 2006. The firm was an adviser as Eircom sold its Heuston Station headquarters to a Derek Quinlan consortium in December 2006 for a staggering €190 million in a sale-and-leaseback deal. It was also involved as heavily leveraged Irish buyers bought up trophy assets on the continent. Jones Lang LaSalle advised on Sean Quinn's €145 million buyout of the Hilton Hotel in Prague in 2004.

In September 2009, Mulcahy was questioned by an Oireachtas committee about the NAMA project and his own background. Mulcahy proclaimed that he had been a 'bear of property for the last four years' and that his negative view on the market had cost him speaking gigs as a result. How bearish was he? In July 2007, just a bit over two years earlier, he said 'the Irish commercial property market is extremely healthy'. Commercial property, of course, was Jones Lang LaSalle's business. He also observed, mildly, that 'the residential property market needs to take some fiscal Solpadeine before returning to wiser ways'.

Reflecting on the 10 per cent increase in office take-up in the first six months of 2007, Mulcahy gushed: 'The prospects for the second half of 2007 and the next year look equally promising, with a number of major users . . . seeking proposals for suitable office accommodation.' In other words, the market was predicted to keep on going strong.

Figures from Mulcahy's former employers show that total returns for commercial property dropped by 36.4 per cent in 2008.

Now, as NAMA's head of portfolio management, one of Mulcahy's key roles was to decide which half-finished developments had potential to make money at some stage and which schemes were complete turkeys. It made him the single most influential player ever in the Irish property sector – the man who would decide which developers would live to fight another day and which ones would have the life support switched off.

But Mulcahy had a problem. And it was a problem that had the potential to completely scupper NAMA and undermine the credibility the agency needed in order to function. In the *Sunday Independent* in April 2010, Nick Webb revealed that Mulcahy held a €2.3 million stake in the listed US parent company of his own former employer, Jones Lang LaSalle. So if Jones Lang LaSalle were to make a bumper profit out of business sent its way by NAMA, its share price would rise, making Mulcahy even richer.

The Oireachtas Joint Committee on Finance questioned NAMA executives over the operation of the monster state agency shortly after the story was published. Labour's Joan Burton asked Brendan McDonagh about Mulcahy's shareholding, suggesting that it 'would seem to be on the face of it a conflict of interest'. McDonagh responded that under 'house rules' Mulcahy would be precluded from involvement in any decisions relating to his former employer. Given that Jones Lang LaSalle would go on to win millions of euros worth of business from NAMA, the house rules promised to leave Mulcahy with an awful lot of free time.

NAMA says that it has clear procedures for managing potential conflicts of interest involving staff members. A spokesman told the *Irish Times* in March 2012:

A key item for any NAMA evaluation group for procurement of services is a declaration by each member that they have no conflict of interest in the outcome of the process. This enables the agency to ensure that potential conflicts of interest in the management of the loan portfolios are managed effectively, and that staff do not participate in decisions which may involve the allocation of work to companies for which they worked previously.

But Mulcahy wasn't the only high-ranking figure at NAMA who had a financial interest in a firm with which the agency was doing business. Limerick accountant Brian McEnery, who had been appointed to the board of NAMA by Fine Gael, was the party's director of elections in Limerick – where Finance Minister Michael Noonan has his seat. McEnery was a partner at Horwath Bastow Charleton, which, according to its website, 'can support businesses in preparing business plans and in dealing with NAMA and their other bankers'. In April 2012, he joined BDO Ireland as a partner. The firm examined developer business plans on behalf of NAMA and is on the state agency's panel of receivers.

In June 2011, McEnery's new employer was appointed as a receiver to developer David Daly's Irish and UK assets. Daly owed €457 million and was one of NAMA's biggest clients. BDO was also a close adviser to one of NAMA's top ten clients, Dundrum Shopping Centre developer Joe O'Reilly. Turlough Flynn, who works at O'Reilly's Crossridge Investments, was listed as a guest of BDO at the Chamber of Commerce dinner in the Four Seasons in February 2012. NAMA chairman Frank Daly was the keynote speaker that night.

NAMA's board is in receipt of commercially sensitive information, the kind of stuff that clients of a firm like BDO would kill for. Having the inside track on an organization as secretive as NAMA would be hugely valuable for dealmakers trying to buy assets from NAMA or even for negotiations with clients. McEnery will need all of his wits to avoid all the potential conflicts of interest that his new career move has brought.

Savills' executive Donal Kellegher became one of the key NAMA portfolio managers in late 2009. Nick Webb would reveal in the *Sunday Independent* that he was also a hefty shareholder in Savills plc, which was actively touting for business from NAMA. The senior executive held over 22,000 shares in the firm, worth close to €88,000, when he joined NAMA.

In early 2010, Ali Rohan – daughter of Ken Rohan, one of the country's wealthiest developers – was recruited by NAMA as a senior manager. She joined from the embattled property investment firm D2 Private, which was run by Deirdre Foley and David Arnold, father of RTÉ star Leigh Arnold. During the boom D2 had put together syndicates of the great and the good to snaffle up trophy assets in Ireland and abroad. Ali Rohan also owned a 15.4 per cent stake in her father's Airspace Investments. Airspace, chaired by former Arthur Cox chairman James O'Dwyer, had bank loans of over €27 million at the end of December 2010, according to filings. Apart from owning a major stake in a property company which had assets worth over €46 million, Rohan herself was a punter on the market. She had a stake in the company that owned the Carluccio's restaurant building on Dublin's Dawson Street, along with investors including former Anglo Irish Bank chairman Sean FitzPatrick's son Jonathan, former AIB chairman Dermot Gleeson and a firm associated with the Crampton building dynasty.

She was also a shareholder in a major UK syndicate which imploded in the downturn. The syndicate, which also included Fergal Quinn, bought the Woolgate building in London for €390m in 2006. In early 2012, the building was sold for a loss, wiping out all of the investors' equity. Now Rohan had been recruited to help fix the Irish property sector.

Kevin Nowlan, who was hired as a portfolio manager, had family connections in the industry. His father, Bill Nowlan, controls the property-focused asset management firm W. K. Nowlan, and his brother Rod works with commercial property outfit Bannon. Nowlan had worked as the managing director of his father's business as well as serving at Treasury Holdings and Anglo Irish Bank. W. K. Nowlan is now one of NAMA's principal advisers, sitting on the panel to provide property management services and valuations as well as doing receivership work. The firm also produced a major report on real-estate investment trusts for NAMA.

Mark Pollard, who joined NAMA as a portfolio manager, had been a development manager at Treasury Holdings, which would become one of NAMA's biggest clients. Hugh Linehan joined NAMA from Aviva, where he had helmed the pension giant's €600 million property investment portfolio. Linehan was involved in Aviva's €177 million purchase of four office blocks at AIB headquarters in Ballsbridge at the top of the market in 2006. Last February, Aviva started to seek a buyer for those office blocks. The price tag was closer to €85 million. It represented a massive loss on Linehan's property punt. The taxpayer must hope that Linehan and his associates will get better results in their new jobs.

Another key appointment to NAMA was Mary Birmingham, who had worked as the project manager for a planned €2 billion mixed-use development in Bray, which was being pursued by the Paddy Kelly-fronted Pizarro Developments. Kelly would become one of NAMA's biggest borrowers; the project would end up being mothballed. Birmingham would become a senior portfolio manager at NAMA, with Treasury Holdings one of her principal responsibilities. Pizarro backers Paddy Kelly and Alanis – the McCormack family investment firm – had been involved with Treasury in a scheme to develop the Blackrock Baths.

Other high-profile NAMA recruits included Paul King, who had helped manage the vast €1 billion real-estate portfolio of Irish Life, one of the largest property investors in the country.

A further round of hires in June 2011 saw Lisney director and former head of valuation Paul McNamara tapped up to join the state agency. McNamara was the guy who provided the Irish property valuations for one of the frothiest real-estate flotations of the entire Celtic Tiger era. Banana company Fyffes and its principal shareholder the McCann family held large blobs of land in Dublin and Louth. In order to capitalize on the rising values, they decided to spin off some of these property interests into a separate listed company called Blackrock Land International. As well as all the Fyffes properties, it would also seek to buy up and develop other projects across Europe. McNamara valued these Irish properties for potential shareholders.

The Blackrock Land International prospectus for admission on to the AIM and IEX markets makes for extraordinary reading. Almost 29 acres of 'development land' near Navan, earmarked for retail warehousing use, was valued at a stonking €24.25 million in 2006, with a warehouse on 1.6 acres in Dublin 7 valued at an extraordinary €25 million. The entire Irish assets of the new company were valued at €139 million by Paul McNamara in May 2006. By the end of 2011, things had gone so badly for Blackrock International that it had even been forced to change its name: the newly retitled Balmoral Land was sitting on Irish property assets worth just over €56 million, according to its financial filings. The values ascribed by McNamara had been miles off the mark. And now he's one of the key people deciding what property is worth for NAMA.

As well as hiring some of the central players in the whole property boom, NAMA saw no difficulty with paying their former firms millions of euros for advice. In March 2012, Michael Noonan told the Dáil that €13.3 million had been divvied out from January 2010 to the end of January 2012 to various estate agents to provide valuation services to NAMA. John Mulcahy's old firm Jones Lang LaSalle got the biggest cheque, earning €1.24 million. GVA Donal O Buachalla was another big winner, bagging €1.2 million. Colliers International earned €978,000, Lisney another €861,000 and Knight Frank picked up €756,000. Others in the top ten included W. K. Nowlan Associates, Cushman & Wakefield, Lambert Smith Hampton, HWBC and Savills Commercial. Noonan added that of the €13.3 million spent by the agency on property valuations, €12.4 million related to one-off property valuations done as part of due diligence on acquired loans. The balance was for valuation required as part of the agency's ongoing management of its portfolio.

In June 2012, in a response to a parliamentary question from Fine Gael's Michelle Mulherin, Noonan revealed that Jones Lang LaSalle had received more than €3.65 million in 'property due diligence' and 'portfolio management fees' from NAMA from the time it was set up until the end of March 2012.

Department of Finance secretary general Kevin Cardiff, right, and senior official Michael McGrath on their way to a hearing at the Public Accounts Committee in 2011. Cardiff, who was the department's top banking official during the period when the banks were running themselves into the ground, was ushered into a cushy new job in Europe – despite a massive error in the accounting of the national debt on his watch. (Gerry Mooney, *Sunday Independent*)

At the DIRT enquiry in 2000: (from left to right) secretary general to the government Dermot McCarthy, clerk of the Dáil Kieran Coughlan, secretary general at the Department of Finance John Hurley and secretary general at the Department of Public Service Management Tom Considine. The DIRT scandal should have been a warning about the Irish banks and regulators, but it wasn't. (Steve Humphreys, *Irish Independent*)

Richard Burrows, then chairman of Irish Distillers, right, chatting with Irish Olympic Council president Pat Hickey in 2001. In 2009, the same year he resigned as governor of the failed Bank of Ireland, Burrows was named to the board of British American Tobacco and to the IMF's Regional Advisory Group for Europe. (Frank McGrath, *Irish Independent*)

Former AIB chairman, former Attorney General and all-round master of the universe Peter Sutherland, right, with former Finance Minister Charlie McCreevy, left, and journalist Marc Coleman at the 2007 launch of Coleman's book about the Irish economy, *The Best is Yet to Come*. (Mark Condren, *Irish Independent*)

Anglo Irish Bank director (and former Bank of Ireland chief executive) Maurice Keane and acting Anglo chairman Donal O'Connor arriving at the Department of Finance, February 2009. (Frank McGrath, *Irish Independent*)

Bank of Ireland chief executive Richie Boucher and governor Pat Molloy at the Bank's AGM in April 2012, at the O'Reilly Hall in UCD. (Frank McGrath, *Irish Independent*)

Tom Parlon moved swiftly and seamlessly from the government – where he had responsibility for the OPW – to heading the Construction Industry Federation. (Frank McGrath, *Irish Independent*)

Olwyn Enright quit politics to spend more time with her family. A month after the 2011 general election, she was back in the game with a public affairs job at Edelman PR. (Tony Gavin, *Sunday Independent*)

As chief executive of the NTMA, succeeding Michael Somers, John Corrigan presides over an agency that has become a byword for stratospheric pay and a lack of transparency. (Frank McGrath, *Irish Independent*)

As managing partner of law firm Arthur Cox, Pádraig Ó Ríordáin had his fingers in a remarkable number of pies, including many that had a major bearing on the public interest. (Damien Eagers, *Irish Independent*)

Ronan Murphy, managing partner of the accountancy and consulting giant PWC.

Tiarnan O'Mahoney – pictured here between Sean FitzPatrick and Willie McAteer in 1999 – was the heir apparent to Seanie's throne at Anglo Irish Bank. In 2005 he left the bank, having failed to secure the top job; by 2007 his firm ISTC had gone spectacularly bust. Neither this nor his part in the Anglo bubble prevented him from holding his position as chairman of the Pensions Board. (Tony Gavin, *Sunday Independent*)

Frank Daly, chairman of NAMA – which has provided extensive employment for professionals from the very firms that contributed to the property crash. (Mark Condren, *Irish Independent*)

NAMA chief executive Brendan McDonagh, left, with John Mulcahy of commercial property giant Jones Lang LaSalle in 2009. A few months later Mulcahy would become NAMA's head of portfolio management – the most powerful job in Irish property. (Frank McGrath, *Irish Independent*)

Supreme Court Judge John Murray, who served seven years as Chief Justice, at the votive mass to mark the commencement of the Michaelmas law term in 2011, flanked by Turlough O'Donnell, SC, and Mr Justice Roderick Murphy of the High Court. (Maxwell Photography)

Among the political operatives and lawyers who worked on behalf of Mildred Fox TD (standing centre, with rosette) at the Wicklow general election recount in 2002 were Fianna Fáil national organizer Sean Sherwin and senior counsel Donagh McDonagh (with beard). McDonagh was later appointed to the Circuit Court by the Fianna Fáil-led government.

Mattie McGrath TD, a rebel within Fianna Fáil, was disconcerted to find himself before Judge McDonagh when he was tried for assault in 2008.

One of the stalwarts of official Ireland, Greencore chairman (and long-time Anglo Irish Bank director) Ned Sullivan. (Mark Condren, *Irish Independent*)

Liam O'Mahony was chief executive of building-materials firm CRH from 2000 to 2008 – remarkably successful years for Ireland's biggest company. O'Mahony is now chairman of the IDA. (Tony Gavin, *Sunday Independent*)

In the sacristy of the Vatican Palace's Pauline Chapel, a plaque acknowledges the generous financial support of some of Ireland's leading businessmen – Sean Mulryan, Derek Quinlan, Johnny Ronan, Sean FitzPatrick, Denis O'Brien and Michael Fingleton – for the restoration of the chapel.

These were the same auctioneers, commercial property firms and valuation specialists who had helped puff the market up into such a catastrophic bubble. They had been dismally wrong in their reading of the market over the last decade and there is no good reason to believe that their specialist knowledge and expertise has made them any more adept at valuing the market nowadays.

Some of the forecasts and predictions of these highly paid advisers have been buried away out of sight. Log on to the website of Savills, Sherry FitzGerald, CBRE or Jones Lang LaSalle to see what these highly esteemed property professionals thought of the prospects for the market before it crashed.

There's nothing there. The research is no longer available.

We've found some excruciatingly embarrassing proclamations, though. Hamilton Osborne King – which would become Savills – published a 'property outlook' twice a year. In the introduction to its spring 2006 edition, its then managing director Paul McNeive triumphantly predicted, 'There is no reason to believe that prices will not continue to strengthen to the end of the decade at least.' Prices started to go south about six months later.

The report arrogantly dismissed concerns about the banks' lending splurge.

> Residential mortgage lending grew at what some consider to be an alarming rate of 29 per cent year on year to the end of December (or by just over €21 billion) and is a cause of regular speculation about over borrowing and the sustainability of growth in the housing market. But the level of mortgage lending last year, taken as a percentage of the amount of money spent on housing in total, gives a reassuring picture.

So the doomsayers were wrong? It gets even more insane.

> This trend is set to continue as all analysts agree that the performance of the economy is on a sustainable path. The question now is: will the Irish be spending €50 billion a year on Irish property by the end of the decade?

The market soon rendered this question laughable – but that didn't stop Savills from purveying the following projection to potential clients and investors in November 2008. Joan Henry, head of research at Savills Ireland, wrote:

> We expect that supply and demand factors have pushed prices close to the bottom and that by mid-2009, prices will have stabilised. What is needed then is a period of at least six months to a year of price stability to allow buyer confidence to be restored which will in turn increase activity levels. Given the extent of the adjustment in the property market and the pain being taken this year, coupled with decisive action by central banks to free up the liquidity situation, we expect the market to bottom out by 2009 and for activity levels to pick up throughout next year, albeit at considerably lower values and volumes.

The desperately tragic thing is that people believed the guff purveyed by the estate agents. Young couples borrowed hundreds of thousands of euros to buy starter homes in new estates. The experts were saying that prices were going to keep rising, so what was the risk? Property sellers have escaped scot-free with no repercussions for their sham advice and forecasts of vast profits as house prices were puffed and puffed. While stockbrokers and investment banks – including Bloxham and Morgan Stanley – have had to pay eight-figure sums in compensation to Irish investors to whom they'd sold pups, the key players in the property sector, far from having to pay for their mistakes, have been richly rewarded.

Despite getting its projections so wrong, Savills is now one of NAMA's key advisers. It has a variety of highly paid roles, including shifting Gerry Gannon's €120 million 'Chrome' portfolio of UK land and buildings and serving as a receiver for the Becbay company which spent €412 million buying the Irish Glass Bottle site in Ringsend; it is also on NAMA's loan sales advisory panel. In its annual return, Savills Ireland, now chaired by Larry Brennan and run by Angus Potterton, described 2010 as a 'turnaround year' for the company, as consultancy work for NAMA and insolvency processes led to the company returning to profit.

CBRE is another major NAMA fee earner that has expunged its boom-time views from its website. But we've tracked down some dangerous predictions and examples of wanton bigging-up of the market just before the crash. At its 'Next decade – Next Challenge' conference in June 2005, CBRE research chief Marie Hunt predicted that the average price of a three-bed semi-detached house would hit €400,000 by 2015, with the average price of a similar house in Dublin closer to €525,000. CBRE also suggested that prime property values could 'double' in value over the next decade. Why wouldn't a young couple buy a house with that kind of outlook for the market?

CBRE's bi-monthly research report of August 2007 viewed the dip in the market as 'a temporary correction phase'. The section on new homes added:

> New homes prices will remain very stable for the foreseeable future, representing a good buying opportunity for many first-time buyers.

Ouch! The 350,000 people in negative equity will feel sick at the thought of CBRE continuing to pontificate on the market.

In January 2008, after a full year of price falls, CBRE's annual property outlook report forecast that Irish commercial real estate would 'weather the storm well'. It figured that domestic investment activity would 'remain strong' but that the bulk of the transaction activity would take place in 'the second half of the year'. It also predicted that there would be 'strong demand for well-located sites' in the development land market. In July 2008, the firm's bi-monthly research report suggested that:

> . . . property defaults and forced sales, which characterised previous downturns in the property market, are unlikely to manifest themselves in this cycle.

Six months later, in January 2009, it told clients that the market was 'very challenging' – but not for long.

> It will likely be 2010 before conditions in the Irish property market improve to any significant degree.

If an investor had taken CBRE's advice on board at any of these stages, they would have lost a fortune. And now CBRE is one of NAMA's principal advisers.

NAMA came at the right time for CBRE, which lost shedloads of money in 2008 and 2009 as lucrative investment property deals dried up. However, it was the only firm to be employed by NAMA to provide valuations in all three of its key markets – Ireland, the UK and America – and by 2010 it was back in the black, with revenues up 60 per cent to €13.6 million and pre-tax profits of €1.7 million.

Jones Lang LaSalle's boom-time end-of-year reviews are no longer available on its website. This is a shame, as they included many pearls of wisdom from its then boss John Mulcahy. Mulcahy's former number two John Moran runs the property firm now. In December 2007, Jones Lang LaSalle was predicting that the amount of money spent by Irish investors on domestic commercial property would actually increase. Just €1.5 billion had been spent in 2007, and the spoofers confidently forecast that €2 billion would be spent in 2008. In fact, less than €500 million was spent in the year as investors fled to avoid the falling knife. In 2009, less than €100m was spent by investors on Irish property.

Jones Lang LaSalle was splattered by the property crash. Revenues slumped from €20.4m in 2007 down to €9.2m at the end of 2010. As the investment market went blue, Jones Lang LaSalle was able to keep afloat through hefty fees from NAMA. In September 2011, John Moran said that the company's work for NAMA 'was relatively good for us in 2010'. He was putting it mildly. John Mulcahy's former firm was the biggest recipient of valuation fees from NAMA, as noted above, earning €1.24 million from 2010 to January 2012. The €1.24 million represented only a portion of Jones Lang LaSalle's income from NAMA. The company also earned €2.8m 'for portfolio management' fees over the same period. Sinn Féin TD Gerry Adams, who was provided with the valuation figures by Finance Minister Michael Noonan, expressed concern about the level of fees being paid by the agency to Mulcahy's former employer. 'The fact that a firm with close links to NAMA management is the top recipient of these fees highlights again the need for closer scrutiny of the work of NAMA,' Adams said. 'I am concerned that NAMA is not properly managing conflicts of interest.'

DTZ Sherry FitzGerald is another enormous fee earner from NAMA. It is part of Mark FitzGerald's Sherry FitzGerald group, which was the largest house seller during the boom. Its pronouncements on property prices carried serious clout until the music stopped. In-house economist Marian Finnegan told the *Irish Independent* in January 2006 that the market was going to continue upwards:

> ... with rises in the second-hand market likely to be closer to 10% nationally and slightly higher in the main cities ... Property still looks like providing fantastic opportunities in the years ahead.

Midway through 2006, she thought that ECB interest-rate rises could slow the market – but not by much.

> The combination of this and the reduction in the gap between supply and demand will facilitate a moderate [sic] of house price growth with current estimates suggesting price inflation will average 15% during the year.

In the summer of 2007, Finnegan wrote a piece for *Finance Magazine* in which she outlined why 'demand for homes and the value of those homes will be sustained for many years to come'. The piece concluded with some of the worst investment advice ever written.

> The combination of a reduction in the gap between demand and supply and the recent upward movement in interest rates will facilitate a moderation of house price growth in the year ahead with current estimates suggesting price inflation will slow to single digit figures in 2007 and into 2008. Such growth rates may be far from the giddy days of the late 1990s when price growth of 10 per cent was achieved in a quarter but they still underwrite a view that residential property offers investors of all types a safe and stable vehicle to invest a relatively small quantity of money and enjoy a very satisfying rate of return.

By July 2008, the country was in desperate straits, with panicked stock markets and property prices in free fall. But Finnegan was like an anti-Cassandra. She released a statement that predicted:

. . . the slowdown in the delivery of new property to the market will facilitate in [sic] return to positive price inflation in the short term albeit at a much lower pace than experienced during the Celtic Tiger period.

House prices would fall another 50 per cent after her toxic forecasts. Strangely enough, Finnegan's views on the market are no longer readily available on the Sherry FitzGerald website. In January 2010, she told the *Irish Times*:

> In my view the market is bottoming out. This is not to suggest a remarkable recovery, rather a stabilisation and a return to a property market serving society, rather than society serving the property market. The indications to this effect outlined above are augmented by anecdotal evidence on the ground.

Residential property prices promptly tumbled 15 per cent in 2010, according to daft.ie, and another 18 per cent in 2011.

Sherry FitzGerald, where Marian Finnegan remains as chief economist, is making lots of money out of NAMA. It has handled some high-profile transactions for the agency, including the €10 million deal to sell Bernard McNamara's home on Ailesbury Road to the family of tycoon J. P. McManus. Having lost €3.79m in 2007, €15.5m in 2008 and €5m in 2009, Sherry FitzGerald returned to profitability in 2010, with pre-tax profits of €2.5m.

The move from moribund state-owned banks or NAMA to the lucrative world of private equity funds was an obvious one for many formerly high-ranking bankers or property professionals. Brian Goggin, who was chief executive of Bank of Ireland when it racked up billions in dumb property loan losses, became an adviser to the €70 billion US private equity giant Apollo – which bought MBNA's Irish and UK credit card operations. Why was Goggin hired? It sure as hell wasn't because Apollo was impressed with his track record in running a bank. But he knew what was under the hood at the Irish banks. Former AIB executive chairman Dan O'Connor became an adviser for Anchorage Capital in Ireland, while Ulster Bank chief executive Cormac McCarthy joined up with Oaktree – the US distressed asset buyout fund that tried to take over the rump of the McInerney building firm. He would later move to become finance chief at Paddy Power bookmakers. Tiarnan O'Mahoney, the ex-Anglo Irish Bank chief operations officer – Sean FitzPatrick's number two for many years – was also linked with a role for the Fortress Investment Group.

Having inside knowledge of the workings of a particular bank and its loan book is exceptionally valuable for any private equity fund targeting potential deals in Ireland. But having someone with the lowdown on NAMA must be like finding a goose that lays golden eggs. Given NAMA's lack of engagement with buyers and the complete lack of transparency over its assets and loan book, the top executives at the state agency must be beating off headhunters and corporate recruiters with sticks.

In April 2012, Nick Webb revealed that NAMA portfolio manager Enda Farrell had left to join US private equity firm Forum Partners. He was to set up its Irish operations. Property companies are on the menu for Forum.

A NAMA spokesman told Nick Webb that the agency didn't have any kind of non-compete clause in employment contracts. Under ethics in public office legislation, senior civil servants must wait a year before joining any private company that operates in the same sphere as their civil service role. This rule, intended to minimize conflicts of interest, does not apply to NAMA. A NAMA employee could spend six months filtering through the assets and loans of a major developer and then simply hop off to a vulture fund with the confidential information. NAMA argued that it only sells assets through a competitive bidding process and with an up-to-date market valuation conducted by one of its panel of advisers. These are the same advisers who were valuing fields in the middle of nowhere at tens of millions of euros six years ago.

NAMA's fear of cocking up a deal by selling an asset too cheaply hasn't stopped it from offloading loans and properties – although 90 per cent of this had happened in the UK and US, which did not experience anything like the drop in values seen in the Irish market. This is a hugely sensitive area for the agency and one which is marked by almost Vatican levels of secrecy. It is also the area where the taxpayer can be hurt most if NAMA gets outfoxed by the giants of Wall Street or wealthy private equity barons. NAMA has a list of rules to protect taxpayers' interests. Developers cannot buy back projects that they've lost control of to NAMA. Staffers in NAMA cannot work with clients or projects that they've dealt with during their previous careers in the private sector. And most importantly, nothing, absolutely nothing, can be sold off without a competitive bidding process and an up-to-date valuation.

In October 2011, NAMA gave the green light to developer Donal Mulryan – a brother of one of its largest borrowers, Sean Mulryan – to sell his property portfolio valued at €250 million. Donal Mulryan used to work in his brother's company Ballymore before branching out with his own West Properties, which owned a number of development sites and several fully finished schemes. Most of the lands and properties were in the north-west of England and London; they included the landmark Skyline Central tower in Manchester, the tallest apartment block in the city and home to local footballers and celebrities. Savills was appointed to sell the assets. The following month, a unit of Morgan Stanley agreed a deal with NAMA to buy the bank loans associated with Mulryan's properties. It was reported that Morgan Stanley – one of the world's biggest and most powerful banks – bought the loans at a 70 per cent discount. Morgan Stanley was one of the advisers to the state on the eve of the controversial bank guarantee scheme and was also hired by the state-owned AIB to help sell off assets.

The *Irish Independent* reported that Donal Mulryan was to be paid to manage the portfolio for Morgan Stanley. NAMA has a rule that no developer is allowed to bid for assets he or she once owned. Mulryan did not put any equity into the Morgan Stanley buyout and thus did not breach the NAMA rule. Even so, here was an overborrowed developer being helped back into the saddle by the taxpayer, giving him a chance to make a fortune again.

One of the real worries about NAMA is that it may end up selling its loans back to the developers who borrowed the money in the first place, netting these speculators huge profits. A newspaper office gets to hear an awful lot of speculation about such things but precious little in the way of hard evidence. Fianna Fáil senator and auctioneer Mark Daly claimed in January 2011 that NAMA was offloading assets below market value to people associated with the original borrower. In June 2011, Taoiseach Enda Kenny, speaking at the British Irish Parliamentary Assembly, expressed concern over these allegations. Several days later, he withdrew his comments and announced that he was satisfied with NAMA's conduct in the disposal of assets. Transparency over the sales of NAMA assets, such as selling prices and details of bidders and advisers, would go a long way towards allaying these fears.

In the run-up to the 2011 election, Fine Gael's manifesto promised that 'details of all non-performing loans acquired by NAMA will be available for scrutiny on a Public Register'. This would also provide much-needed transparency. But the vote-grabbing promise has simply been shelved.

NAMA has occasionally moved quickly, and controversially, to sell property. In July 2011, writing in the *Sunday Independent*, Ronald Quinlan revealed that billionaire industrialist Martin Naughton had bought Derek Quinlan's luxury penthouse at the Merrion Hotel from a NAMA-appointed receiver weeks after NAMA took control of the apartment. Documents in the Property Registration Authority showed that Naughton completed his purchase on 3 June 2011 – several months after NAMA took ownership of the 2,500 square foot pad, and before the NAMA-appointed receiver to the property placed it on the open market. According to the report, Naughton paid €2.2 million for the apartment. The property was never advertised for sale.

'A receiver has a statutory responsibility to achieve the best price possible in the disposal of an asset and we have no doubt that this was achieved to the benefit of the taxpayer,' a NAMA spokesman told us in April 2012. NAMA declined to discuss the sales process. The agency won't, of course, say if there have been any other similar deals done without a competitive bidding process.

In January 2012, NAMA agreed to sell a 125-acre block of land at Curraheen, Co. Cork to the Munster Agricultural Society and University College Cork. The land had been bought by developer John Fleming in 2005 for €17 million; NAMA sold it seven years later for closer to €4 million. 'The land, while not advertised for sale, was on the market and had appropriate signage on the arterial, western route into the city,' according to the examiner in January 2012. A few 'for sale' signs in a field in the middle of nowhere? It's hardly the best way to drum up a competitive sales process.

In April 2012, a block of 450 acres near Cork was sold by NAMA for around €7 million. The purchaser is thought to be a local farmer. Castlelands Construction, a local property development firm, had spent close to €100 million putting the land bank together during the boom. Savills acted for NAMA and the land owners in the sale of the land. It was not advertised on the open market. Savills said that the bidding was competitive and recommended the sale. NAMA commented that 'the sales process was independently managed by Savills, on behalf of the debtor, and was designed to obtain the best achievable price for the property', adding that it was 'a competitive process and this is reflected in the fact that the final price achieved was above that which was considered feasible prior to sale, having conducted an independent valuation'. It would be easier to believe this if the land had been advertised and sold with more transparency.

Apart from the utter lack of transparency, the failure to provide pricing clarity to the domestic market through asset sales, and the massive costs incurred, NAMA has also failed the few property players who didn't over-borrow and who aren't corporate corpses. But few in the industry were brave enough to speak up about it and even fewer were in the position to actually do anything about it – until Bill Durkan's UK-based construction firm Durkan Brothers decided it had had enough. In an unprecedented move, Durkan decided to pay off €43 million in NAMA bank loans rather than continue to deal with the necrotic state agency. According to Durkan Group documents obtained by Nick Webb in January 2012:

On December 23, 2010, NAMA advised that it had acquired the Durkan Group loans (all good loans). The group was left in the invidious and unfortunate predicament of having to engage in a cumbersome, costly and time-consuming exercise with an agency whose ultimate aim is the realisation of loans on behalf of the Irish Government. Negotiations with NAMA over facilities and the repayment of the loans proved to be unsatisfactory and would have been most uneconomic if accepted.

The documents further noted:

By July 2011, it had become abundantly clear to the group that NAMA was not in a position to facilitate the reasonable requirements as set out in our comprehensive business plan submitted to NAMA on March 31, 2010. On August 2, the group repaid its entire indebtedness to NAMA.

While NAMA's initial and unofficial response was to welcome the fact that it had got a borrower off its books, it completely missed the point. NAMA was seen as an obstacle to recovery. Of course, few other property developers or construction moguls had the resources to pay off their loans, and banks weren't exactly lining up to offer to refinance borrowings held on NAMA's books.

The central objective behind NAMA was that it would strip out the loss-making property loans from bank balance sheets, enabling them to function properly and start lending again. Irish Banking Federation figures show just how badly it has failed in its primary role. There has been a massive contraction in mortgage lending, from €39.8 billion in 2007 to €2.46 billion last year. In May 2012, the IBF/PwC mortgage lending survey revealed that €450 million had been lent in new mortgages in the first three months of 2012.

But consumers aren't just being starved of credit for mortgages. Businesses are struggling too. In the first three months of 2012, the Credit Review Office, which hears appeals from SMEs that have been refused credit, found that lending transactions had fallen a scary 15 per cent from the first quarter of 2011. The ongoing credit crunch is starving the economy.

'NAMA has destroyed the property market. The Minister should call the people from NAMA into his office and tell them to put €2 billion or €3 billion of property on the market at fire sale prices. These may be sold too cheaply but at least that would establish a floor in the property market and people would start again. Currently everybody is watching prices currently falling and nobody will get into the market. They believe prices will fall further and are waiting for the bottom.' This quote isn't from some crackpot academic or media whore. It was Michael Noonan, speaking in the Dáil when in Opposition in 2010.

As Minister for Finance since early 2011, Noonan's attempts to change the way the agency operates have been weak. A review by Irish-born former HSBC boss Michael Geoghegan suggested that it lacked entrepreneurial zeal. Cosmetic changes occurred in late 2011, when Northern Irish accountant Peter Stewart and then former Bank of Ireland executive Michael Connolly stepped down from the board. Noonan sought to create a new advisory board above the NAMA board which would have his ear. It didn't exactly bowl people over when it emerged that the advisory board was to be made up of Geoghegan, NAMA chairman Frank Daly, and a Northern Irish quantity surveyor called Denis Rooney. There was a little bit of jigging around with executive levels, with John Mulcahy's role being tweaked slightly and the establishment of a number of new divisions including Asset Management, Asset Recovery and Strategy and Communications. The civil service mentality remained unchallenged.

The creation of NAMA was a dramatic gesture by Brian Lenihan. Apart from cleansing the banks, it was supposed to bring about seismic change. But it has just maintained the status quo. The professional classes have been bailed out and even the property developers are being kept afloat. The helicopters have gone but they aren't shopping in Aldi yet. Since NAMA started it has extended €55 million to 41 developers in 'overheads' which include their salaries. That's around €1.3 million in 'overheads' for each of the developers – far, far more than the average €70,000 to €100,000 per year that most NAMA developers are supposed to be getting as a wage. Three developers are receiving salaries of €200,000 per year – or about the same as the Taoiseach.

The last time anybody looked, there weren't swathes of property developers writhing in agony on crucifixes lining the Bray Road. In December 2010, an explosive *Prime Time* programme showed secret camera footage of NAMA top ten developer Gerry Gannon sweating profusely as he lugged bags of shopping from Brown Thomas to his Range Rover. Another massive borrower, Michael O'Flynn, was filmed taking an Augusta helicopter from his home to watch his horses run at Down Royal. There had been some carefully managed and high-profile removal vans. Paddy Kelly – one of the first developers to go splat – moved out of his home on Shrewsbury Road. He travelled about a mile and a half away to another large red-brick in the heart of Dublin 4. Bernard McNamara also moved from his Ailesbury Road palace – the one with a retractable dance floor. He flew off to the Gulf to start building again. Noel Smyth's 400-piece art collection – including a set of Harry Clarke stained-glass windows – was sold off, as were Sean Mulryan's racehorses. But by and large the developers remain wealthy and comfortable.

In March 2012, NAMA developer Michael O'Flynn was pictured at Cheltenham watching his horse China Rock race in the Gold Cup. O'Flynn had entered other horses in various Cheltenham races – hardly the actions of a cash-strapped developer. The following month, China Rock romped home in the Punchestown Gold Cup, which had a prize fund of €86,000, bringing the nine-year-old's career earnings past the €246,000 mark. Michael Cotter of Park Developments spent a large chunk of the spring of 2012 sailing his luxury €1 million yacht *Whisper* in the Caribbean.

While you can't get a loan from your bank and the taxman is decimating your pay packet, developers are sailing in the Caribbean or cheering on their racehorses at Cheltenham. Sales of BMWs, so beloved of the professional classes, are creeping back up.

As usual, the little guy is getting stuck with the bill.

NAMA is not doing what it says on the tin.

8. The Judges: JAABs for the Boys

How the Judiciary Win Their Wigs

Mattie McGrath was the full Fianna Fáil shilling.

His father fought in the War of Independence and on the Republican side in the Civil War, and was imprisoned by the pro-treaty side for fourteen months for his pains. He went on to be a founding father of Fianna Fáil in the village of Newcastle, near Clonmel, in South Tipperary.

Growing up in Newcastle, Mattie became active in the party when he was sixteen. He rose through the ranks by fighting local elections, and served as a county councillor from 1999 until 2007. McGrath's energy was welcome within Fianna Fáil – so long as his ambitions were confined to council level. It was when he decided to have a run at the Dáil that he suddenly met fierce, local internal party opposition.

McGrath decided to make his charge on Dáil Éireann for the 2007 general election. An opening had appeared when Noel Davern, who had held a seat for Fianna Fáil for a total of thirty-two years, decided to step down. Noel was the son of Michael Davern, TD for Tipperary South from 1948 to 1965. Michael's son (and Noel's brother) Don had succeeded his father for three years but died unexpectedly while in office in 1968. Noel in turn took over from Don and after a short break in the European Parliament (where he lost his seat) he returned to the Dáil in 1987 to enjoy another twenty-year stint.

In 2007, for the first time for fifty years, no Davern was pitching for the Dáil seat. McGrath made his move.

McGrath was not part of the Tipperary South succession plan at Fianna Fáil headquarters in Dublin's Lower Mount Street. They would have favoured another Davern, but none was offering in 2007. Mount Street's favourite, in the absence of a Davern, was Martin Mansergh. He had been an insider in Fianna Fáil under three Taoisigh; he had served as special adviser to Charlie Haughey, Albert Reynolds and

Bertie Ahern. Mount Street had already helped Mansergh to a Seanad seat in 2002. Now, in 2007, they wanted the Mansergh brand in the Dáil. There could not have been a bigger contrast in style or outlook than there was between Mansergh and McGrath. Mansergh was an English public schoolboy, an Oxford-educated Protestant who played a role in the Church of Ireland General Synod. McGrath was a devout Catholic, a loose cannon who shot from the hip.

The Davern dynasty was opposed to McGrath's nomination. If Mattie once set his foot in Dáil Éireann he would be difficult to dislodge – he was only fifty, against Mansergh's sixty. But McGrath fought like a terrier for the nomination. Unfazed by the opposition of the Daverns and totally impervious to the pressures from Mount Street, he was hell-bent on taking his fight to the convention floor. He had no quarrel with Mansergh (the two men speak highly of each other), but they were chalk and cheese. Mansergh was the career insider; McGrath was the maverick whom party headquarters and the Daverns wanted to stop in his tracks. Their opposition looked hopeless when McGrath topped the poll at Fianna Fáil's candidate selection convention in February 2006. But Mount Street refused to ratify him. Mansergh and the other candidate, Siobhán Ambrose, were given the all-clear.

Six months after the convention, in August 2006, Mattie's opponents were handed a timely gift when the aspiring Fianna Fáil TD was caught in a fracas outside a pub in his home village of New-castle. His supporters insisted that he was attempting to keep the peace. His enemies suggested that he had been involved in an assault. In February 2007, two squad cars arrived at McGrath's home and served him with summonses for unlawful violence and threatening behaviour.

One or two aspects of the case were deeply disturbing to McGrath. He claimed the local media had contacted him with detailed knowledge of the charges to be brought before they were served on him. He was further aggrieved by the gleeful behaviour of some of his internal political foes at the prospect of his demise. He lodged a complaint with the Garda Complaints Board. McGrath felt that dark forces were working against him.

As the election approached, and with a legal cloud now hanging over McGrath, Fianna Fáil still delayed ratifying the selection convention's choice. McGrath, protesting his innocence, headed for Mount Street with his barrister in tow. He demanded to be ratified, threatening a clash in the High Court. Only weeks before polling on 24 May 2007, the party gave McGrath the nod. On election day, he outpolled both his Fianna Fáil colleagues and captured a seat in Dáil Éireann. Mansergh squeaked in on the last count, thanks to transfers from McGrath; Ambrose, whom Mount Street had preferred to McGrath, didn't make it.

But McGrath's biggest hurdle was yet to come. If convicted on the charges arising from the pub brawl he faced a possible jail sentence. A sentence in excess of six months would automatically cost him his Dáil seat, threatening an early end to a parliamentary career that had barely begun.

The case was not heard until November 2008. From the ranks of the 'unassigned' judiciary – those who are not attached to any particular circuit – the judge appointed to the case was Donagh McDonagh. Judge McDonagh was a strange choice to preside over the trial of a thorn in the side of the Fianna Fáil establishment. McDonagh's own connections with Fianna Fáil were not the most closely guarded secret down in the Law Library.

The judge in McGrath's case was called to the Bar in 1977 after studying in Trinity College Dublin and a spell in the army, where he served as an officer. In 1984, he was called upon to defend Fianna Fáil TD Liam Aylward and party colleague Senator Martin Joe O'Toole after they had been charged with being drunk and disorderly, a breach of the peace and resisting a garda in the execution of his duty. During the proceedings the Fianna Fáil duo engaged McDonagh and Hugh O'Flaherty in their defence. Both members of the Oireachtas were released on probation.

In 1988, McDonagh was appointed by the Haughey government as its observer at the highly sensitive Gibraltar inquiry into the deaths of three IRA activists who had been shot dead by the SAS while planning to detonate a bomb in the colony. On 12 September 1988, under the headline 'Leftie Spies Pack SAS Gib Inquest', the *Sun* published an article grossly defamatory of McDonagh. The barrister sued for defamation in Dublin. He claimed that the headline referred to him, that it was deeply damaging to him professionally and sought compensation in the High Court. Justice Lynch awarded him a massive IR £90,000. The *Sun* appealed the decision to the Supreme Court, where chief justice Thomas Finlay upheld the award, although admitting that it was 'at the top end of the appropriate range'.

In 1990, Haughey's Minister for Justice, Ray Burke, had to deal with a crisis on the Legal Aid Board. The chairman, Nial Fennelly, a senior counsel with no suspected Fianna Fáil leanings, had resigned because of a lack of resources, especially for hearing the cases of those refused legal aid. He had been joined in his exit by barrister Fidelma Macken, Incorporated Law Society president Ernest Margetson and senior counsel Denis McCullagh, leaving only four members – and just one lawyer – on the eight-person board. Burke chose McDonagh, together with Jack Marrinan (former general secretary of the Garda representative body), solicitor Tony Taaffe and barrister Vincent Landy – as chairman – to fill their places. Marrinan was later to be a Fianna Fáil candidate for the Seanad and Taaffe was later to be a Fianna Fáil councillor. Taaffe also ran as an 'Independent Fianna Fáil' candidate in the 1997 general election after failing to get the party nomination.

In September 1991, McDonagh was appointed to the coveted post of Judge Advocate General (JAG). The JAG is supposed to give general advice to the government on military matters and specifically on courts martial. With his background in the army McDonagh had a credible claim to the part-time job. The appointment is made by the President on the advice of the government. McDonagh was the incumbent for nearly ten years. During the nineties, then, he was a rare creature – a practising barrister, simultaneously holding two state positions courtesy of the Fianna Fáil government.

McDonagh was one of a group of lawyers who volunteered their services to Fianna Fáil in Mount Street at election times. These included the former Attorney General, and later Chief Justice, John Murray, the barrister Luigi Rea and the future European Commissioner and Attorney General David Byrne. McDonagh would often join the team of lawyers who manned the telephones at election headquarters in the evenings, answering queries from the public, specifically if a lawyer was needed.

He was conspicuously active during recounts, turning up to assist Fianna Fáil candidates in cliffhanger battles where a lawyer was needed. In 1992, he represented Fianna Fáil TD Ben Briscoe at the ten-day recount against Eric Byrne of Democratic Left. His job was to challenge any doubtful votes for the opposition, to check and re-check ballot papers, to dispute spoiled votes, to quote the Electoral Act at the returning officer and to fight for every single vote to secure a victory for Briscoe. Briscoe eventually won the Dublin South Central contest by five votes. For the first time in the state's history an original count result had been reversed. The lawyers at the scene, including McDonagh, were given due credit for vigilance, knowledge of the Electoral Act and pure bottle.

McDonagh, who became a senior counsel in 1999, was again part of the Fianna Fáil legal squad at a recount in 2002, when he headed for the Sports Hall in Arklow Town to bolster the hopes of Mildred Fox, an independent who had provided crucial support for the Fianna Fáil-led government in the previous Dáil. Fox was fighting to save her Wicklow seat in a tight race with Labour's Nicky Kelly. Among others accompanying McDonagh at the Wicklow count in their joint quest to ensure Fox's re-election were Sean Sherwin, the Fianna Fáil National Organiser, and Derek Mooney, a long-time Fianna Fáil loyalist and future adviser to Willie O'Dea. The *Irish Independent* reported that at one point during the heated recount there were too many Fianna Fáil lawyers present for the taste of the returning officer, Breda Allen. She restricted the number of supporters allowed to inspect the ballots to three per candidate.

Once again, McDonagh was on the winning team. Mildred Fox won by nineteen votes.

In 2004, McDonagh was appointed to one of four seats vacant on the Circuit Court. Fianna Fáil was again in office; the appointing minister was their coalition ally, Justice Minister Michael McDowell. McDonagh had been one of eighty-two applicants for the four

Circuit Court seats. He was now on a salary of €135,000 with a gold-plated pension, lengthy holidays and freedom from any more election-count slogging in the interests of Fianna Fáil.

That was the route that led Donagh McDonagh the ordinary barrister to become 'His Honour' Mr Justice Donagh McDonagh. There is no reason to believe that his work for Fianna Fáil at elections, or the string of appointments he had received from the party, made him professionally unqualified or a bad judge. But it is natural to question whether, given his history with Fianna Fáil, he was a good choice as the judge in a case involving a maverick Fianna Fáil TD, the outcome of which would have ramifications for the party pecking order in Tipperary South, and which could force a by-election.

McDonagh was presumably chosen for the case in the usual manner by the president of the Circuit Court, Mr Justice Matthew Deery. The allocation of particular judges to particular cases by the presidents of the various courts is carried out behind closed doors under a procedure not subject to public scrutiny. It is not known whether the president of the Circuit Court was aware of the extent of McDonagh's links to Fianna Fáil or whether it would have mattered if he had been aware. It was in any case open to McDonagh to spell out his history vis-à-vis the party to the allocating judge and to suggest that the case might be more appropriately taken by another. He evidently did not regard that history as a hindrance.

Discussions among judges about who should take specific cases, and decisions by judges to recuse themselves from cases in which they may have a real or perceived conflict of interest, rarely come into the public spotlight. But we do know that it is rare in Ireland for judges to pull out of cases after they have started. McDonagh was a rare example of a judge who had done exactly that in a very different trial only three years earlier.

In November 2005, McDonagh spent ten days in the Dublin Circuit Criminal Court as judge in the trial of the so-called 'Shannon Five', the celebrated anti-war protestors accused of damaging a US military transport plane at Shannon Airport. According to Harry

Browne's book on the Shannon Five, McDonagh intervened during legal submissions to make a point about the political views expressed in the trial.

> I have one problem with the language that has been used throughout this case and the slant that has been put throughout this case, that this was a war that was being perpetrated on the Iraqi people without ever a mention from anybody of what had been perpetrated on the Iraqi people by their own leaders . . . It is so one-sided, the approach to this, that I am actually concerned.

McDonagh's sentiments sounded uncomfortably political to the defendants' counsel. According to Browne, Brendan Nix, one of the defence lawyers, took it upon himself to give McDonagh a dressing down.

> The prosecution is here to take care of their side, the defence is here to take care of ours. You're the man in the middle and you have no concern except to show a fair trial, for the five people, not for the American army or George W. Bush or Tony Blair. There are five people on trial here, they are your only concern.

On the tenth day of the trial, McDonagh ruled that the jury could not consider the defence's central claim that the five protestors had had a 'lawful excuse' to damage the US plane. It was a blow to their chances. On foot of this ruling, defence lawyers took a new tack. Seemingly out of the blue, they asked McDonagh if he had, as a barrister in the mid-nineties, attended a conference in Texas and been photographed at it with the defendants' bête noire, George W. Bush. They pushed the Bush button even further by asking if McDonagh had attended his first inauguration as US President in 2001 and had turned down an invitation to his second inauguration in 2005 from the Texas congressman Tom DeLay, who, according to defence counsel Michael O'Higgins, 'has had recent difficulties'. (DeLay had been Republican House Majority Leader from 2003 until 2005, when he resigned because of criminal money-laundering charges in connection with a campaign finance investigation. In 2011 he would be convicted and sentenced to three years in prison, but freed on bail pending appeal.)

According to Browne, the judge was 'unamused and said his personal life was not a matter for this court'. When challenged about his visit to Texas and the inaugurations, according to Browne, 'McDonagh responded that the information was "basically correct" though he also said it was "half right".' The defence counsel's team were at pains to emphasize that they were concerned about the 'perception', not the reality, of bias. O'Higgins insisted that the trial process should 'be seen to be untainted' and added that the 'purity of the system must be to the fore. The personality of George W. Bush is part of this process whether one likes it or not.'

According to the *Irish Times*, McDonagh said he would not 'give detailed analysis' in response to the questions about his ties to Bush in open court and called a short recess. After fifteen minutes, according to Browne, the judge returned 'looking flushed with anger', summoned the jury and declared that the trial was over. Browne writes that McDonagh 'gave them no explanation, adjourned the case and flew from the room'.

McGrath's case did not come to trial until November 2008, more than two years after the Newcastle incident and a year and a half after McGrath had been elected a TD. His legal team never raised Judge McDonagh's past work on behalf of Fianna Fáil. The TD says that he was not aware of it at the time.

At one point during the three-week trial, McDonagh humiliated McGrath by ordering him out of the courtroom. According to the *Irish Times* report:

> Proceedings came to a halt at Clonmel Court as Judge McDonagh looked towards McGrath (50) and asked him 'Are you chewing gum?' McGrath nodded and added 'yes' to which Judge McDonagh replied: 'Get out of my court.' McGrath apologised to the court and left the room for a number of minutes before returning and telling the court he was chewing gum because he had a sore throat.

At the end of the trial, as McGrath stood in front of the judge awaiting the outcome, there was a hiccup. The judge was unable to read the jury's verdict. There was a delay while it was sorted out. After a pause, the jury's verdicts on all charges were read out, one by one. All six defendants were acquitted. Judge McDonagh left the courtroom. There was an eruption of triumphant relief from the crowd in the court. Mattie McGrath, their local hero, had been declared an innocent man. His two-year ordeal was over.

McGrath's relationship with Fianna Fáil headquarters deteriorated further as he took an increasingly strong stand against the leadership of Brian Cowen. Just before the 2011 general election, he decided to run as an independent. He and Fianna Fáil parted ways. At the February poll McGrath was re-elected while his former party colleague, Martin Mansergh, lost his seat.

McDonagh is still a Circuit Court judge. As recently as March 2012, he was back in Texas – at a conference of the Texas Irish Lawyers Association on the subject of 'Comparative Litigation and the Administration of Justice: Texas, US and Ireland'. There were ten contributors billed – eight from Texas, two from Ireland. Interestingly enough, both speakers from Ireland bore the name McDonagh. His Honour Judge McDonagh was one of a panel of five that discussed 'The Effect of Budget Constraints on the Administration of Justice'. His four fellow panellists were District Court justices from Texas, all Republicans.

The second speaker from Ireland called McDonagh was a little-known young barrister by the name of Ciara-Elena McDonagh. She just happened to be the daughter of Donagh McDonagh. Ciara-Elena, a barrister of just over two years' standing, gave a half-hour analysis of 'Congressional Investigations in Ireland and the US' to the learned judges and others.

Political pedigree does not mean that candidates for the judiciary make bad judges, but it certainly helps them to reach the top. It often compensates for lack of family connections in the legal profession, traditionally a prerequisite to a good start.

Some are blessed with both. The following announcement appeared in the *Irish Times* 'Social & Personal' column on Friday, 12 April 1968.

MR J. L. MURRAY BL

MISS G. WALSH

Mr Justice Walsh and Mrs Walsh, 'Tullyheron',
Howth Road, Clontarf, Dublin, have pleasure in announcing
the engagement of their daughter, Gabrielle, to John, eldest
son of Mr and Mrs John Cecil Murray, Carraigerra House,
O'Callaghan's Strand, Limerick.

Gabrielle Walsh was the daughter of Brian Walsh, a Supreme Court judge and friend of Charles Haughey, then Minister for Finance; John Murray was an ambitious young barrister.

John Murray's links with the legally lofty Walsh family and the rising political star of Haughey in the late sixties did him no harm. He reached early prominence at the Bar when, as a junior counsel with just three years' experience, he was engaged to defend Neil Blaney, Haughey's co-defendant in the 1970 Arms Trial. All charges against Blaney were dropped before the case went to trial, giving Murray a success in the highest-profile court battle in Ireland since Independence. In 1974, Murray stood for Fianna Fáil in local elections in the south Dublin suburb of Ballybrack, narrowly failing to take a seat.

Murray earned a good living as a junior counsel in the seventies, much of his earnings coming from work for the state. He became a senior counsel in 1981, and the following year he got a lucky break. After murderer and fugitive Malcolm McArthur was arrested in the Dalkey apartment of Attorney General Paddy Connolly, Haughey – now Taoiseach – was looking for a rapid replacement for the most senior law officer in the land. Most of the party loyalists at the Bar had sided with Jack Lynch in the Arms Trial battle, leaving few legal figures of stature upon whom Haughey could rely. Murray was on vacation in France when he received the call. Still under forty, he broke his holiday and headed home to assume the office of Attorney General.

His tenure was brief, because the government fell four months later, but it did not lack political incident. He agreed to chair Fianna Fáil's election convention in Haughey's own constituency of Dublin North Central in early November, dragging the supposedly independent office of Attorney General deep into the political arena. According to journalist Olivia O'Leary in the *Irish Times*, Haughey's backup team in this election included 'former Bord Fáilte boss Joe Malone . . . Mr Frank Wall, party general secretary, the Attorney General John Murray and other legal experts'.

Murray also became involved in a policy row during the campaign. He rubbished as unconstitutional a Fine Gael proposal to set up an all-Ireland court and police force to prevent terrorists from playing ducks and drakes with the law in the two jurisdictions. He may have been right, but Fine Gael was incensed that he had used the Fianna Fáil press office to issue his rebuttal of their stance, and called for his resignation. As the short-lived 1982 government was going out of office he even became involved in an unseemly, but not uncharacteristic, attempt by Haughey to install Vivian Lavan – a 38-year-old with just two months' experience as a senior counsel – at the High Court. Lavan had joined Fianna Fáil in 1974 and had run their communications department over several general elections and two European contests.

Unfortunately for Haughey and Murray, the government had jumped the judicial gun, announcing the appointment of Lavan to the High Court although no vacancy existed! The Cabinet hoped that a serving High Court beak would step aside in Lavan's favour and take the vacant chair at An Bord Pleanála, a position reserved for High Court judges. None volunteered, leaving Murray and Haughey with a problem. Lavan himself was reported to have declined a compromise solution whereby he would take the chair of Bord Pleanála.

According to a report by *Irish Times* journalist Frank McDonald at the time:

> Acutely embarrassed by its blunder, the Government refused to comment on the situation yesterday. Despite lengthy consultations between the Attorney General John Murray and the head of Government Information Services, Mr Noel Gilmore, a GIS spokesman said later, 'We have nothing to say.'

Haughey as Taoiseach and Murray, as adviser to the Cabinet on judicial appointments, emerged with egg all over their faces. Lavan stayed at the Bar.

After Fianna Fáil lost power in the November 1982 election, Murray returned to the Law Library to pursue his career as a barrister. At the general election in 1987, when Haughey's son Sean was in a nail-biting battle against the Workers' Party candidate Pat McCartan for the last seat in Dublin North-East, Murray showed his loyalty to family and party, heading for the Mount Temple School count centre along with barrister Luigi Rea to assist the once and future Taoiseach's son in his hour of need. Sean Haughey was eventually defeated by 235 votes, but John Murray was reappointed Attorney General a few weeks later when Sean's father formed the next government.

Murray's 1987–91 spell as Attorney General was less controversial than his first stint in the office, but his mood was unfailingly in line with the policies of his masters. His most controversial decision – not to extradite IRA sympathizer Fr Patrick Ryan on explosives charges – caused uproar in the UK but was popular among his cabinet colleagues and Fianna Fáil backbenchers. A scathing personal attack on Murray by Margaret Thatcher raised his stock in nationalist circles. Boiling with rage at Murray's failure to arrest Ryan on the back of British extradition warrants, the British Prime Minister told MPs that the UK had provided all the necessary documentation. Then she thundered:

> Despite this, no action was taken by the Irish Attorney General to serve provisional warrants or to endorse the original warrants. The failure to secure Ryan's arrest is a matter of very grave concern to the Government. It is no use governments adopting great declarations and commitments about fighting terrorism if they then lack the resolve to put them into practice.

Michael Mates, vice-chairman of Westminster's Anglo-Irish Parliamentary Group, went one step further, saying that many people feared that Ireland was a 'safe haven' for terrorists.

Less than a fortnight after Thatcher's outburst in the Commons, Murray announced his decision not to extradite Ryan to the UK.

He cited the statements in Westminster and the prejudicial media coverage. He insisted that Ryan could not now receive a fair trial in Britain.

Labour leader Dick Spring argued in the Dáil that:

> . . . the failure of the Attorney General to take this course [i.e. extradite Ryan] will inevitably be seen by many as evidence of the further politicization of what ought to be a judicial process.

Fine Gael spokesman Sean Barrett suggested that the perception had taken hold overseas that the involvement of Attorney General Murray (rather than the less politicized Director of Public Prosecutions) in extradition cases meant that the government's political agenda would decide the result. Both Spring and Barrett warned of the long-term dangers of such a decision, but – acutely aware of public opinion running strongly against the UK's attitude – were careful not to support the UK's position.

The British were incensed, but Murray's decision undoubtedly pleased Haughey. Murray was reappointed as Attorney General by Haughey after the 1989 election. Two years later, he was appointed a judge at the European Court of Justice. In 1999 the Fianna Fáil government of Bertie Ahern asked him to return home to fill a vacancy on the Supreme Court. He served five years as an ordinary member under Ronan Keane before becoming Chief Justice in 2004.

Two years later, Murray faced his biggest test. In May 2006, the Supreme Court ruled that the section of the 1935 Criminal Law Amendment Act on statutory rape was unconstitutional. A man in his early twenties, known as 'CC', had brought a constitutional case to the Supreme Court after he was accused – when he was eighteen – of taking sexual advantage of a fourteen-year-old who, he claimed, had consented to intercourse and had told him she was seventeen, above the age of consent. He sought a declaration that the law on statutory rape was unconstitutional because he was not allowed to plead the defence that he had made an honest mistake about the victim's age. The Supreme Court unanimously found in his favour and declared the relevant section of the Act to be unconstitutional.

Within a week, another man, a convicted rapist known as Mr A, applied to the High Court seeking immediate release from prison. Mr A was serving a three-year sentence, having pleaded guilty to unlawful carnal knowledge of a twelve-year-old girl whom he had plied with alcopops.

Justice Mary Laffoy ordered Mr A's release on the basis of the previous week's Supreme Court decision. According to her ruling, the implication of the Supreme Court's decision in the 'CC' case was that the statute under which Mr A had been convicted, and which the court had found unconstitutional, could now effectively be said not to have existed when Mr A raped the child or when he was convicted or sentenced – or indeed at any time since the 1937 constitution was enacted.

All hell broke loose. A queue of convicted rapists, seeking release, began to line up to appeal their cases in the Four Courts. Pressure piled on to the government. Public opinion was at boiling point as victims of rape went on the radio. In the Dáil, Opposition leader Enda Kenny reflected the furious popular mood when he declared, 'As a public representative and a father, I am appalled by today's decision by the High Court which releases a pervert back into society.' The government was accused of having failed to anticipate the danger. In the middle of the controversy, Tánaiste Mary Harney admitted to an outraged Dáil that a top civil servant at the Department of Justice had been told about the original constitutional court challenge by the Chief State Solicitor's Office as early as November 2002. According to Justice Minister Michael McDowell, nobody had ever informed him of this.

The atmosphere in Leinster House was electric. A media frenzy fuelled the already fragile fears of public opinion. The mother of a rape victim appeared on the popular *Liveline* programme on RTÉ Radio. The equally influential Gerry Ryan radio show piled on the pressure. TDs began to panic and the government wobbled. According to the *Sunday Tribune*, one Fianna Fáil deputy from Dublin, on returning home from Leinster House, was met by his wife: 'Can you lot do anything right?' she asked.

While McDowell frantically prepared emergency legislation to ensure that the Mr A situation could not be repeated, the government appealed the High Court's decision in the Mr A case to the Supreme Court. On Friday 2 June, the dramatic news came through to a highly charged Leinster House that the state had won its appeal. A warrant was issued for the re-arrest of Mr A. The crisis was over. McDowell triumphantly relayed the news to the Seanad in the middle of the debate on the new legislation.

The Supreme Court had saved Fianna Fáil and the Progressive Democrats from a crisis that threatened to topple their coalition.

The reasons for the ruling failed to convince several observers. Many felt that the panic in political circles and the horrific prospect of further releases had convinced their lordships to take a pragmatic, populist decision. Public revulsion at the prospect of a flood of rapists stalking the streets had, according to this theory, sent massive vibrations all the way down to the Four Courts.

Legal experts were divided on the legal merits of the decision. In an analysis of the verdict, *Irish Times* legal affairs correspondent Carol Coulter pointed out that the Supreme Court had 'limited the consequences of its own earlier decision' and departed 'from the retrospectivity previously applied'. In other words, according to Coulter, the court had broken with precedent relating to the status of people convicted under laws subsequently found to be unconstitutional:

> ... based on past decisions of the court, once a law was found to be unconstitutional, an unconstitutionality dating from the enactment of the Constitution in 1937, then effectively it never existed. If previous decisions were followed, this meant that all decisions taken under it were now void.

She went on to quote the case of Murphy versus Attorney General, in which 'the constitutionality of the taxation regime for married couples was successfully challenged and found to be retrospectively inoperative'. If that precedent had been followed by the Supreme Court, Coulter asserted, Mr A and others would have been released.

The state's case, as articulated in court by senior counsel Gerard

Hogan, was primarily that Mr A had never pleaded that he believed that the girl he raped was older than twelve. He had pleaded guilty. He had never raised a constitutional issue. Hogan advocated that only those who had challenged the law on constitutional grounds should benefit from the Supreme Court's ruling on the 1935 law. The principle of retrospectivity should apply only to those who might have been successful if they had challenged the law on constitutional grounds in their own cases.

He maintained that to release Mr A would be 'a triumph of abstract logic over justice'.

In the words of Coulter, 'Clearly the Supreme Court agreed.'

Another who took a critical view of the Mr A ruling was a former High Court judge, Sean O'Leary. A diehard Fine Gael loyalist who had been appointed to the judiciary by his old party, O'Leary wrote an article, published in the *Irish Times* shortly after his death in late 2006, in which he lambasted his fellow judges for their 'harsh, populist approach to those persons who stand accused of socially unacceptable crimes'. With regard to the Mr A case, he wrote:

> The lengths to which the Supreme Court went to obfuscate the fact that the continued detention of a prisoner in an Irish jail (in fact the re-arrest of a released prisoner) for an offence that did not exist in law at the date of his conviction, smacks of an attempt to curry favour with a potentially hostile media.

Had the judges made a sound decision on the legal merits?

The question was left hanging in the air. Specialists differ about the answer to this day. There are strong legal arguments on both sides. But all five of the judges who heard the Mr A case, including the Chief Justice, were appointed by Fianna Fáil. Their ruling had halted a crisis that was threatening the survival of a Fianna Fáil-led government. The scepticism in the media about the reasons for the verdict was fuelled, quite understandably, by the embedded political patronage that has long poisoned Ireland's system of judicial selection.

John Murray's seven-year term as Chief Justice ended in 2011, but he retains his place on the Supreme Court until 2015. In 2011, Murray was described by journalist Michael Clifford in the *Examiner* as 'the highest paid judge in the world'. Clifford's statement was based on a 2008 study by the Council of Europe into the pay of judges in forty-five developed countries.

Apart from his €295,000-a-year salary for the Chief Justice's job, he had picked up a few pensions on the way. As a two-time Attorney General he simultaneously drew a pension of €67,686. As a judge at the European Court of Justice from 1991 to 1999 his annual retirement package was reliably estimated at €70,000. At one point in 2011, his rewards from all three judicial posts came to approximately €440,000 a year.

Esmond Smyth was director of policy and research for Fianna Fáil from 1973 to 1977, in advance of Jack Lynch's landslide victory in 1977. He was expected to be rewarded with a Seanad nomination by Lynch but was surprisingly not among the Taoiseach's eleven nominees.

In 1990, he was made head of Brian Lenihan Senior's campaign for the presidency. His candidate was defeated by another barrister, Labour's Mary Robinson.

In 1992, Smyth accepted a nomination to be a judge of the Circuit Court, where he served as an ordinary member until he was elevated to its presidency by Fianna Fáil in 1998. He served a full seven-year term as president of the court before resuming his duties as an ordinary judge. He retired in 2012.

Like Murray, he picked up quasi-judicial gigs from the government. He was appointed chairman of a committee to advise Fianna Fáil's Minister for Justice, Dermot Ahern, on how to implement the findings of the Morris Tribunal about Garda behaviour. In 2008, the Fianna Fáil Minister for Education, Mary Hanafin, made him chairman of the Residential Institutions Redress Board. He received no pay for this post while still a serving judge, but he was entitled to a healthy fee afterwards – being the difference between his pension and the salary of a High Court judge. He has waived half of that fee.

Smyth never reached the dizzy heights achieved by Murray, but their career patterns were not dissimilar. If there was ever a breach arising from their respective loyalties to the warring Fianna Fáil leaders Lynch and Haughey, it was healed on Saturday, 28 May 2011, when a notice appeared in the 'Social & Personal' column of the *Irish Times* announcing that two barristers with famous names were going to be wed.

LEONORA SMYTH
BRIAN MURRAY
Esmond and Odile Smyth, Monkstown, Co. Dublin
are delighted to announce the engagement of their daughter
Leonora to Brian, son of John and Gabrielle Murray,
Greystones, Co. Wicklow.

One of the most controversial judicial appointments in Irish history was made on 21 May 1991, when Taoiseach Charles Haughey's government appointed the president of the High Court, Liam Hamilton, as the sole judge in the investigation known as the Beef Tribunal. Haughey had resisted demands for a full inquiry from the Progressive Democrats, his partners in government. He had initially suggested that his Attorney General could carry out a probe, but the Progressive Democrats insisted on a proper judicial inquiry. Haughey caved in and went off in search of a judge.

Eventually, Hamilton – and Hamilton sitting alone – was put in charge of the most politically explosive inquiry in the state's history up to that point. He was instructed to investigate allegations of illegal activity, fraud and malpractice in the beef processing industry. Fianna Fáil was in the dock at the Beef Tribunal. So were Haughey and Albert Reynolds, both suspected of having an unhealthy relationship with beef baron Larry Goodman.

Charles Haughey and Albert Reynolds, whose activities would be reported on by Hamilton, were appointing the judge in their own case.

Hamilton was originally a Labour Party protégé, but he had long ago shed his socialist credentials. He was a gregarious man with friends in all parties. The real problem was that Hamilton wanted desperately to be Chief Justice. The government on whom he was being asked to give a verdict would very likely be making the appointment.

One Fianna Fáil source told us that at the time of his appointment to the Beef Tribunal Hamilton spent several hours 'locked in private discussion with Charlie'. A few months after he made his report giving Fianna Fáil, Albert Reynolds and Haughey the benefit of much doubt in the face of accusations made against them, Hamilton was made Chief Justice by Reynolds. By this time Fianna Fáil was in coalition with Labour. According to the *Irish Times*:

> The Labour Ministers who had made the allegations that led to the inquiry, were less pleased and only agreed to the elevation with reluctance.

By this time the Labour Party, formerly Hamilton's patron, was disillusioned with its protégé. The tongues in political circles wagged wildly. One politician called Hamilton's report, which exceeded a thousand pages, 'the longest job application in history'. It was widely criticized as a whitewash or praised as a piece of masterly evasion, depending on the political view of the speaker. Albert Reynolds, Taoiseach by the time of publication, greeted its publication by claiming that he was vindicated.

It was an incredible situation. A man with high hopes of becoming the highest judge in the land was asked to decide the fate of those politicians who would decide whether those hopes would be realized. Hamilton's report was a godsend to Fianna Fáil.

Judges frequently emerge from the ranks of failed politicians, but it is rare, if not unknown, for members of the bench to abandon their posts in favour of politics. It is one-way traffic. First they make the political connections; next they network and help the party; finally they receive preferment.

John Murray was a good networker both in politics and in his social life, but he had never been as good at getting elected as he was at securing appointments or profitable briefs. He tended to lose popularity contests. Apart from his defeat in the local elections in Ballybrack in 1974, he lost another contest in his youth when he stood for the auditorship of the Law Society in University College Dublin. He was beaten by none other than his successor many years later as Attorney General, Harry Whelehan.

The career of Harry Whelehan probably provides the most dramatic example of what is wrong with the Irish judiciary.

In his student days, Whelehan was defeated for the chair of UCD's Fianna Fáil cumann by Gerry Collins, later to become a cabinet minister and party grandee. After UCD and the King's Inns he enjoyed a highly successful career in the Law Library. He initially specialized in personal injuries on the Midlands circuit. In 1990 he was part of the legal panel for Brian Lenihan Senior's presidential campaign. An *Irish Times* profile of Whelehan in 1991 quoted one colleague as saying that Whelehan was 'respectable Fianna Fáil – and goodness knows there aren't many of those'. Prior to his appointment he had received many high-profile state briefs, including the Ballycotton Inquiry and the Beef Tribunal. He was a keen yachtsman and was known to hunt and shoot at his Offaly country house.

When Murray headed for Europe in 1991, Charlie Haughey needed a new Attorney General. After Haughey's disastrous choice of Paddy Connolly (the Attorney General found with a murderer in his flat), he had learned to be more careful. This time he opted for Whelehan, knowing him to be a Fianna Fáil supporter with a reputation for having 'a safe pair of hands'. Haughey could not have been more mistaken.

Whelehan fell into big trouble in February 1992, when he sought and secured an injunction in the High Court preventing a fourteen-year-old girl who had been raped from travelling to the UK for an abortion. The girl won on appeal, but the affair caused a national outcry. Whelehan's reputation was damaged.

He caused further political bedlam in July when he secured an order from the Supreme Court preventing the Beef Tribunal inquiry from discovering the details of cabinet meetings. The Opposition insisted that he was protecting his friends in Fianna Fáil from investigation. Fine Gael's Jim Mitchell even declared him 'unfit for office', a charge he later withdrew. But a pattern of accusations against Whelehan, branding him as a socially conservative Fianna Fáil follower, had gained currency in the ranks of the Labour Party, by then Fianna Fáil's partners in government.

The split was not long coming. In 1994, the promotion of Liam Hamilton to the position of Chief Justice left the presidency of the High Court vacant. The Taoiseach, Albert Reynolds, wanted to give Whelehan the position, but his coalition partners in the Labour Party baulked at the idea that someone with Whelehan's conservative record should be given such a powerful post. Dick Spring and the Labour Party were quietly promoting the cause of Susan Denham. The government was split along party lines on a theoretically non-party issue, the appointment of a judge. An already nasty political row became lethal when it was discovered that an RUC warrant seeking the extradition of Brendan Smyth, a paedophile priest, had lain idle in the Attorney General's office for seven months. Labour blamed Whelehan. Reynolds and Fianna Fáil defended him, denying to the Dáil that the matter raised any questions about his fitness for the job. The Taoiseach dismissed the mistake as merely 'an administrative matter in his office'.

After weeks of wrangling, Reynolds took a gamble: he and his Fianna Fáil cabinet members nominated Whelehan, disregarding the views of their Labour colleagues. After presenting his credentials to Mary Robinson at Áras an Uachtaráin, Whelehan headed for the High Court as its officially appointed president.

The two government parties were on a collision course. Various efforts at a resolution were attempted, but ultimately they all failed and the government collapsed over the matter. Reynolds was removed from office by his own party and a new coalition of Fine Gael, Labour and the Democratic Left was formed without an election. Harry Whelehan lasted all of six days in the High Court before he resigned, claiming that he did not want to politicize the judiciary!

Two days before his ultimate resignation, Whelehan had been verbally thrown to the wolves by his champion, Reynolds, as a last-minute sacrificial lamb to save the sinking Taoiseach's own political skin. In a desperate effort to appease his Labour opponents Reynolds told the Dáil that he agreed that 'there was an unacceptable delay in handling the Smyth extradition case'. Reynolds continued: 'On my own behalf and on behalf of the government I wish to express my deep regret to the Irish people.' He had ordered an immediate review of the office of Attorney General; he expected a radical reorganization of the office. He sunk the knife deep into Whelehan's ribs when he conceded that the importance of the case had not been realized in Whelehan's office. And in a final coup de grâce against his former ally, he declared: 'In relation to the seven-month delay, with great regret I have to tell the house there is no really satisfactory or adequate explanation I can give the house.' He was dumping on Harry Whelehan to save himself, desperately trying to crawl back into favour with the Labour Party. The ploy failed. Within forty-eight hours he had resigned.

Harry Whelehan returned to the Law Library humiliated. He was no longer Attorney General; he had been a six-day wonder as president of the High Court. His legacy was a fallen government, destroyed not by ideology or principle, but by a political row about the appointment of a judge.

At one point during the crisis, a new system for selecting judges had been provisionally agreed between Spring and Reynolds. The creation of a Judicial Appointments Advisory Board (JAAB) was announced by the Minister for Justice, Máire Geoghegan Quinn; this was seen as the price that Labour had extracted from Fianna Fáil for agreeing to Whelehan's nomination to the High Court. At last, the old ways of nod and wink, of cross-party deals in the Leinster House members' bar about the next judicial vacancy, and of reward for party loyalty, were to be abolished. The JAAB was to comprise senior judges, the chairman of the Bar Council and the president of the Law Society. It would then submit names to the government for approval. Geoghegan Quinn promised that the new system would provide 'greater transparency in the appointment by government of the judges'. Committees of the JAAB would submit between three and five names to the minister for selection for each vacancy. Labour's departure from government meant the JAAB as conceived in 1994 did not come into being, but the seeds had been sown for a reform of the way judges are appointed.

The seeds withered rapidly. The potion cooked up by Labour, Fine Gael and Democratic Left when they passed the Courts and Court Officers Act in 1995 proved even less potent than the reforms agreed by the previous government.

The board was to be chaired by the Chief Justice and include the president of the High Court, the president of the Circuit Court, the president of the District Court and (unlike the 1994 version) the Attorney General – political appointees to a person. Alongside them there were two less-partisan appointees, a solicitor and a barrister, both nominated by their own regulatory bodies. And, in another departure from Geoghegan Quinn's Bill, there were to be:

> . . . not more than three people appointed by the Minister, who shall
> be persons engaged in, or having knowledge or experience (being
> knowledge or experience that the Minister considers appropriate) of
> commerce, finance, administration or persons who have experience as
> consumers of the services provided by the courts that the Minister
> considers appropriate.

The wording of the legislation was gloriously vague, but it was crystal clear what type of creature the minister would consider 'appropriate'.

When a bench vacancy arose, the JAAB would advertise it and invite applications. The JAAB would then consider the suitability of the applicant without interview. The legislation specified that the JAAB must decide whether the candidate's record as a barrister or solicitor showed a competence and probity necessary for the judiciary; whether the candidate was suitable on the grounds of temperament and character; and whether the applicant was otherwise suitable and complied with other miscellaneous requirements of the Act. Few applicants were likely to stumble at such undemanding fences. Law Library wags joked about 'JAABs for the boys'.

Following the initial screening process, the JAAB would send at least seven names to the minister, who would take the list to his cabinet colleagues. The Cabinet would then either choose from the list or, if none of the candidates were to their taste, send for more names. We know how many applicants there are each year, but the secretive nature of the process means that we never know how many reach the minister. In the words of one senior minister speaking to Carol Coulter of the *Irish Times* in 2002, 'You'd have to be a complete dodo not to get on that list.'

The innocuous nature of the brave new dawn in judicial appointments became even clearer when it emerged that sitting judges seeking promotion would not have to suffer the indignity of applying to the JAAB for preferment. Minister for Justice Nora Owen explained this to the Dáil by claiming, 'I do not believe that it is necessary for people who have proven themselves as judges to go through this procedure.'

The Bill came under attack in the Dáil. Brian Cowen described it as a 'smokescreen' while Fianna Fáil justice spokesman John O'Donoghue pointed out that the three political nominees to JAAB were never in the Fianna Fáil–Labour Bill. He was withering:

> I can only assume it was decided that three persons would be appointed by the Minister in order to ensure that all three partners in the rainbow coalition would have a say in the recommendations which would be made to the Minister on appointments to the Judiciary. The naked political fact is that in order to minimise any possibility of the appointment of an individual who is not politically correct, the Government decided to take a 40 per cent shareholding in the board. This is in stark contrast to what the Labour Party and its leader sought this time last year. At that time they did not seek to have the Attorney General or three political appointees on the board. What changed in the meantime? Sceptics and cynics will make up their own minds about this, but it is notable that the chairman of the Law Reform Commission, who would be relatively independent, is now excluded from membership of the board.

Fianna Fáil, for so long master practitioners at stuffing the judiciary, for so long experts in setting up quangos to reward their supporters, could spot the cynical stroke pulled by the new government a mile off.

Fianna Fáil, arriving back in power in June 1997, found the JAAB chock-a-block with Fine Gael and Labour supporters. The Attorney General's ex-officio place had been held by Fine Gael supporter Dermot Gleeson, and the president of the High Court was a former Fine Gael cabinet minister, Declan Costello. Two of the three political nominees' slots were held by John McGilligan, the son of a former Fine Gael minister for finance, and Evelyn Owens, a former Labour Party senator, trade union activist and chairwoman of the Labour Court; only Jennifer Guinness of the Irish Association of Victim Support was not known to have any connection with a party.

In 1999, when the original appointees' three-year terms ran out, the rainbow government's nominees were replaced by Tadhg O'Donoghue, Olive Braiden and John Coyle. O'Donoghue was the former director of elections for Fianna Fáil in Dun Laoghaire-Rathdown. Fianna Fáil also put him on the boards of both Aer Rianta and the ESB. Braiden had once stood for Fianna Fáil in the European elections. Coyle was a well-known supporter of the Progressive Democrats. At one point, the JAAB included not only O'Donoghue, Braiden and Coyle but also Chief Justice John Murray, a former Fianna Fáil candidate; Central Court president Esmond Smyth, a former Fianna Fáil press officer; District Court president Peter Smithwick, once a director of elections for Fianna Fáil in Carlow-Kilkenny; and Attorney General Rory Brady, a lifelong Fianna Fáil zealot.

The Whelehan affair had left the selection of Ireland's judges as politicized and lacking in transparency as ever. JAAB did little more than create new patronage opportunities for politicians. The new system invited more, rather than less, lobbying for seats on the bench. After the applications were made, the lobbying began. It was a sham.

Former members of the Oireachtas are well represented among the ranks of the judges. Defeated Fianna Fáil TD for Longford-Westmeath, Henry Abbott, lost his seat in 1989, but found himself in the High Court in 2002. Michael O'Leary, former Tánaiste and Labour Party leader, gained early promotion to the bench after his departure from politics in 1997. Democratic Left TD Pat McCartan returned to his solicitor's practice after narrowly losing his Dáil seat in 1992. His talents were rapidly recognized by the incoming Fine Gael–Labour–Democratic Left administration when he was bounced into the Circuit Court.

Sometimes Fianna Fáil surprised the pundits in the Law Library. Defeated Fine Gael TD George Birmingham was put in the High Court, not by Fine Gael but by the outgoing Fianna Fáil–Progressive Democrats government in 2007. The Justice Minister at the time, Michael McDowell, is credited with breaking the mould on other occasions, like when he appointed two Fine Gael supporters, John MacMenamin and Frank Clarke, to the High Court in 2004. Sceptics pointed out that MacMenamin was a cousin of McDowell's, but few argued with the merits of either his or Clarke's elevation. Fianna Fáil diehards apologetically explained away the promotion of Birmingham, Clarke and MacMenamin by saying that, after so many years in power, they had run out of Fianna Fáil lawyers to appoint. There was nobody left.

Not every judge has a political pedigree. A few are difficult to pigeonhole. The current Chief Justice, Susan Denham, has managed to avoid being branded in a partisan way. Nevertheless it is widely believed that she would never have been given the job by a Fianna Fáil-led government. Although she was appointed to both the High Court and the Supreme Court by Fianna Fáil, it would have caused shudders in political circles if someone perceived as so culturally different to Fianna Fáil had been gifted such a politically pivotal position by that party. Denham is a Protestant, a daughter of former editor of the *Irish Times* Douglas Gageby and perceived to have a progressive, liberal outlook.

Insiders insist that despite the patronage system, the standard of judgements in the three higher courts is nevertheless impeccable. They protest that once a judge is appointed he or she instantly abandons any past political allegiances and 'goes native'. They point at the lack of concrete evidence of any political interference with judicial decisions or of misconduct on the part of judges. But this does not change the fact that a patronage-driven system not only means that we are unlikely to get the best possible judges, but also creates an unhealthy pall of suspicion and cynicism around the entire system.

The case of Philip Sheedy is perhaps the most dramatic example in recent times of critically bad judgement by members of the judiciary – and there is reason to believe that party politics may have played a part in the fiasco. Philip Sheedy was an architect who became drunk, drove his sports car recklessly and killed Anne Ryan at the Glenview Roundabout in Tallaght in March 1996. His case came before Circuit Court Justice Cyril Kelly in October 1997. Sheedy pleaded guilty. Kelly took the case, but asked fellow judge Joe Mathews to step in and sentence Sheedy.

That much is agreed, but the details of what Kelly said to Mathews are a matter of dispute. Mathews' version of events – related by him to a later inquiry before the Chief Justice, Liam Hamilton – was that Justice Kelly claimed that he was handing over the case because he had become too close to it and had entered into private discussion with counsel for both sides. Mathews recalled that Kelly told him that he had even discussed the possibility of the payment of compensation as a way of resolving the case. Kelly, however, insisted to the inquiry that he had had no meetings with counsel for either side.

According to Mathews, Kelly told him that this was a tragic case of death from drunken driving, but that the accused was a 'graduate' from a good family and could afford to pay compensation to the Ryan family. Mathews asserted that Kelly suggested that this was a suitable case for a suspended sentence. Kelly, however, denied that he had made the suspended-sentence suggestion. Again according to Mathews, after he had looked at the file, he told Kelly that he could not impose a suspended sentence for such a serious offence. Kelly, according to Mathews, simply stretched out his arms as if to say Mathews could do as he saw fit. Mathews proceeded to sentence Sheedy to four years in prison, plus a twelve-year driving ban.

Sheedy had good Fianna Fáil contacts. According to Geraldine Kennedy in the *Irish Times*, in 1997, while out on continuing bail, he was referred by his solicitor to psychologist and Fianna Fáil senator

Don Lydon. Lydon prepared two psychological reports for him – one in 1996 and the other in 1997 – both prior to the trial. Kennedy discovered that Sheedy's mother played bridge with the wife of former Fianna Fáil TD Jim Tunney. Jim Tunney arranged for Sheedy to meet the new Fianna Fáil TD for Dublin West, Brian Lenihan, who gave Sheedy a character reference after a meeting in the Dáil bar, barely a week before his trial.

Having spent six months in Mountjoy, Sheedy found himself in the open prison of Shelton Abbey. One of his more interesting visitors there was Joe Burke, a Fianna Fáil supporter and one of Bertie Ahern's closest mates. Burke, who would later be appointed chairman of Dublin Port by Bertie, had employed Sheedy as an architect for his building firm. In July 1998, after Sheedy had spent nine months in jail, there was a sensational development. Bertie contacted his own Justice Minister, John O'Donoghue, through their private secretaries, requesting day release for Sheedy. Unhappily for Sheedy, he was not eligible for day release. Sheedy's political options were exhausted.

Three months later, in October 1998, Supreme Court Judge Hugh O'Flaherty was walking near his Donnybrook home when, 'entirely by chance', he met a neighbour's son, who was accompanied by Sheedy's sister. She explained her brother's plight to O'Flaherty. She insisted that he was very vulnerable in prison and that his mental condition was deteriorating, and she asked O'Flaherty's advice. The judge, a humane man, was sympathetic. Fatally for himself, he decided to convert his sympathy into action. O'Flaherty called the Dublin County Registrar, Michael Quinlan, into his chambers and asked if anything could be done to have Sheedy's sentence reviewed.

Justice Hamilton found in his report that Quinlan rang Sheedy's solicitor, Michael Staines, to ask him when his application for a review of Sheedy's sentence was coming and to say that Judge Cyril Kelly was 'awaiting' it. (Quinlan claimed that Staines approached him.) Staines said that he was advised by Quinlan to make the application in Court 24, where Kelly was sitting, on 12 November 1998. When the surprised solicitor asked Quinlan what this was all about, he was told 'you do not want to know'.

Staines contacted the Sheedy family, who indeed wanted him to pursue the application for review. Within two weeks, Sheedy was in front of Kelly, who made a rapid statement expressing his 'grave concern' about Sheedy's mental condition and suspended the balance of his sentence. The hearing took less than ninety seconds. A later report into the incident by the state solicitor, Michael Buckley, acknowledged that no representative of the state solicitor was present when Judge Kelly called the Sheedy case out of sequence. The state solicitor's representative present in the Four Courts that day was probably taking a telephone call at the time. The same report noted that there was no obvious reason why Justice Kelly called the Sheedy case out of turn.

Judge Kelly's concerns about Sheedy's mental condition were based on the two old psychological reports, prepared by Don Lydon, that were part of the original trial. There was no new psychological report on which Judge Kelly could base his decision to suspend Sheedy's sentence. Yet despite the lack of any new evidence of Sheedy's mental state, Justice Hamilton's report on the affair found that:

> . . . the learned judge announced that he had had the benefit of a 'psychology report' and that he had grave concerns in relation to the mental condition of the accused 'at the moment'.

According to a letter from Staines to Justice Hamilton, Luigi Rea, the barrister who had represented Sheedy in court, was subsequently approached by Judge Kelly. The judge asked Rea to ask Staines to have a new report prepared 'by a psychiatrist' which would:

> . . . set out Philip Sheedy's psychiatric/psychological condition as of 12 November 1998, as the Medical Report on the Court file was from a psychologist and out of date. This new report was then going to be put on the Court file. I indicated that I was not prepared to do this.

Hamilton described Judge Kelly's attempt to commission a new and backdated psychiatric report for the court file as 'manifestly improper'.

The Sheedy case might never have come to light if a member of the Ryan family had not spotted him going to work after his release in November 1998. The authorities were alerted and, in February 1999, the Director of Public Prosecutions appealed Kelly's decision to release Sheedy. The DPP was given permission to apply for an order quashing Kelly's suspension of the balance of the sentence. Questions were asked in the Dáil. The media, scenting a judicial-political scandal, began to run daily bulletins on the Sheedy story. Chief Justice Hamilton launched his investigation. In late March, three weeks before Hamilton's report was published, Sheedy threw in the towel. He decided not to contest the DPP's appeal, and returned to prison.

Hamilton's report found that O'Flaherty's conduct had been 'inappropriate and unwise'. While acknowledging his humanitarian motives, Hamilton described his Supreme Court colleague's behaviour as 'damaging to the administration of justice'. Hamilton was even harder on Kelly. He concluded that Kelly's 'handling of this matter compromised the administration of justice' and was scathing about his decision to suspend Sheedy's sentence on the basis of psychological evidence which was out of date. He condemned Kelly as having 'failed to conduct the case in a manner befitting a judge'.

On the day that Hamilton's report was delivered, Minister for Justice John O'Donoghue wrote to Judges O'Flaherty and Kelly giving them little room for manoeuvre short of resignation. Failing that, they faced the prospect of being impeached by both houses of the Oireachtas. O'Flaherty resigned the day after Hamilton's report was released. Cyril Kelly delayed for one more day before falling on his sword.

Michael Quinlan took the same course on the same day. A separate Department of Justice inquiry running parallel with Hamilton's report found that Quinlan's behaviour 'fell short of the standards that could reasonably be expected of a person holding his position of County Registrar'. It stated that Quinlan had presented a 'false and misleading' account of what had happened due to a belief that protecting the 'confidentiality' of his contact with Justice O'Flaherty took precedence over 'his obligations to ensure that the Minister was in a position to give a factual account to Dáil Éireann'. Specifically, it found that he had initially contacted the defence solicitors, upon being approached by O'Flaherty, whereas the impression given in his earlier letters had been that the initiative had come from the defence lawyers.

The heads on plates took the heat out of the political furore. O'Flaherty and Kelly had been appointed by Fianna Fáil; the Opposition had drawn blood.

There was an unhappy twist in the tail for O'Flaherty. A year after he resigned over the Sheedy affair, Minister for Finance Charlie McCreevy attempted to recognize – in the normal Fianna Fáil way – that he believed O'Flaherty had been wronged. McCreevy nominated O'Flaherty as Ireland's nominee for the post of vice-president of the European Investment Bank. There was another public uproar, and the nomination was withdrawn. O'Flaherty was humiliated.

The Philip Sheedy affair shook public confidence in the judicial system. For a brief period the curtain was lifted on what goes on behind closed doors at the Four Courts. It raised still unanswered questions about how cases are allocated. How did Cyril Kelly come to be allotted the Sheedy review? As Hamilton noted:

> . . . there is no practice in the Circuit Court whereby a Circuit Court judge can review, in a criminal case, the final order of a judge of equal jurisdiction who is available or is likely to become available. Insofar as Judge Kelly thought that such a practice existed he was mistaken. Insofar as he followed such an alleged practice himself, he was wrong.

Judges O'Flaherty and Kelly resigned on threat of impeachment – but no judge in Ireland has ever actually been impeached.

Brian Curtin probably came closest. Curtin, a barrister from Tralee, was made a judge of the Circuit Court in November 2001. Like so many others appointed to the Circuit Court, he had been active politically. While he was at Trinity in the 1970s, he had joined Fianna Fáil but had later switched to the Progressive Democrats and stood unsuccessfully for them in local elections in Tralee. Not surprisingly, his talents were rewarded when he was elevated to the bench by fellow Kerryman John O'Donoghue, at the time Minister for Justice in a Fianna Fáil–Progressive Democrats government.

In May 2002, just six months after Curtin was made a judge, his home in Tralee was raided by gardaí brandishing a search warrant. The raid was part of Operation Amethyst, aimed at over a hundred individuals suspected of child pornography offences. Information on suspects in Ireland – including Brian Curtin's name, address and credit card details – had been received from Interpol and US authorities. Gardaí leaving his Tralee home took away a desktop computer and various components.

In November 2002, Judge Curtin was charged with possession of child pornography. When the case came up in Tralee courthouse in January 2003, an adjournment was granted due to Curtin's ill health. Eventually, in June 2003, under threat of an arrest warrant being issued, Curtin attended court and was returned for trial. The case against Curtin was finally heard in April 2004. Lawyers for the state claimed that images of children in explicit sexual acts had been found on his computer. Curtin pleaded not guilty.

Curtin's lawyer was Paddy McEntee, one of the finest barristers in the country, a man famous for his eloquence and success in securing acquittals in high-profile cases. McEntee argued that the warrant to search Curtin's house was a day out of date, and that the evidence provided by the seized computer was consequently inadmissible. He insisted that as the entry to Curtin's house was unconstitutional, the computer's contents were not allowable as evidence.

A day later, Judge Carroll Moran ruled in Curtin's favour. The judge was acquitted. The public outcry at Curtin's acquittal spurred the government into action. Four days later, the Cabinet despatched a letter to the judge asking him to explain the background to the case. The letter warned him that under the Constitution, the Oireachtas has powers to impeach a judge for stated misbehaviour. In his response, Curtin eyeballed his former patrons, refusing to offer the explanation demanded.

Just two weeks after his acquittal, Curtin was arrested in Tralee for drink-driving. A urine sample showed that his blood-alcohol level was three times the legal limit. His solicitor later pleaded the stress of the trial and the hostility of the media as extenuating circumstances. He was banned from driving for two years and fined €250.

In July 2004, spurred on by a demanding media and an outraged Opposition, the government began to move towards impeachment proceedings. A motion for impeachment of the judge was laid before both houses of the Oireachtas. Denis O'Donovan, a solicitor and Fianna Fáil TD, was selected to chair a seven-person Oireachtas committee to inquire into Curtin's conduct. The stage for the first successful impeachment in the state's history was being set.

Curtin's lawyers pleaded that he was medically unfit to appear before the Oireachtas committee. Next, they challenged the committee's procedures in the High Court, especially its demand that Curtin hand over the computer with the offending images of child pornography. If its contents were unconstitutional as evidence in court, they asked, how could they be admissible as evidence to an Oireachtas committee? Curtin's lawyers also challenged the right of the Oireachtas to investigate their client's fitness to be a judge.

The High Court found that the committee was constitutionally established and that the computer should be handed over. Judge Curtin's counsel, former Attorney General John Rogers, appealed the decision to the Supreme Court. By the time the appeal was heard, the proceedings of the Oireachtas committee had been adjourned for eighteen months. It was now October 2005, a full three and a half years since the original search of Curtin's house in May 2002.

Five months later, in March 2006, the Supreme Court found against Curtin. The committee was free to go ahead with its inquiry. But the TDs and senators were now involved in a race against time. If the committee had not concluded its work and the impeachment process was not completed before the next general election – due in spring 2007 – the whole process would collapse. The committee would expire with the Dáil.

Curtin was still clinging on to his judicial post; although he had not heard any court cases since the search of his house, he was still drawing his €149,461 salary and building up his pension entitlements. He had produced numerous certificates documenting illnesses ranging from depression to heart problems to organic brain damage. In September, the committee was briefed by the lead US investigator in the probe that had fingered Curtin. Further legal delays led to a statement from O'Donovan that the committee was 'determined' that the Curtin case would proceed amid growing doubts and further adjournments.

Another milestone was reached in November 2006. Curtin had by that point served as a judge for five years – and thus qualified for a pension of €19,000 a year plus a lump sum on the grounds of ill health. Under the Courts Act of 1961 any judge who had served five years or more was entitled to retire on the grounds of age or permanent infirmity with a pension and lump sum.

The shape of the final outcome was becoming clearer. Curtin did not want his dirty linen washed in public. Early on the morning of 13 November, John Rogers appeared before the impatient Oireachtas committee with a final plea to stop the inquiry. He revealed that Curtin had recently been diagnosed with 'organic brain damage'. He suffered from short-term memory lapses and confusion about his location. O'Donovan granted an adjournment, but refused to halt the impeachment proceedings. The senior counsel returned with the news that Curtin had resigned as a judge, almost four years to the day after his arrest on child porn charges.

The impeachment proceedings were over. The Oireachtas was off the hook, avoiding the prospect of a vote in both houses on an impeachment. No legislator wanted to sit in judgement over a judge. There were no procedures for a 'trial' in the Oireachtas. The details of the case were sordid. And the spectre of long days and nights away from the normal legislative and constituency work spooked them.

In April 2007, Curtin's lump sum was set at €57,447, and his €19,000 pension was backdated to the date of his resignation. The Department of Justice accepted the medical evidence that he was unfit to serve as a judge, thus allowing him to qualify for the pension on the grounds of ill health.

The Supreme Court had ruled that Curtin was entitled to have his legal costs covered by the state, but the Oireachtas committee was shocked when a bill for nearly €2 million arrived. Lawyers for the

Houses of the Oireachtas billed for an additional €1 million. A cheque for €977,000, sent by the commission that funds the Houses, was rejected by Curtin's lawyers and a protracted dispute began. Finally, in April 2012, Curtin's legal team accepted the lower figure and called it a day.

It is questionable whether Curtin would ever have reached the Circuit Court were he not a former Progressive Democrat candidate for election and a one-time Fianna Fáil member. Was he suited to be a judge? Could his failings have been detected in a searching interview or a thorough screening by outsiders? The much-delayed impeachment process begs serious questions about the difficulty of removing a judge under any circumstances.

While misdemeanours in their duties have surfaced more often than the judiciary would have wished, criminal charges against judges are very rare. Curtin's case was exceptional, especially from a judge of the Circuit Court. Errant behaviour from a member of the District Court would have caused less of a stir.

The lowest layer of judges are a motley crew. Most District Court judges are former solicitors. Many of them are from small firms in the country towns of Ireland. Many of them are appointed on unapologetically partisan political grounds. The job is widely regarded as a doddle.

Two solicitors who had some involvement in Bertie Ahern's tribunal travails were appointed District Judges by Bertie while he was Taoiseach. Both Hugh O'Donnell and David Anderson had been involved in the sale of Manchester businessman Michael Wall's house to Ahern in 1997. The sale attracted the attention of the Mahon Tribunal and both District Judges were listed for appearances in 2008. There was speculation that some of the conveyancing paperwork was missing or incomplete, but it appears this was not the case, and they were not called as witnesses in the end.

Not least of the embarrassments popping up in the same jurisdiction was the story of District Court Justice John Lindsay (the son of former Fine Gael TD and Master of the High Court Pat Lindsay, and brother of Alison Lindsay, a judge of the Circuit Court). John

Lindsay, a solicitor, was made a judge in 2007. In early 2010, the Disciplinary Committee of the Law Society published some damning findings about his activities while practising as a solicitor. It found him guilty of misconduct on twelve different counts. Lindsay was fined €10,000, censured and ordered to pay legal costs.

The case had been ongoing for seven years. This did not stop his upward march: despite the probe, he was cleared for approval by the JAAB and appointed days before the 2007 general election. It is not known if the JAAB inquired into the progress of the probe into Lindsay's activities as a solicitor.

Lindsay was being investigated for his delay in discharging the administration of an estate, but his equally serious sin was to treat the inquiry in a cavalier fashion. He was found guilty of frustrating the Law Society in resolving the matter and of breaching an undertaking to the disciplinary committee. His failure to attend a series of meetings left the Law Society exasperated with his lack of cooperation. Despite the ongoing inquiry, Lindsay was appointed a judge in 2007. Despite the publication of the adverse findings in 2010, he remained a judge. Lindsay sat tight. Here was a man who had been censured by his fellow solicitors, but was good enough to be a judge of the District Court.

Lindsay was a minority breed in the District Court: he was born and bred Fine Gael. Among his colleagues – at least before the change of government in 2011 – the most obvious characteristic running through the judges squatting on the bottom rung of the ladder was a connection to Fianna Fáil. The number of District Judges from the Fianna Fáil gene pool puts the political shenanigans of the appointments to the Circuit and High Court to shame. The political bias, so prominent in the identity of many of the lucky winners of the consolation prizes, is even more unacceptable when the massive number of applications for the jobs is examined.

From the establishment of the JAAB in 1995 until the end of 2010 there have been 45 vacancies on the District Court. During that period there were 3,953 applications for the jobs – or an average of 88 per opening. Why do so many solicitors aspire to such heights? What is wrong with the world of a traditionally lucrative profession that so many are gagging to leave it?

Well, what could attract stressed lawyers languishing in a struggling practice more than a well-paid public service position, a guaranteed pension, short hours and good holidays? Moreover, the job involves power and social status, and there is not a hope in hell of dismissal. Successful applicants have no awkward colleagues to deal with as they are now kings of their own courtrooms. They need no special qualifications, provided they passed solicitor's or barrister's exams all those years ago. If they are not up to date with the modern law, no one need know. They will not be interviewed for the job. No wonder there are so many battered solicitors seeking salvation in the warm womb of the District Court.

In 1998, Mary Devins, wife of Dr Jimmy Devins, who would serve as Fianna Fáil TD for Sligo from 2002 to 2011, was appointed a beak. In August 2012, she was forced to make two public apologies after describing social welfare as 'a Polish charity'.

In 1999, Sean MacBride, former Fianna Fáil member of Donegal County Council, was given the nod. He had been a key figure for Fianna Fáil in the Donegal North-East 1996 by-election when Cecilia Keaveney was elected. Fianna Fáil TD Jim McDaid subsequently lobbied hard for MacBride, admitting in a letter to Justice Minister John O'Donoghue that he was 'under enormous pressure regarding MacBride's appointment to the District Court'.

MacBride has consistently attracted unwelcome media attention in the court. In 2011 he issued a statement after a *Sunday Times* article had named six lawyers who had reached the District Court following political lobbying. He took offence at the piece, denouncing its tone and context as 'derogatory, defamatory and deeply offensive to me and the office I hold'. He went on to list his academic qualifications. He pointed out that he was 'twice recommended by the Independent Judicial Appointments Board'. He ended, 'I was appointed on merit.' He read out his statement in open court.

As recently as April 2012, a defendant brought a successful High Court challenge after the former Fianna Fáil man had refused to grant him bail. According to the *Irish Independent*, the appellant alleged that MacBride told him that he would 'swallow him up and spit him out', that he was 'mentally and psychologically superior to him' and that he would 'put manners' on his solicitor. It was agreed in the High Court that the case would not be heard by MacBride.

In 2001, MacBride was followed into the District Court by his Sligo neighbour Conal Gibbons, the son of a former Fianna Fáil TD for the area, Hugh Gibbons. Other successful applicants included Tim Lucey, who was appointed following representations from the Fianna Fáil leader in the European Parliament, Gerry Collins, while another winner, Gerard Furlong, received strong support for his nomination from John McGuinness TD after he had applied through JAAB.

Many of the appointments were rewards for lower-profile Fianna Fáil supporters and fund-raisers; but as it reached the melting months of its long term in government, the bigger partner in coalition became more shameless in its promotions. In October 2009, eighteen months before the general election, Seamus Hughes, principal in Mayo solicitors Seamus F. Hughes & Co, was parachuted on to the bench. Hughes just happened to be the man who had flown the flag for Fianna Fáil as the TD for Mayo West from 1992 to 1997 before losing his seat to party colleague Beverley Cooper Flynn. In 2010, he made it into the newspapers when he heard the case of a Donegal man who had told a garda 'to go back to Mayo'. Hughes ordered the man to climb Croagh Patrick and to come back to the Donegal court in a month's time with evidence that 'you did the four stations of Croagh Patrick and say a few prayers'. In a show of sensitivity at the defendant's insult to his native county, the judge declared, 'You then might have a different impression of County Mayo and its people, and it will be in recognition of your fellow Irish people especially those in the line of duty.'

As the February 2011 general election approached, and with it the certain end of Fianna Fáil's fourteen-year run in power, the exercise of patronage became more naked. In December 2010, Paul Kelly, a former Fianna Fáil councillor and a 2002 candidate for the Dáil from Kildare, landed the jackpot when he was picked to sit in judgement over his fellow citizens. Kelly was even fortunate enough to duck the

10 per cent pay cut applying to new judges by just a few days. The timing meant an extra €14,700 to his take-home pay.

The same pattern applies in Dublin. In 2008 Dermot Ahern and Brian Cowen slotted Dermot Dempsey, their cabinet colleague Noel Dempsey's brother, into one of the vacancies in the Dublin Metropolitan Court. In 2010, solicitor Patricia McNamara was slipped into a vacancy. Justice Patricia McNamara turned out to be Mrs Cyril Kelly, wife of the High Court judge who had lost his job in the Sheedy controversy. She had represented one of Albert Reynolds's sons and had also sat on the Hepatitis C Compensation Tribunal with Leonie Reynolds, daughter of Albert.

Politicians regard the District Court circus as part of the normal political merry-go-round. Their relentless pursuit of this agenda has undermined the independence of the judiciary. Fine Gael and Labour have wreaked revenge on Fianna Fáil on the battlefield of the District Court. If anything, in their first year in power their behaviour was even worse than their predecessors'. Their pre-election promises of an end to cronyism were jettisoned.

The first five appointees of the new government were closely linked to the two parties in power. Gráinne Malone was a particularly interesting choice. A solicitor who had run her own practice until a merger with another small firm in 2007, Malone was one of three well-connected sisters who were promoted by the Fine Gael–Labour alliance within months of each other. No doubt her success had nothing to do with her close relationship with Labour junior minister Joe Costello – who is married to Gráinne Malone's sister Emer.

Emer Costello herself, quite coincidentally, enjoyed her own stroke of political luck in early 2012 when Labour veteran Proinsias de Rossa suddenly decided to retire from the European Parliament. She was the first substitute and headed for Strasbourg to fill the vacancy.

Good fortune came in threes. Emer's and Gráinne's sister, Mary Moran (née Malone), was also blessed with political favour in 2011 when Labour leader Eamon Gilmore made her a senator. She was lifted into the Seanad as one of the Taoiseach's nominees. And Joe Costello himself, having been overlooked for a place in the new government's original Cabinet, was slotted into the spot as minister of state at the Department of Foreign Affairs after his Labour colleague Willie Penrose's resignation had created an opening. Four strikes in a row for the Costello clan.

Gráinne Malone was joined on the bench by Michael Coghlan, another solicitor running a small firm. He had been lucky enough to serve on the Employment Appeals Tribunal and the Valuation Tribunal in the eighties and nineties. More importantly, he just happened to have been election agent for Labour MEP Nessa Childers in her successful campaign for a seat in the European Parliament in 2009.

The third Fine Gael–Labour nomination to the District Court was a conversation-stopper. Patrick Durcan was as true blue a Fine Gael supporter as could be found from Donegal to Kerry. Durcan was a principal in the solicitors' firm founded by his father. He had been on JAAB's list for the District Court for many years before he was finally picked for the job in 2011. A possible explanation for the change of attitude to Durcan's ambitions lies in the simultaneous change of government. Durcan was from Mayo, had been Enda Kenny's running mate in four elections and was on one occasion sitting TD Michael Ring's election agent. A Fine Gael trustee, he had himself been a Fine Gael senator, nominated by Garret FitzGerald, in the eighties. The pedigree does not come purer than Patrick's. His eventual promotion in 2011, after so many years of waiting, spoke volumes about the selection process.

Prior to the District Court appointments, the coalition had made two changes to the High Court. Another member of Fine Gael's Lindsay family – Kevin Cross, the husband of Patrick Lindsay's daughter Alison Lindsay, a circuit court judge – was sent to the High Court, while a former Workers' Party colleague of Eamon Gilmore's, Michael White, was promoted from the Circuit to the High Court. White's earlier promotion to the Circuit Court had taken place under the previous rainbow government in 1996. Not surprisingly, he had received no preferment during the fourteen years of Fianna Fáil rule.

Optimists suggested that the first wave of appointments would also be the last example of blatant partisanship; that the Kenny–Gilmore partnership would draw the line after paying off a few debts and showing their troops that they too could share the fruits of battle. The hopes of such naive observers were dashed with the next set of appointments. In March 2012, just before the St Patrick's Day weekend, the government named another self-indulgent list of twelve new judges.

This time it was Fine Gael's turn, after Labour's disproportionately large share of the spoils five months earlier. At least five of the twelve carried obvious Fine Gael links. David Riordan, who was elevated from the District to the Circuit Court, had been a candidate for the party twenty years earlier in 1991. He had failed to win a seat in that year's local elections in Cork North-West but had been given a District Court perch in 1995 by the earlier Fine Gael-led government. Since then, like so many others, he had waited patiently for the return of Fine Gael for his next break. Another Fine Gael councillor, solicitor Alan Mitchell, scrambled up the ladder on to the District Court. Mitchell had been the Fine Gael leader on Longford County Council for over ten years and was credited with the success of Fine Gael stalwart James Bannon's election as a TD.

Three others who made the cut on the same day in March 2012 included barrister Kevin Staunton, who had chaired Fine Gael's Wicklow organization in the past. Less well known was that Staunton's uncle was a Fine Gael councillor in Enda Kenny's Mayo heartland. Pauline Codd, sister of Wexford Fine Gael councillor Kathleen Codd-Nolan, made it to the Circuit Court, where she was joined by Keenan Johnson, a loud supporter of Fine Gael's Sligo-based minister of state, John Perry.

Fine Gael and Labour were not pulling their punches. They were playing catch-up with Fianna Fáil. And they still had a long way to go. Nevertheless, they were taking no chances. When it came to refreshing the toothless JAAB, Justice Minister Alan Shatter managed to find a place for Karen Dent, a Fine Gael activist in his own constituency, and another for Valerie Bresnihan, a one-time member of the Labour Party. To his credit, the minister also selected a rare creature, a man with no known party allegiance, Dr Simon Boucher, an Irish Management Institute employee.

By May they were back in the old groove. Solicitor John O'Connor, a member of a loyal Fine Gael family from no less a county than the Taoiseach's Mayo, was appointed to the District Court. O'Connor's brother Pat was director of elections for Fine Gael in Mayo in 2002. On the same day Iseult O'Malley, a granddaughter of Fine Gael founder Kevin O'Higgins, filled a vacancy in the High Court. Iseult had broken with the family tradition when she joined Labour, becoming a prominent member of the Labour Lawyers Group; her coalition credentials were perfect.

June 2012 brought a summer flourish of Fine Gael comradeship, when Colm MacEochaidh, a prominent Fine Gael barrister, was given a High Court post. MacEochaidh, who rose to prominence in 1995 when he and another barrister, Michael Smith, offered a £10,000 reward for anyone providing information leading to convictions for corrupt land rezoning, had run for Fine Gael in Dublin South-East in 2002.

The new government moved its two pet pupils, John MacMenamin and Frank Clarke, up to the Supreme Court. Down in the District Court's ranks, Fianna Fáil's dominance will take many years to break even if the Soldiers of Destiny have to endure a long absence from power. Judges there may serve until the age of sixty-five. Many of them were far from retiring age. All appointees were guaranteed security of tenure in this coveted sanctuary until they collected their comfortable pensions.

Judges at every level are untouchables par excellence. They need to undergo no interview for their appointments. They are not obliged to declare their commercial or other interests. They are well paid, and almost impossible to remove. There is no mechanism available for the public to complain about judicial actions.

Even accountants, solicitors, auctioneers and other professionals of doubtful repute have regulatory bodies that at least give the impression that they are vigilantly policing their members' activities. These bodies have complaints procedures, admittedly tortuous and woefully inadequate, as outlets for public complaints against their members. Not the judges. They have not yet even discovered self-regulation. For a group that enforces the law, they are the most lawless profession of all. There is no code of conduct, no rules. The only sanction for a judge's misdemeanour, major or minor, is impeachment. And that has never happened.

The Philip Sheedy case sent up some green shoots of reform. Probably in response to the consequent public unease, Chief Justice Liam Hamilton asked Justice Susan Denham to chair a committee on the judiciary. Denham's committee proposed the creation of a Judicial Council. It would have the power to review complaints against judges. But it would be controlled by the judiciary. It would consult with the Attorney General, the Minister for Justice, the Bar Council, the Law Society and 'any other body deemed appropriate'. It would round up the usual suspects. Hardly a template for radical reform. The judiciary had nothing to fear.

The following year, Hamilton's successor as Chief Justice, Ronan Keane, sent proposals for a Judicial Council Bill to the government. Keane's report recommended the establishment of three committees, dealing with judicial conduct and ethics, judicial training, and the pay and conditions of judges. It suggested the establishment of sanctions for breaches including admonishment, a private reprimand, a public reprimand and, the ultimate penalty, the removal of a judge by the Oireachtas. These were the measures that Justice Minister Michael McDowell was using as a basis for his Judicial Council Bill. But Judge Brian Curtin rode to the rescue of the reactionaries. Progress was halted. Neither party felt able to pursue the reform agenda until the Curtin case had closed. There were fears that the legal challenge launched by Judge Curtin to the Oireachtas inquiry might muddy the waters of the proposed judicial legislation. So it was put on ice.

The end of the Curtin affair reopened the clamour for reform of the code of judicial behaviour. Curtin was perceived as having beaten the system. Once Curtin had resigned, McDowell announced that plans for the Judicial Council Bill would go ahead. In December 2006, seven years after it was first mooted, a draft Judicial Council Bill was sent to the judges for comment. Relations between the two powerful arms of the state had been deteriorating. McDowell had got right up their lordships' noses when he publicly criticized their stance on bail and sentencing policy. According to the *Irish Times*, several top judges boycotted the minister's Christmas drinks in protest against his belligerent attitude to them being 'soft on bail'.

The stand-off between judges and government over reform lasted another two years. The judges fought a masterly rearguard action. Politicians trod warily, as they feared being seen to be treading over the line that defined the separation of powers. Although they had always controlled judicial appointments, they did not want to be pilloried for influencing the administration of justice itself.

In 2009, now ten years after the initial moves for reform, the Chief Justice John Murray and Justice Minister Dermot Ahern started fresh negotiations on another draft Bill. In 2010, Dermot Ahern published the General Scheme of a Judicial Council Bill. It was a walk in the park for the judges. The auctioneers and accountants would have been proud of them. They had completely wiped the government's eye.

A Judicial Council was to be set up embracing every member of the judiciary, all the way from the Chief Justice down to the humblest member of the District Court. Beneath the council would sit its nine-member board, again consisting exclusively of judges. The heads of all four court jurisdictions would either sit on the board as ex-officio members or would nominate substitutes. Other members were to be elected by their peers in the four jurisdictions. There would be no laymen on the board. It was a clean sweep for the judges. They had managed to keep outsiders away from having any say over their conduct.

The crux came with the composition of the Judicial Conduct Committee, the most sensitive element of the proposed Bill. Two members of each jurisdiction of the courts were to serve on this committee, including the heads of all four jurisdictions or their nominees. A second judge at each level would be elected by their peers. The committee would consist of two Supreme Court, two High Court, two Circuit Court and two District Court judges. Added to these eight would be another judge co-opted by the original eight. Insiders from the Four Courts were set to hold an iron grip on the Judicial Conduct Committee; but there was a chink of light in the proposed make-up of the eleven-member group. Two lay people were to be appointed by the minister. According to the blueprint for the Bill, the three must be of 'standing in the community'.

It was all beginning to sound a little familiar. Just as with the JAAB, there were to be three 'lay members' chosen by none other than the minister. A recognizable formula was reappearing. As in the case of the JAAB, the conduct committee was to be chaired by the Chief Justice. There was no reason to believe that the lay members would be any different from the normal gang of party appointees installed in the JAAB. A code of conduct for judges was to be drawn up by judges. Complaints against judges were to be heard by judges. Advice to judges about judicial conduct was to be provided by judges. The procedure for complaints into judges' behaviour was to be written by judges.

Complaints were to be heard by a Panel of Inquiry. The panel would be composed of two judges and only one lay person, who must be 'of standing in the community'. Cynics would be forgiven for suggesting that they might more accurately be described as people of 'standing with the party in power'. One of the judges chosen for the panel was specifically to be a judge of the same court as the judge under investigation. The chances of the defending judge and the chosen panel member from the same court being cronies were high, a danger that could not possibly have escaped the notice of those behind the legislation. The investigations were to be held in private. Any court proceedings taken as a result of these investigations were to be held in camera.

In the draft Bill, the Panel of Inquiry reports to the Judicial Conduct Committee. It can make its decision public when it wishes, but the identity of the judge must be kept secret. So must the identity of the complainant. Nor can the annual report of the Judicial Complaints Committee give anything more than the bare facts and figures. The judges' dirty linen would never be washed in public. The hierarchy which ruthlessly exposed the conduct of others to public view was not to be subjected to the same treatment. Just to make doubly sure, the draft Bill contained prohibitions of any exposure of the proceedings to the Freedom of Information Act or the Data Protection Act. No record or any documents in the possession of the Judicial Conduct

Committee or a member of the Inquiry Panel or an investigating judge could be released under a freedom of information request.

The power of the Oireachtas to impeach a judge was again cited in the draft Bill as the ultimate weapon, a power that has never been exercised. Far from making the judges more accountable, the Bill provided them with additional protection. Once again they were building an ingenious smokescreen.

The putative Judicial Council Bill lapsed with the fall of Brian Cowen's government in 2011. The new government declared its intention of introducing yet another version to address the issue. After sixteen months in office there was no sign of it. Spokesmen for the Department of Justice explained that it was not a priority because they needed first to publish and pass the Personal Insolvency Bill. More tellingly it was not on the list of 105 priority Bills from the new government.

Even Chief Justice Susan Denham seemed embarrassed by the endless delay in reform. In November 2011, she set up an interim Judicial Council pending legislation promised in 2012. It was modelled on the 2010 draft legislation. It embraced the idea of a board of two judges from each court jurisdiction plus one co-opted judge. One would be an ex-officio member, the other elected by the judges of that jurisdiction. No lay people were envisaged on the interim council.

Progress was slow. In late April 2012, the secretary of the Interim Judicial Council conceded that 'the matter of principles or guidelines for holders of judicial office is under active consideration'. Five months after the announcement of the interim body, its key objective was still 'under active consideration'. According to Carol Coulter in the *Irish Times* in November 2011:

> Among the likely committees is one which will draw up draft ethical guidelines which would be considered by the Council when it is set up on a statutory basis. They will also provide the benchmark against which complaints against judges will be examined.

There was still little sense of urgency. They could wait for the statutory body before tackling the thorny bits.

The judges guarded their sanctuary more feverishly than any other profession in Ireland. They saw their position through a totally different prism from the rest of the population. If they ever came under pressure to submit themselves to normal scrutiny they protested that their independence was sacrosanct, that outside interference or pressure could compromise their ability to give impartial judgements. The argument carried a thread of credibility until they stretched it too far by using it against efforts to reduce their pay to bring them in line with ordinary mortals. It was an equally unconvincing line of defence against critics seeking to discover what happened behind closed doors in the Four Courts.

The response to all demands for more transparency was always that any invasion of their privacy was an attack on their independence. It had worked for years. Judges can plausibly point to several cases where the higher courts handed down verdicts that caused fury in government circles. A good example of this is the decision of the Supreme Court in the celebrated Crotty case, which specified that any material change in European treaty rules requires a referendum; this ruling has caused nightmares in Government Buildings.

So have others. An attempt by a Fianna Fáil government in 1959, bringing in electoral legislation to change the constituencies, was judged unconstitutional by Justice Gardner Budd in the High Court. Opponents saw it as a stroke by Fianna Fáil, aimed at giving them the ability to gerrymander the boundaries, as it potentially allowed more seats per head of the population in the West of Ireland than in Dublin. So did the judges. The state did not even bother to appeal the judgement. A new Bill without the offending parts was introduced in line with the constitution. The judges were momentarily positioned as defenders of democracy against stroke politicians.

Undoubtedly judges have made many honourable judgements that displeased the people who had appointed them and who held the power to promote them. But in the eyes of the world outside the Four Courts they inhabit a different planet. They lost much goodwill when they resisted attempts to cut their pay in line with other public servants. They were seen to have provoked a referendum on judges' pay in 2011 because of their lofty resistance to sharing the nation's pain, a vote which they lost overwhelmingly.

Chief Justice John Murray was completely wrong-footed when he decided to challenge the government on judges' pay. In late June 2011, he told the new Taoiseach Enda Kenny in a memo that the idea of a referendum to cut judges' pay was 'fundamentally deficient and would compromise the substance of judicial independence'. He attempted to give the impression that he and his colleagues were concerned about their independence rather than their salaries. Details of a private meeting between the Chief Justice and the new Taoiseach found their way into the media. Murray was reportedly upset that a new €2.3 million cap on pension pots would greatly increase judges' tax liabilities, including his own. He had been shafted by a leak to the press.

Murray's clash with the government on a reduction in judges' pay was without precedent. He and the president of the High Court, Nicholas Kearns, published the judiciary's criticisms of the government's plans in a report on the Courts Services website. Their principal argument was that leaving the decision on judges' pay to politicians might subject them to political pressure, compromising their independence. They wanted an 'independent body' to decide their pay and conditions. It was a difficult angle for political nominees to promote. The public challenge from two protégés of Fianna Fáil governments went too far for the Kenny–Gilmore regime – they were forced to remove the item from the website by a furious Cabinet. If Fianna Fáil had been in power, things might have been so different.

As part of the judges' campaign, eight former Attorneys General wrote a letter to the *Irish Times* that reeked of self-importance and self-interest, and all the more so in the middle of a crippling recession.

Sir,

We are strongly opposed to the current proposals to amend the Constitution for the following reasons.

The proposal in relation to Oireachtas enquiries seriously weakens the rights of individual citizens, firstly to protect their good names, and secondly to have disputes between themselves and the Oireachtas concerning their constitutional rights (especially their rights to fair procedures) decided by an independent judiciary.

The proposal to allow proportionate reductions in judicial remuneration (which we support in principle) provides insufficient protection for the independence of the judiciary.

Yours etc.,

Patrick Connolly

Peter Sutherland

John Rogers

Harold Whelehan

Dermot Gleeson

David Byrne

Michael McDowell

Paul Gallagher

C/o The Law Library,

Dublin 7.

Here were legal plutocrats, who had benefited from political patronage and financial largesse in the Four Courts, loudly defending their privileges. The public gave the judges their answer in the referendum on pay by a margin of four to one. Supreme Court judges' pay was reduced from €257,872 to €198,226 while High Court judges took a cut from €243,080 to €186,973, both reductions of 23 per cent. Newly appointed judges were to see their pay cut by a further 10 per cent.

Possibly for the first time in the state's history, the judiciary was on the back foot against the government. They had been flushed out of their ivory tower, incensed by having been hit in their pockets. For the first time ever the 'untouchables' had been touched; but in reality it was a very light touch. They had been subjected to equal treatment on pay and the pension levy with the rest of the public service. Their basic position of entrenched privilege remains. Successive attempts to address complaints against them have been stymied. Impeachment is the only available sanction against a judge, and the existence of this never-enforced penalty has protected them from any lesser remedies.

The concentration on the absence of a complaints procedure has proved a red herring, cleverly masking the real problem of political appointments. Judges are still being promoted and picked on the basis of cronyism and political colour. The abuse is stronger than ever. It is practised by Fine Gael and Labour as much as it ever was by Fianna Fáil.

One former Fianna Fáil senator told us that the judicial appointments system was the 'best racket' in Irish politics. He is right. Good judges are undoubtedly lost to the courts as a result. Phoney remedies, like the JAAB, have provided camouflage for political patronage. The fundamental problem of cronyism has not been tackled. The citadel is as strong as it ever was.

Just as the banks were run for the bankers, the judiciary is run for the judges – and their political patrons.

9.   The Directory

Ross and Webb's Handy Guide to Ireland's Golden Circle

There's nothing more certain to cause a good row than a list. Our list of the key insiders and influencers in Ireland includes those right at the centre of power now, plus a few who have stepped back from the front lines but still quietly exert significant influence. Some of the bankers, like Sean FitzPatrick, David Drumm and Michael Fingleton, aren't here: their jobs and influence are gone, and FitzPatrick faces criminal charges. We know all about the bumbling Financial Regulator Pat Neary, hapless Central Bank governor John Hurley and king of the mandarins Dermot McCarthy; they are now whiling away their time with massive state payouts, and are not included either. We haven't included sitting politicians, as they are removable by the electorate; but a few ex-politicians figure in new roles. There's no Michael O'Leary, Dermot Desmond, Tony O'Reilly or Denis O'Brien: they are massively wealthy and powerful, but they are also very much in the public eye. Our focus is on those people you may never have heard of, but who have their hands on the controls in the public or private sector – or, in some cases, both.

These are the people we want to bring blinking into the light.

Peter Bacon

Economist for hire Peter Bacon was one of the principal advisers to the Fianna Fáil-led government when it came to the property market during the boom, and he retained his influence after the crash, when he was tasked by Brian Lenihan with running the numbers on the creation of a bad bank. Bacon gave the thumbs up to the creation of the body that would become NAMA. In June 2012, Bacon proclaimed that NAMA should be sold off as it was veering off course and failing to realize value for the taxpayer. These claims came in a report commissioned by Treasury Holdings, which was locked in a legal battle with NAMA. Bacon also earned good money from the property industry, having served as a board member of Sean Mulryan's Ballymore business.

David Begg

The bearded trade-union kingpin was at the forefront of the social partnership movement when the Fianna Fáil-led government agreed to the lunatic wheeze of benchmarking that saw public sector pay zoom miles out of whack with anywhere else in Europe. Begg supped at the top table during the boom: he was a director of the Central Bank from 1995 until 2010, years when it completely failed to rein in the out-of-control banks. Begg was also a serial quango appointee during the years of social partnership with roles at the National Economic and Social Council and on the Advisory Board for Development Cooperation Ireland. The former Concern Worldwide chief sits on the board of stock-market-quoted airline Aer Lingus as well as being a governor of the Irish Times Trust.

Ron Bolger

The former KPMG managing partner is Ireland's Honorary Consul to Singapore. But it's his involvement with some of the most powerful players in corporate Ireland that gives him such clout. Bolger is a close associate of beef baron Larry Goodman and serves as vice-chairman of his ABP Group, which is one of the biggest meat processors in Ireland and the UK. Goodman owns C&D Foods, the Longford dog food business formerly run by ex-Taoiseach Albert Reynolds, and a chunk of the Blackrock Clinic; Bolger sits on the boards of both. Bolger is on the UCD Governing Authority as well as serving as a director of listed aviation leasing company Aercap. He is also involved with the Carluccio's restaurant business. The chartered accountant is a former board member of the EBS and an ex-chairman of Telecom Éireann.

Richie Boucher

How many lives does Richie Boucher have? The Zambian-born banker headed up Bank of Ireland's Irish retail business, which shovelled out billions of euros in loans to madcap developers. Now the taxpayer is picking up the tab. The Rockwell-educated Boucher wrote a letter to the planning authorities supporting developer Sean Dunne's proposal to build a skyscraper in the heart of Ballsbridge. Despite being one of the central players in a bank that lost the run of itself, Boucher was chosen as the new chief executive when the hapless Brian Goggin resigned in 2009. Boucher was paid €831,000 in 2011. He managed to sell a stake in Bank of Ireland to a group of North American investors including billionaire Wilbur Ross. For more details, see Chapter 2.

Gillian Bowler

What on earth was a travel agent doing running a major bank and insurance company during the boom? Gillian Bowler may have been pretty useful at shifting holidays but her appointment as chairman of Irish Life & Permanent in 2004 didn't work out so well. Bowler survived the scandal of the €7 billion window-dressing transaction with Anglo Irish Bank, which accounted for her chief executive Denis Casey. She stepped down as IL&P chair in late 2010. Bowler also retired from a non-executive role at Grafton Group and set up an online travel firm, Clickandgo.com.

Patrick Brady

The Central Bank's director of policy and risk since March 2010, Brady previously served as head of insurance supervision at the Financial Regulator from May 2006 onwards. Quinn Insurance blew up in the month Brady took his promotion.

John Bruton

He was lampooned mercilessly for his lack of charisma during his two-and-a-half-year stint as Taoiseach and he never led his party to victory in a general election, but the Meath man has remained close to various centres of power. His LinkedIn profile describes him as an 'Independent Government Relations Professional'. Bruton's little brother Richard is Minister for Enterprise and Employment; there must be plenty to talk about at Sunday lunch as John is now the tsar of the IFSC, promoting the Irish financial services sector abroad. Bruton was a highly effective EU ambassador to the US; when his term ended he moved into the corporate sector, becoming a board member of Ingersoll Rand, a multinational valued at €10 billion which has headquarters in Ireland. The Clongowes-educated Bruton is also an adviser to Brussels-based lobbying firm Cabinet DN.

Richard Burrows

The Howth man can add cigarettes to a career that has encompassed booze (Pernod Ricard), poison (Rentokil) and toxic debts (Bank of Ireland). After presiding over the near destruction of Bank of Ireland, where he had been governor during the boom, he was appointed as chairman of UK-listed tobacco giant BAT. In June 2012, he was appointed to the €131,000-a-year post as a director of ENRC, the Kazakh mining company that had faced a series of corporate governance issues. For more details, see Chapter 2.

Breffni Byrne

NCB Stockbrokers chairman Breffni Byrne spent most of his career at Arthur Andersen before the global accountancy firm was vaporized in the wake of the Enron scandal. Byrne was a longstanding director of Irish Life & Permanent, joining the board in 2004.

He retired in 2011 as the state stepped in to pick up the pieces. There are also boardroom positions at semi-state forestry company Coillte, oil distributor Tedcastle Holdings, drug firm Hikma and listed recruitment outfit CPL Resources.

David Byrne

One of Ireland's lowest-profile EU commissioners, he held the health and consumer protection brief from 1999 to 2004. The Newbridge College-educated barrister had previously been the Attorney General in the Bertie Ahern-led government elected in 1997. He was a board member of Irish Life & Permanent from 2004 to 2008. Despite the snafu at the Permo, Byrne is now chairman of the advisory committee to the National Treasury Management Agency. He's also a board member of Kingspan and Chancellor of Dublin City University. For more details, see Chapter 4.

Brendan Cahill

Cahill served as managing partner of one of the state's largest legal firms, William Fry, during the crazy part of the boom. He took over the baton from Owen O'Connell in 2004 and ran the show until 2008, when he was succeeded by Myra Garrett. William Fry advised bankers and builders alike, and now makes money from NAMA. It was also involved in the sale of a near 35 per cent stake in Bank of Ireland to Wilbur Ross, Fairfax and Fidelity in 2011.

Kevin Cardiff

The massively overweight former secretary general of the Department of Finance, who was in charge of the banks during the boom and then helped make a mess of the economy. Cardiff was moved out to a handsomely paid gig at the European Court of Auditors. For more details, see Chapter 1.

Paul Carroll

The solicitor led top law firm A&L Goodbody from 2001 to 2010, serving three consecutive terms as managing partner of the Docklands-based practice. A&L Goodbody advised AIB, EBS and Irish Life & Permanent as well as playing a key role in the €412 million Irish Glass Bottle site deal. Now the firm is on the panel for NAMA. Carroll was appointed to the board of investment company One51 in April 2012 and is a former director of Eircom. He was spotted in Gdansk during Euro 2012 in the company of beef baron Larry Goodman.

Peter Cassells

The former ICTU general secretary is now one of the most influential lobbyists on the Labour Party side of the house. Years of being fêted by the Bertie Ahern government as a social partner leader have given Cassells quite remarkable levels of access, and he knows which buttons to press. Along with former Labour press officer Tony Heffernan, Cassells runs DHR Communications, which is beginning to pick up crumbs from the new Fine Gael–Labour establishment. DHR now advises the Broadcasting Authority of Ireland – once the remit of Fianna Fáil-linked PR consultancy Q4. Cassells has a lengthy list of quangos to his name. The former Forfás chairman also fronted the Digital Hub and the National Centre for Partnership and Performance, and is a board member of the National Economic and Social Development Office. He has also advised semi-states such as An Post, Aer Rianta, ESB, Fáilte Ireland and RTÉ. In June 2012, the lobbyist was appointed to the board of the IDA by the government he lobbies.

Noel Cawley

The former chief executive of the Irish Dairy Board has embarked on a tour of the non-executive director circuit. Cawley is chairman of Teagasc, the agricultural and food development quango, and has also been a chairman of the Irish Horse Board. There's also a board job at An Bord Bia and one at IBRC – formerly Anglo Irish Bank. He's also a board member of One51.

Bernard Collins

The Galway-based businessman, who was instrumental in building up multinational pharma company Boston Scientific's operations in Ireland in the 1990s, is a key citizen of quangolia. He was the chairman of semi-state health insurer VHI from 2003 until July 2012 and joined the board of Irish Life & Permanent as it fell into state ownership in 2010. Collins is also on the board of the IDA.

Ciaran Conlon (and other special advisers)

Fine Gael and Labour preach the gospel of austerity. Belts must be tightened. Unless of course you are inside the tent. Not only did the new establishment dole out jobs for the boys when it took power by plonking key advisers into highly paid government jobs, but it also got them better pay deals than anyone else. In December 2011, Ken Foxe in the *Mail on Sunday* revealed that Enda Kenny had personally intervened to ensure that his former adviser Ciaran Conlon received a sweetheart deal of €35,000 more than the agreed salary cap for special advisers. Kenny told the Dáil that Conlon, who was an adviser to Richard Bruton, had a relevant master's degree and political experience which made him suitable for the position, saying that 'in particular circumstances . . . technical expertise was required' to fulfil the role.

Conlon wasn't the only adviser who had got a special deal far and above the agreed cap. Public Expenditure Minister Brendan Howlin approved breaches of the pay cap for his adviser Ronan O'Brien – a former Labour Party insider, with Simon Coveney's adviser Fergal Leamy and Joan Burton's adviser Ed Brophy also getting a pay boost. Despite the outcry over the special deals for these advisers as austerity measures bit deep, some government members simply ignored public opinion to look after their inner circle. In June 2012, it emerged that Fine Gael Health Minister James Reilly had contacted Public Expenditure Minister Brendan Howlin seeking to hike the pay rates of his special adviser Sean Faughnan and his personal assistant.

Hugh Cooney

Cooney, educated at St Finian's in Mullingar, was one of the high-profile accountants of the last two decades. His career took him through the doors of Stokes Kennedy Crowley (now KPMG), NCB Corporate Finance, Arthur Andersen and BDO Simpson Xavier. Now he is chairman of state grant aid and business support outfit Enterprise Ireland. Cooney is a director of Aon MacDonagh Boland, which puts him at the table with former Anglo director and current Smurfit Kappa boss Gary McGann. He's also on the board of listed agri-food firm Origin Enterprises. Cooney was the chairman of debt-laden satellite TV installer Siteserv, which was bought by Denis O'Brien for €45 million, leaving its banker Anglo, aka the taxpayer, nursing big losses.

John Corrigan

The former stock-picker at AIB Investment Managers became the highest-paid civil servant in the country in December 2009 when taking over as chief executive of the National Treasury Management Agency following the retirement of Michael Somers. Corrigan had joined the NTMA in 1991 and had been involved with the setting-up of the National Pensions Reserve Fund, which would be looted by the government to bail out the banks. His central role is to sell Irish bonds so that we can fund the day-to-day running of the country. It's been a hard job given that we've been locked out of the markets since the EU/IMF/ECB troika arrived in December 2010. Corrigan sits on the National Development Finance Agency, with Stewart Harrington of Stafford Holdings and technology backer Peter McManamon. The former Department of Finance official is also on the board of NAMA. Corrigan earns around €416,500 – more than Enda Kenny and Michael Noonan combined. For more details, see Chapter 4.

Pat Cox

The former current affairs broadcaster bent over backwards in his attempt to become President of Ireland. The one-time Progressive Democrat TD for Cork South Central went as far as joining Fine Gael in hope of securing the party's nomination. But Fine Gael's grass roots didn't buy it and plumped for the unfortunate Gay Mitchell instead. Cox, who had served as president of the European Parliament from 2002 to 2004, remained close to the blueshirts despite this rejection. He was involved in the creation of Fine Gael's 'First 100 Days' strategy, which led to ministers ditching their Mercs and not much else.

Cox briefed top bankers and business people on the European financial crisis and the need for austerity at a private dinner in the Shelbourne Hotel in February 2012. In April, the Cork man joined Certus – the company managing Bank of Scotland (Ireland)'s bombed-out mortgage loan book – as a special adviser. There are a lot of other advisory roles, too. He's a member of Microsoft's European Advisory Council and part of the Pfizer Europe Advisory Council. There's also a gig on the international advisory board of lobbying outfit APCO Worldwide and a role with Michelin.

CRH

Cement Roadstone Holdings became Ireland's most valuable company through selling lots and lots of buildings materials in Ireland, Europe and the Americas, but it has a dark history. Following the Ansbacher report in 1999, CRH was forced to launch an internal investigation into the activities of its former chairman Des Traynor and a large number of directors. Among the items on the agenda were the circumstances which saw Traynor, who was also Charles Haughey's bagman, operating an illegal bank from the company's headquarters on Fitzwilliam Square. CRH chairman Tony Barry and director Jim Culliton confessed to having been involved with tax evasion through the use of accounts at Traynor's secret banking operation.

The links between CRH and Haughey were examined at the Moriarty Tribunal. The tribunal examined a 1990 deal in which CRH bought a 147-acre site at Glen Ding in Wicklow for £1.25 million. The sale never went to a public tender. Then there was the illegal dumping scandal at its Blessington lands, where for ten years nobody at CRH noticed large-scale illegal dumping. Then there's the near monopoly that it operates in Ireland, where it controls over 60 per cent of the cement market.

In 2005, CRH said that it had 'no involvement or awareness at all' of an allegation that the firm asked a Polish businessman to bribe a government minister. CRH had a 40 per cent stake in Holding Cement Polski. The other sharcholder in the company, Marek Dochnal, told a Polish parliamentary inquiry that he had paid some €825,000 to a key political figure ahead of the privatization of a major cement plant. Dochnal has been arrested by Polish authorities. In 2007, it emerged that CRH had made a €125,000 donation to a charity fronted by the wife of the Polish president. During parliamentary hearings into the privatization of state assets, she was questioned about this donation and denied that it had anything to do with a takeover by CRH of a cement plant. CRH said that the payment was fully above board and was publicized when it was made.

John Cronin

Law firm McCann FitzGerald has always been seen as the practice with the best Fine Gael credentials. Former Fine Gael senator Alexis FitzGerald was one of its earliest partners. McCann FitzGerald has kept in with the new establishment and was listed as a donor to a golf fund-raiser in aid of current Health Minister James Reilly. Cronin is the chairman of McCann FitzGerald and was appointed to his second term in office in January 2012. He succeeded Ronan Molony, who had been in the hot seat for a decade. Cronin, a banking and financial services specialist, is also involved with NAMA negotiations. McCann FitzGerald is one of NAMA's main law firms and has also been involved with a probe into failings at Michael Fingleton's Irish Nationwide. McCann FitzGerald is AIB's law firm and was involved in all manner of deals during the boom, ranging from the *Irish Times* €50 million acquisition of property website Myhome.ie to various transactions for Irish Nationwide, DEPFA and Ulster Bank in 2006.

Frank Daly

The former chairman of the Revenue Commissioners was appointed by the late Brian Lenihan to be the first chairman of NAMA. Daly had briefly served as a public-interest director of Anglo Irish Bank, where he was instrumental in the major clear-out of key players. Daly has come under fire for the lack of progress at NAMA. He's also involved with a Switzerland-based Catholic charity.

Catherine Day

Eurocrat Catherine Day is part of the so-called 'murphia' in Brussels. Since 2005 she has been secretary general of the European Commission, i.e. the EU's top civil servant. The UCD-educated administrator worked with Investment Bank of Ireland before joining the Commission in 1979. She was part of Peter Sutherland's Cabinet when he was EU commissioner in the 1980s before moving to the top ranks of the Commission. Last January, she made a speech at the Institute of International European Affairs in Dublin urging Ireland to be more active in getting behind the European Commission.

Sean Dorgan

The IDA is a stepping stone to serious wedge in the private sector: former chief executives tend to land plum jobs in industry on their retirement. Cork man Sean Dorgan ran the IDA for eight years until retiring aged fifty-six in 2007. He was a career civil servant, having been a former secretary general of the Department of Tourism and Trade. Sandwiched between his time in the civil service and the IDA was a stint as the chief executive of the Institute of Chartered Accountants. After departing the IDA he was signed up by Tesco to be chairman of its Irish operations. Ulster Bank also hired him as its chairman, although he was invisible during the bank's IT meltdown in July 2012, when up to 600,000 customers of the bank were left high and dry as computer systems crashed. Diaries of former Department of Finance secretaries general David Doyle and Kevin Cardiff revealed that they had met with Dorgan on several occasions during the financial meltdown.

Dorgan also became a director of the country's biggest domestically owned insurance company, FBD. He's also on the board of financial software firm FINEOS and Belfast aviation and defence firm Shorts. Dorgan is also plugged into the education sector, serving as chairman of the Governing Body of Dublin Institute of Technology.

Alan Dukes

The Drimnagh-born economist, a former leader of Fine Gael and finance minister, lost his Kildare seat in 2002. He became the head of the Institute of International and European Affairs, a think tank, and hooked up with Wilson Hartnell as a consultant and a director. After the Anglo Irish Bank meltdown, Brian Lenihan appointed Dukes as a public-interest director of the bank; he later became the €200,000-a-year chairman. The board of the zombie bank also includes former Bank of Ireland chief Maurice Keane and Elan director Gary Kennedy.

Jim Farrell

Having become a member of the board of the Financial Regulator in 2002, Farrell took over as chairman in May 2008. The former Citibank chief also held senior positions with the National Treasury Management Agency and helped to establish the National Development Finance Agency, serving as its first chief executive. In 2011, Citibank appointed Farrell as a director of one of its European subsidiaries. 'It [Citibank] would know my record when I served on the board of the Regulator and also when I took over as chairman just before the whole thing blew up, and what I did to try to steady the ship at that stage,' he told the *Sunday Independent* in October 2011. 'Our reliance on the boards and management of credit institutions to meet their corporate governance and risk management responsibilities was misplaced,' he wrote in 2008.

Pat Farrell

Former Fianna Fáil apparatchik Pat Farrell is the head of banking lobby group the Irish Banking Federation. It would be hard to find two more toxic affiliations. Farrell was general secretary of Fianna Fáil from 1991 to 1997 and was appointed to the Senate by Albert Reynolds in 1992. Farrell's role during the boom was to pressure the government over banking regulation, so he must be considered a central figure in the regulatory disaster that sank the country. He is still out batting for the banks. During Fianna Fáil's reign, Farrell was appointed to buckets of quangos by his buddies, picking up juicy fees from the HSE, the VHI and the Dormant Accounts Commission. He's also on the board of the UCD Global Finance Academy with former bankers including Bank of Ireland's Paul Haran and Ulster Bank's Cormac McCarthy.

Irial Finan

Finan is becoming one of the newest 'must haves' for any self-respecting corporate board. He's moved far from Roscommon to become one of the most senior executives in the global Coca-Cola empire. Finan was one of the attendees at the Farmleigh Global Irish Economic Forum in 2009, which produced some nice photos and a lot of hot air but precious little else. Finan is also hooked in with the Ireland Fund, and was an award winner at the 2011 American Ireland Fund annual backslapfest. As a director of the Galway University Foundation, Finan sits alongside aviation tycoon Domhnal Slattery, former EBS chairman Brian Joyce, Burren Energy's Finian O'Sullivan and former government press secretary P. J. Mara. He keeps a house in Ireland and was appointed to the board of Gary McGann's Smurfit Kappa in February 2012.

Marian Finnegan

The Sherry FitzGerald economist was one of the strongest advocates of an ever rising property market. We're all kicking ourselves now for thinking that Finnegan could predict the future. For more details, see Chapter 7.

John FitzGerald

The Economic and Social Research Institute is the state-funded economic think tank. The body has proved about as useful as a wooden frying pan. We're still waiting for the 'soft landing' it kept predicting. FitzGerald, a research professor at the ESRI, has the ear of those running the country now that Fine Gael is in power. The Dublin-born economist is a son of the late Garret FitzGerald and brother of Sherry FitzGerald's Mark FitzGerald. The UCD-educated economist worked with the Department of Finance before joining the ESRI in 1984. He was plonked on to the board of the Central Bank by Brian Lenihan in September 2010.

John Fitzgerald

A Limerick man, Fitzgerald was Dublin City Manager for ten years until 2006. In 2007 he was appointed to front the €3 billion Limerick regeneration project, which has been subsequently scaled back due to a lack of funding. Fitzgerald was also handed the role of chairing the Grangegorman regeneration scheme, a grandiose white elephant that stalled due to the economic malaise. In 2008, Communications Minister Eamon Ryan appointed Fitzgerald as the new chairman of An Post. He is also a board member of the HSE, chairman of the National Transport Authority and the vice-chairman of InterTradeIreland.

Mark FitzGerald

Under the leadership of the son of Garret FitzGerald, Sherry FitzGerald was one of the great cheerleaders for the ridiculous notion that property prices would simply keep on rising. Mark FitzGerald also sits on the boards of new construction industry lobby firm Property Industry Ireland and of the country's largest oil distributor, Tedcastles. For more details, see Chapter 7.

Eileen Fitzpatrick

The chemistry PhD swapped the cosy world of academe for the cosy world of banking, working at AIB for sixteen years, ultimately heading up its investment management unit. She also did time with NCB and Goodbody stockbrokers before moving to the NTMA. Fitzpatrick was appointed to the extremely plum post of chief executive of NewERA – the monster quango tasked with selling state assets and managing the government's strategic investment fund. There was no competition or interview for the job of running the quango within a quango.

Frank Flannery

The Galway man has been at the core of Fine Gael from the 1980s, when he served as a key handler for Garret FitzGerald. Flannery authored a report into Fine Gael's disastrous election showing in 2002 and was among Enda Kenny's principal advisers as the party was rebuilt from within. He was the party's director of elections for the local elections of 2009 and helped in the final push for power in the 2011 campaign. Soon after Fine Gael was elected, it emerged that Flannery had become an adviser of public affairs and lobbying firm Insight Consultants. He has enviable contacts in the corridors of power.

Jim Flavin

Jim Flavin was one of the country's top business heavyweights. He built up DCC, with interests ranging from console games to KP nuts and natural gas, into one of the most valuable companies on the Irish stock market. DCC owned an 11 per cent stake in listed banana company Fyffes, on whose board Flavin sat. In February 2000, DCC sold its stake in Fyffes for €106 million – a month before Fyffes issued a profit warning. The Fyffes share price fell sharply; Fyffes took a case against Flavin and DCC over the share dealing. In 2005, the High Court ruled in favour of Flavin, but two years later the Supreme Court ruled that the High Court had been mistaken in deciding that DCC had not been in possession of price-sensitive information when selling the Fyffes shares. Despite this damning judgement, the board of DCC, which included former AIB chief executive Michael Buckley and former Bank of Ireland chief Maurice Keane, rowed in behind Flavin.

In May 2008, over eight years after the sale of the Fyffes shares, ODCE chief Paul Appleby announced that he'd be going to the High Court to have an inspector appointed to examine the DCC share trading. Flavin resigned. DCC agreed to pay Fyffes €41 million in compensation. In 2010, a report for the ODCE by senior counsel Bill Shipsey concluded that Mr Flavin was guilty only of 'an error of judgement' and that he 'genuinely believed' he was not in possession of price-sensitive information when he sold the shares.

Donal Forde

Forde headed up AIB's Irish retail operations from 2002 until May 2009. He was one of the central players in the orgy of unwise lending that destroyed the bank. Forde joined the Irish Red Cross as chairman in May 2011 – but he'll have to singlehandedly end famine in Africa and cure cancer before his slate is wiped clean.

Michael Geoghegan

As chief executive of HSBC, Michael Geoghegan was the world's top Irish banker. Having retired in 2010, he is now one of Finance Minister Michael Noonan's key confidants on all things banking-related, especially with regard to the festering sore that is NAMA. In a report he produced for Noonan in late 2011, the marathon-running former banker suggested significant changes at the €80 billion bad bank. Board changes and a tweak of the executive ranks ensued. Geoghegan was then appointed to a kind of super NAMA board – a group above the board that was set up to advise the minister. Geoghegan is joined on this new body by NAMA's John Mulcahy, NAMA chairman Frank Daly and Northern Irish chartered quantity surveyor Denis Rooney. In July 2012 it emerged that Geoghegan had been named in a US Senate subcommittee report in connection with its allegation that HSBC concealed Iranian banking transactions from the US authorities.

Dermot Gleeson

The former AIB chairman returned to practice as a barrister not long after the failed bank was nationalized. In early 2010, he turned up as the chairman of private equity owned Travelport, a travel software company, that announced plans to float on the stock market. Wobbly stock market conditions saw the plans shelved. In January 2012, he sold his opulent Shrewsbury Road home for a little over €5 million. For more details, see Chapter 2.

Brian Goggin

Foxrock Golf Club has been well trod by Goggin since he left Bank of Ireland with a bumper pay-off after almost running it into the ground. Goggin has been signed up by US private equity firm Apollo as a special adviser. The fund bought MBNA's Irish and UK credit card operations in February 2012. For more details, see Chapter 2.

Sean Gorman

Secretary general of the rejigged Department of Jobs, Enterprise and Innovation, Gorman left the civil service in mid-2011 with a €634,088 exit package. Gorman's department was responsible for jobs and training during the boom; its skewed focus on churning out tens of thousands of builders and other construction workers critically unbalanced the economy and contributed to a situation where many of the 430,000 unemployed are critically under-skilled. Gorman was one of the guests in FÁS's infamous Croke Park outing when a bunch of middle-aged men rocked the night away to the sound of Robbie Williams . . . at the taxpayers' expense. Gorman's department oversaw the deal whereby FÁS boss Rody Molloy left the state agency with a bumper pay package after the expenses scandal.

Paul Haran

The fingerprints of the former secretary general of the Department of Trade, Enterprise and Industry are everywhere. Haran spent thirty years in the civil service, working as a board member of Forfás, the National Economic and Social Council of Ireland, the National Economic and Social Forum and the Top Level Appointments Commission. He also did the spadework for the setting-up of Science Foundation Ireland. Soon after leaving the civil service in 2004, he was recruited to the board of Bank of Ireland. Despite the disaster that unfolded on his watch, Haran is in demand in both the public and corporate sector. He sits on the boards of listed food company Glanbia and the Mater Private Hospital, and chairs booze firm Edward Dillon & Co. Haran also has a decent quango collection, including roles at the National Qualifications Authority of Ireland and the Road Safety Authority. He chairs the UCD Michael Smurfit Graduate Business School, which has an advisory board including former Arthur Cox chairman James O'Dwyer , PwC managing partner Ronan Murphy and Google's John Herlihy.

Nicky Hartery

A chartered engineer, Hartery was European vice-president for Dell at its Limerick operations before the calamitous pull-out in 2008. In February 2012, he bagged the biggest part-time job in the Irish business community when he was picked to succeed Kieran McGowan as €337,000-a-year chairman of CRH. Hartery is a non-executive director of Musgrave Group, the company behind Supervalu and Centra, and of Eircom, which went into examinership in April 2012.

Anne Heraty

The only woman chief executive of an Irish stock-market-quoted company, Heraty runs listed recruitment firm CPL. She was appointed to the board of Anglo Irish Bank in 2006. She was also on the boards of the Irish Stock Exchange, Forfás and Bord Na Móna, resigning two months after Anglo was taken over by the state.

John Herlihy

Herlihy is Google's man on the ground in Ireland. He joined the domestic corporate circle by joining the board of listed food company Greencore, where he sits with Eircom chairman Ned Sullivan, hotel veteran Pat McCann and Elan director Gary Kennedy.

John Hogan

Hogan was the managing partner of accountancy firm Ernst & Young from 1994 to 2000. The Anglo debacle wasn't his fault. But Ernst & Young had form in failing to shout when it found something wrong. The Public Accounts Committee investigation into the DIRT scandal heard how, in 1992, Hogan had told ACC that it had a £17.5 million liability in relation to unpaid DIRT tax. Hogan told the PAC that no provision was made in ACC accounts over the potential DIRT exposure because it was believed that 'a liability . . . would not be looked at by the Revenue'. Ernst & Young was not censured for its failure to reveal ACC's facilitation of tax evasion. Hogan went on to become a non-executive director of McInerney, the listed building firm that was wound up after being crushed by a mountain of debt in 2009. He's also a board member of drinks firm C&C.

Guy Hollis

Hollis moved from Hong Kong to take over the Irish operations of property adviser CBRE in October 2007. The timing was pretty awful, as the market had just started to tumble over a cliff. Hollis replaced Pat Gunne, who had run the business during the boom, putting together some of the largest commercial property transactions of the Celtic Tiger years. The market is deathly quiet these days, but CBRE is making handy money from providing consultancy and other services to NAMA.

Con Horan

Career public servant Con Horan was head of banking supervision at the Central Bank until 2007, when he was promoted by Financial Regulator Patrick Neary to the role of prudential director. When the useless Neary was shuffled out the door, Horan – who had been in charge of the day-to-day dealings with the banks – was appointed as a special adviser to Neary's replacement, Matthew Elderfield. This meant that Horan was involved with 'supervisory matters, leading supervisory projects and assisting in supervisory crisis management'; the new role also saw him appointed as deputy chairman of the Central Bank's Supervisory Risk Committee as well as chairing an advisory risk expert panel on financial regulation. In his wide-ranging report on the causes of the banking crisis, Central Bank governor Patrick Honohan noted, 'It is clear that a major failure in terms of bank regulation and the maintenance of financial stability occurred.'

In April 2011, it emerged that Horan was moving to London, having landed a plum job in the European Banking Authority (EBA), the new EU body for banking supervision. This is the outfit that may have a starring role in the proposed European banking union. Not bad for a man who was part of a complete regulatory fiasco.

Rose Hynes

The Limerick solicitor became chairman of Bord Gáis in 2009, having served on the board for three years. It's a phenomenally well-connected board that includes former Bank of Ireland governor Laurence Crowley, Anglo Irish Bank director Adrian Eames, lawyer Laurence Shields and SIPTU general secretary Joe O'Flynn. Hynes joined the board of Bank of Ireland Mortgage Bank in 2004 and served all through the property boom as the bank shovelled out billions in property loans. She was elevated to the full board of Bank of Ireland in 2007, stepping down as part of the general clear-out of pre-bailout directors in 2011.

Despite her links with a crippled bank, she's a hugely active member of the boardroom elite. Hynes sits on the board of Fyffes spin-off Total Produce, where the board includes Carl McCann and KPMG former managing partner Jerome Kennedy (with whom she also served on the Bank of Ireland board). The former Guinness Peat Aviation executive's CV also includes stints as a board member of Fyffes, Shannon Airport Authority, Northern Ireland Water, Aer Lingus Group and Concern.

Michael Jacob

Jacob joined the board of Anglo Irish Bank in 1998, serving until the bank was nationalized in 2009. His eleven years on the board coincided with the most reckless lending splurge ever unleashed by a bank. He was also a director of Dolmen Securities until January 2012. Jacob has been a board member of beef baron Bert Allen's huge Slaney Foods Group since October 2006 and major drink wholesaler G. H. Lett & Co.

Maurice Keane

Maurice Keane was chief executive of Bank of Ireland from 1998 to 2002. He left the bank in decent shape. The Kerry man was appointed to the board of Anglo Irish Bank as a public-interest director in 2009 as the likes of Gary McGann and Anne Heraty headed for the exit. The banker was appointed by the then Finance Minister, Brian Cowen, to the board of the National Pensions Reserve Fund Commission in February 2007. He's on the board of IFSC-based Axis Capital Holdings and is a former chairman of BUPA Ireland. Keane was also one of the directors of DCC, which rowed in behind chief executive Jim Flavin during the landmark Fyffes insider dealing case. For more details, see Chapter 2.

Gary Kennedy

After Eugene Sheehy pipped him in the race to be AIB chief executive in 2005, Kennedy left the bank with a €3 million package. He remained as an 'adviser' to the bank, which soon went bust. He is a board member of Elan, Greencore and financial services firm Friends First. He's also involved with Cork biotech group Radisens Diagnostics. Kennedy, who had advised AIB on 'risk', was subsequently appointed as a board member of the nationalized Anglo Irish Bank. For more details, see Chapter 2.

Patrick Kennedy

The Gonzaga old boy and former McKinsey consultant is the boss of Paddy Power bookmakers, earning a staggering €6.97 million in 2011. Kennedy's father David became head of Aer Lingus aged just thirty-five, before becoming a board member at Bank of Ireland, CRH, Jurys Doyle, Mount Juliet Estate and Drury Communications, so there's clearly something in the genes. Kennedy followed in his father's footsteps by joining the Bank of Ireland board in July 2010. He is also a director of Elan.

Angela Kerins

As soon as Fine Gael was swept to power in the 2011 election, a secretive group of wealthy and powerful business tycoons released a major report entitled 'A Blueprint for Ireland's Economy'. It called for pay cuts for workers, reform of the public sector and renewed efforts to fix the banking sector. Angela Kerins, the €260,000-a-year boss of disability organization Rehab, co-chaired the group with former One51 boss Philip Lynch. The other members of this new business lobby included Goldman Sachs' Peter Sutherland, billionaire Dermot Desmond, Glen Dimplex chief Sean O'Driscoll, NAMA developer Michael O'Flynn, telecoms and media tycoon Denis O'Brien, FBD's Michael Berkery and former NTMA chief Michael Somers. The group was also peopled with political insiders such as John Bruton, Dick Spring and Fine Gael national handler Frank Flannery. Kerins has a stack of quango roles to her name including ComReg's Consumer Advisory Panel, the Department of Foreign Affairs NGO Committee on Human Rights, and the Equality Authority.

Pat McArdle

McArdle was Ulster Bank's top economist from 1996 until his departure in May 2009. The bank embarked on an orgy of unwise borrowing during the boom with its customers saddled with the most toxic financial product of recent years – the 100 per cent mortgage. The bank clearly thought the good times would continue for ever. McArdle has become a media commentator since his departure, penning pieces for national newspapers about the economy. He's also a board member of the Chartered Accountants Regulatory Board.

Eugene McCague

As chairman of Arthur Cox, legal adviser to the state during the banking crisis, McCague was at crucial meetings ahead of the ruinous bank guarantee. McCague, who sold his Ailesbury Road pad in early 2012, was also on the board of the HSE. Arthur Cox won the bumper HSE legal services contract despite having a more expensive tender. Needless to say, McCague was not involved in the deliberations.

Cormac McCarthy

You would have thought that the banker who brought Ulster Bank's 100 per cent mortgages on to the market would be corporate poison. Not so. After stepping down as chief executive of Ulster Bank – which had clocked up around €10 billion in loan losses – McCarthy joined the boards of listed bookmaker Paddy Power and BWG (owner of Spar and Mace) in 2011. He was also a consultant to the €60 billion private equity fund Oaktree, which had been nosing around distressed financial and property assets in Ireland. In 2012 Paddy Power appointed him chief financial officer. The holders of Ulster Bank 100 per cent mortgages who are now in negative equity must feel sick as dogs.

John McCarthy

McCarthy is the senior economist at the Department of Finance's economic forecasting and analysis unit. If anyone should have seen the signs of the impending crisis coming, it was him. He didn't. The WikiLeaks cables revealed that McCarthy had briefed US embassy officials about the financial crisis in December 2008 and told them 'forecasting anything in the current uncertain environment is almost impossible'.

Gary McGann

The former Aer Lingus chief executive joined the board of Anglo Irish Bank in 2005. He obviously thought that the bank's chief executive cum chairman Sean FitzPatrick was amazing, as the banker was appointed chairman at McGann's Smurfit Group in March 2007. McGann was part of the infamous fourball at Druids Heath with Seanie, the economist Alan Gray and Brian Cowen that ultimately brought about Cowen's resignation and speeded the demise of the government. McGann left the board of Anglo after FitzPatrick's loan scandal blew up and the bank tumbled towards nationalization. He also stepped down as chairman of Dublin Airport Authority. The Coláiste Mhuire-educated accountant is also a board member of United Drug, where he serves with former ICON plc chief Peter Gray and ex-Kerry Group chief Hugh Friel. In his spare time, McGann is chairman of major insurer Aon MacDonagh Boland, where board members have included former Taoiseach Albert Reynolds and Enterprise Ireland chairman Hugh Cooney.

Kieran McGowan

Kieran McGowan has been one of the biggest cheeses in the Irish business community for more than a decade. The Foxrock man headed up the IDA just as the economy was beginning to kick off in the 1990s and multinationals such as Microsoft, Dell and Intel made major investments here. When departing the IDA, he was sought after by blue-chip business. He joined the board of CRH in 1998, becoming chairman in 2007. McGowan retired from the €337,000-a-year job in 2012. He's also a board member of drug company Elan, along with former Anglo Irish Bank chairman Donal O'Connor, Anglo Irish Bank director Gary Kennedy, Paddy Power and Bank of Ireland's Patrick Kennedy and Davy Stockbrokers' Kyran McLaughlin. McGowan's other gigs have included the presidency of the Irish Management Institute and chairing the Governing Authority of

UCD. In July 2011, it emerged that McGowan had become involved with Property Industry Ireland, a new builder-funded lobby group.

Dan McLaughlin

Bank of Ireland economist Dan McLaughlin was one of the most bullish economists of the boom, along with fellow cheerleaders AIB's John Beggs, KBC's Austin Hughes, Davy's Robbie Kelleher, Goodbody's Dermot O'Leary (now an uber-bear) and Bloxham's Alan McQuaid (now at Merrion). They were all wrong to varying degrees. And worse still, we believed most of their guff. McLaughlin was perhaps the most bullish of the lot. He is still Bank of Ireland's group chief economist.

Kyran McLaughlin

Davy's joint boss Kyran McLaughlin is the 'rainmaker in chief' at the stockbroker and has been involved in some of the biggest transactions this country has ever seen. Davy's client list includes the likes of Smurfit Kappa, Ryanair, Kerry Group, NTR, Glanbia, Elan, CRH and Bank of Ireland. As well as advising on potential takeovers, buyouts and other deals, Davy manages what remains of the fortunes of many of the country's richest people. That gives the firm extraordinary access to some of the most influential players in the country. He was chairman of drug firm Elan until 2010 and is a long-serving board member of Ryanair.

Heather Ann MacSharry

Sligo's Heather Ann MacSharry was Irish country manager of consumer goods firm Reckitt Benckiser, which sells Dettol and Cillit Bang here. Her career had previously seen her run Boots chemists in Ireland. She's now highly in demand for non-executive boardroom posts. In March 2012, she was appointed to the board of CRH. She was a board member of Bank of Ireland as it began to implode from 2007 onwards. She's a former member of the UCD Governing Authority and sits on the board of the IDA. There are also huge networking links from her time on the Governing Council of the Institute of Directors which features the likes of HP's Irish chief Martin Murphy, William Fry's managing partner Myra Garrett, former NTMA chief Michael Somers and Elan's Liam Daniel. Her father, Ray MacSharry, was Fianna Fáil Minister for Finance and is a non-executive director of Irish Life & Permanent.

Anne Maher

Maher served as a board member of AIB from January 2007 until July 2011. She served as chief executive of the Pensions Board before becoming a serial non-executive director and resident of quango land. Roles have included board memberships of the Irish Airlines Pensions, Health Insurance Authority, the Retirement Planning Council and the Fiscal Policy Research Centre of Ireland. She's a director of AIB's staff pension fund.

Pat Molloy

There's no escape from the banks. Pat Molloy ran Bank of Ireland from 1991 to 1998, during which time the bank got into all kinds of trouble relating to DIRT and non-resident accounts. It was hugely embarrassing stuff, but corporate Ireland closed ranks. Molloy was one of the best-connected boardroom directors of the noughties, picking up well-paid roles as chairman of CRH and Enterprise Ireland as well as peachy roles at Eircom and Waterford Wedgwood. In late 2009, Molloy returned to become chairman of Bank of Ireland. A shareholder threw an egg at Molloy at the bank's AGM but missed. Molloy stepped down from the role in June 2012. He's also on the board of the posh Blackrock Clinic along with beef baron Larry Goodman and former EBS deputy chairman Ron Bolger.

John Moran

Not the new secretary general of the Department of Finance but the Blackrock College-educated managing director of property consultancy Jones Lang LaSalle. Moran replaced John Mulcahy when he moved to front NAMA's property operations in mid-2009. Jones Lang LaSalle was one of the central players in the commercial, retail and industrial property market during the boom. It was involved in €1.6 billion worth of overseas deals involving Irish investors in 2007 alone. While many of its former clients have bitten the dust, Jones Lang LaSalle has returned to profit, fuelled by sizeable fees from NAMA. Moran's company is now the biggest recipient of valuation fees from the hulking state agency.

Matt Moran

Anglo Irish Bank's director of finance moved on following the nationalization of the bank. In February 2010, Moran joined the Luxembourg-based wealth-management firm Lombard International Assurance as its finance chief. The company is part of the Resolution group. In February 2012, Moran was promoted to chief executive of Lombard.

Mark Mortell

A key Fine Gael strategist who played a pivotal role in the party's resounding general election victory in 2011, he is a director and head of consulting for PR firm Fleishman-Hillard. The former councillor has been close to Enda Kenny for the best part of thirty years. The link with Kenny gives Mortell unmatched access to the decision-making processes, and puts him top of the list for corporate lobbying prowess. The close links between Fine Gael and the lobbying firm came under scrutiny days after the new government took office as it emerged that Fleishman-Hillard was awarded a massive consultancy contract from FÁS. For more details, see Chapter 3.

John Mulcahy

As NAMA's number-one property guy, the Porsche-driving Ballsbridge resident is the most influential player in the property market. He decides which developments get funded or sold and which don't get financed. Given that he was a major blower as the property bubble inflated faster and faster, his influential position in the agency created to sift through the rubble marks an unusually neat transition from poacher to gamekeeper. Mulcahy was managing director of Jones Lang LaSalle, which was involved in some of the largest property deals conducted during the boom. The firm was involved in the valuation and sale of the €412 million Irish Glass Bottle site. He was also appointed by Bertie Ahern to the ill-fated Campus and Stadium Ireland Development Company in 2000. Mulcahy owned shares in Jones Lang LaSalle worth €2.3 million when joining NAMA, leading to suggestions that he faced a potential conflict of interest.

Kevin Murphy

The Irish Life & Permanent chief executive who replaced the hapless Denis Casey in 2009. Murphy, who comes from the Life side of the business, had been a main board member of IL&P since 1999. One of the last remaining bank heads who had been a top executive prior to the crash, Murphy has announced that he will step down at the start of 2013.

Ronan Murphy

Bertie Ahern clearly trusted PwC's managing partner Ronan Murphy, as he was one of the people tasked with sorting out the finances of the then Taoiseach's St Luke's accounts. He was also involved in one of Bertie's pet projects, the National Aquatic Centre. PwC is also schmoozing the other side now: it was represented at a Fine Gael golf fund-raiser in the K Club in 2010, and Enda Kenny was a guest speaker at the accountancy firm's annual business dinner in 2011.

PwC, which lost the job auditing AIB after rogue trader John Rusnak lost €690 million on its watch, is now directly involved in the running of the nationalized bank.

Dan O'Connor

Former General Electric high-flyer O'Connor returned to earth with a bang when he assumed the role of executive chairman of AIB in late 2009, having served on the board since 2007. Along with Colm Doherty, he stood down with 'immediate effect' in October 2010 as part of the cull of pre-bailout directors. O'Connor has continued the tradition of cross-fertilization of the boardrooms of AIB and CRH, acting as a director of the cement company since June 2006. O'Connor is now believed to be an adviser to US private equity firm Anchorage Capital, which has been scouring the Irish market for distressed assets.

Donal O'Connor

The electric-guitar-playing former senior partner of PwC was one of the country's top corporate advisers during the boom. He ran PwC from 1995 to 2007, as the audit firm bagged millions from the banks. O'Connor's fortunes were inextricably linked with those of Anglo Irish Bank. O'Connor became chairman of Anglo Irish Bank in December 2008 in the wake of the Sean FitzPatrick loan scandal, and held the post until March 2010. He'd served for a number of years on the Dublin Docklands Development Authority with FitzPatrick and another Anglo director, Lar Bradshaw. O'Connor sits on the board of Elan – along with Anglo (now IBRC) director Gary Kennedy – and is now in a senior advisory role at Sherry FitzGerald.

Mary O'Dea

The former consumer director of the Central Bank was tasked with making sure that we all knew what a tracker mortgage was. Clearly the education process didn't prevent Irish consumers from loading themselves up with unsustainable mortgages and credit-card debt that may never be paid back. O'Dea acted as the temporary head of the Financial Regulator after Patrick Neary was put out to pasture. In July 2011, she moved to Washington DC to take the job as 'alternative executive director' of the IMF. 'I'm really looking forward to what I know will be a challenging role, especially at a time when Ireland is itself in an IMF/EU programme,' she told the *Sunday Independent*. Rather ironically, after her role in the failure of regulation of the banking sector, she has a liaison role between the IMF and the Irish government.

Jim O'Hara

The Dublin-born engineer headed up Intel's Irish operations in Leixlip from 2002 until 2009, during which time he also served as president of the American Chamber of Commerce Ireland. He was appointed to the board of Enterprise Ireland in 2009 and was involved in the Research Priorities Report which will serve as a 'road map' for state investment into research over the next decade. A key adviser to the state on all things technological, O'Hara is also on the boards of AIB and Fyffes, which puts him in a spider web with the likes of former Arthur Cox managing partner James O'Dwyer, former DAA chief Declan Collier, ex-Bank of Ireland director Declan McCourt and former Labour leader Dick Spring. O'Hara was prominent in trying to persuade the country to vote for the Lisbon Treaty, with Intel spending an estimated €300,000 on the campaign.

Tiarnan O'Mahoney

Sean FitzPatrick's right-hand man at Anglo racked up losses of €820 million with his finance company ISTC in 2008 – a record for an Irish company until the banks went bust. Despite this corporate calamity, he served as chairman of the Pensions Board until 2010. O'Mahoney is now believed to be scouting deals for US private equity firm Fortress. For more details, see Chapter 6.

Liam O'Mahony

Tipperary-born O'Mahony joined cement company CRH in 1971, when it had sales of €26 million per year. He stayed with the business, serving as chief executive from 2000 to 2008. CRH is now Ireland's biggest company, with a global reach that stretches from the USA to China and Africa. He remained on the CRH board until the end of 2011. After the Sean FitzPatrick loan scandal broke in December 2008, O'Mahony replaced the disgraced banker as chairman of Smurfit Kappa group. In early 2010, he was recruited as chairman of the IDA. A circle was completed, as O'Mahony's chairman at CRH had been former IDA boss Kieran McGowan. The CRH–IDA connection was further strengthened by the arrival of IDA board member Heather Ann MacSharry on to the board of CRH in early 2012. The King's Inns-educated O'Mahony is also a board member of Project Management Holdings alongside former Enterprise Ireland chief Dan Flinter.

Peter O'Neill

The Dubliner took over as general manager of IBM's Irish operations in 2010 after the departure of long-serving chief Michael Daly. While IBM plays a crucial role in the Irish economy, O'Neill has bigger clout as the president of the American Chamber of Commerce

Ireland, which represents the country's most powerful vested interest – the US multinationals. There are over 600 such firms operating in Ireland, ranging from long-established behemoths such as Microsoft, Pfizer and Intel to newer arrivals such as Twitter and Facebook, and they directly employ over 100,000 people. The Chamber of Commerce role sees UCD-educated O'Neill put the armlock on the government over issues as diverse as the corporate tax rate, Europe and education.

Pádraig Ó Ríordáin

The former Arthur Cox managing partner pops up all over the place. He was a key legal adviser to Brian Lenihan, and his firm was central to negotiations on the bank guarantee, the bank bailout and the creation of NAMA. Arthur Cox was appointed to advise the government on the financial crisis without the contract going out to tender. In January 2012, Ó Ríordáin was appointed chairman of Dublin Airport Authority by Transport Minister Leo Varadkar. Arthur Cox acts for both DAA and one of its biggest clients, Aer Lingus. The UCC-educated Ó Ríordáin also studied at Harvard. He served as chairman of the Fianna Fáil-led government's Financial Legislation Advisory Forum. Once touted as a possible Attorney General, Ó Ríordáin is now a director of Paddy Power and TVC Holdings. For more details, see Chapter 5.

Terence O'Rourke

The Monaghan-born accountant has been managing partner of the country's biggest accountancy and consultancy firm, KPMG, since 2006. O'Rourke does more than just tot up ledgers, as KPMG advises some of the country's wealthiest people and biggest companies on how to pay less tax, or on corporate strategies. It lobbies hard on behalf of its clients, with the retention of the 12.5 per cent corporate tax rate top of its agenda. KPMG was the auditor of AIB over the last decade, earning €49.9 million in fees. At the same time, the audit firm was also advising many of the top developers, including Liam Carroll. Neither of those jobs worked out swimmingly but KPMG is back at the table, raking in huge fees as an adviser to NAMA. It also advises central government and state agencies on such things as the innovation taskforce. O'Rourke is serving his second term as KPMG chief. He also sits on the KPMG global executive team. You can see him in the photograph of Enda Kenny and Denis O'Brien ringing the New York Stock Exchange bell that made all the head-lines in March 2012.

Brian Patterson

It wasn't my fault – we're all to blame for the mess. That was the gist of the speech that former chairman of the Financial Regulator Brian Patterson gave to the Kilkenny Chamber of Commerce president's dinner in October 2010. Patterson was chairman of the watchdog from 2002 to 2008 – a period marked by a catastrophic failure of over-sight by the authorities. He told diners at the Kilkenny beano that the blame for Ireland's economic mess should be shared by everyone who bought a house or punted on shares. 'We were all responsible,' he repeated over and over again. The former Vodafone chairman is now a board member of advertising firm Ogilvy & Mather, having served as a director of The Irish Times Ltd, Waterford Wedgwood, the National College of Ireland and the Irish Management Institute.

Maurice Pratt

Pratt was the housewives' favourite when fronting TV ads for yellow-pack products at Quinnsworth. The marketing whizz moved to head up listed cider maker C&C but made a complete hames of it by shovelling money at major expansion as the cider market contracted. He resigned in October 2008. In March 2006, Pratt became chairman of Bank of Scotland (Ireland), replacing Phil Flynn, who stepped down following a Garda raid on his home during an investigation into money laundering after the Northern Bank robbery. Under Pratt's watch, Bank of Scotland (Ireland) shovelled out loans to developers and home buyers and clocked up close to €7 billion in losses. The bank exited the Irish market with its tail between its legs. In 2009, Pratt was appointed by Fianna Fáil to head up the Tourism Renewal Body. Pratt was also chairman of Uniphar, the chemist group that hit turbulence over its excessive borrowings. He's a past president of IBEC, and chairman of the European Movement Ireland think tank.

Deirdre Purcell

Charlie McCreevy must have whacked his head on something before deciding that a novelist would be a good appointment to the Central Bank board. Deirdre Purcell was appointed to the board in 2003 and served on the audit and risk committee. At the same time, she was also a board member of the Financial Regulator. From 2003 until she stepped down from the Central Bank in 2010, she published books including *Last Summer in Arcadia* (2003), *Children of Eve* (2005), *Tell Me Your Secret* (2006), *Somewhere in Between* (2007), *Jesus and Billy Are Off to Barcelona* (2008) and *Days We Remember* (2008). Purcell is still writing and contributing to the 'What it Says in the Papers' slot on *Morning Ireland*. Here's what most of them have said: inept regulators helped lead the country to collapse by failing to rein in the banks. The country faces further austerity.

Stan Purcell

The important guy at Irish Nationwide you never heard of: Purcell was group finance director and secretary to Michael Fingleton during the boom, and the only other executive director of the building society during the lending binge. Some €5.4 billion was injected by the taxpayer into Irish Nationwide before it was merged into Anglo.

Purcell got €340,000 for six months' work in 2010, including €62,000 in lieu of notice and €98,000 in holiday pay. He has set up a specialist finance company called Private Financial Management which advises clients on how to deal with their bank debts.

Liam Quirke

Quirke is managing partner of law firm Matheson Ormsby Prentice, which advises some of the country's most powerful tycoons and companies. He is also a former member of the Taoiseach's Committee on International Banking and Treasury and played an important role in the creation of the legal framework for the IFSC which enabled lucrative international securitization and repackaging transactions to take place in Dublin. MOPs, as the law firm is familiarly known, is also well connected with the major multinationals and advises on corporate and tax strategies. In 2005, the *Wall Street Journal* reported that MOPs housed a low-profile Microsoft subsidiary that helped the computer giant shave at least $500 million from its annual tax bill. The slowdown in Ireland has seen MOPs target overseas expansion, and it is pulling up trees to grow its UK business. Quirke is married to Arthur Cox partner Grainne Hennessy.

Ann Riordan

It was a different world when Ann Riordan stepped off the landing craft in 1990 to set up a beachhead for Microsoft in Sandyford, south Co. Dublin. The country grew and so did Microsoft, benefiting hugely from the low tax rates designed to lure foreign direct investment here. Riordan left in 2001 and has picked up a number of influential roles over the last decade or so. She is a trusted government adviser on technology issues and has served on the Information Society Steering Committee and the Irish Council for Science, Technology & Innovation. A president of the Institute of Directors in Ireland, she's planted a flag in quangolia with positions at Dublin

Regional Tourism Authority and the National Standards Authority of Ireland. She's also held boardroom jobs at Tourism Ireland and a public-interest directorship at the bailed-out EBS.

Tom Savage/Terry Prone/Anton Savage

The Savage/Prone family's Communications Clinic works for politicians, government departments, blue-chip corporates and broadcasters. Terry Prone has long been a favourite of Fine Gael, and her firm worked on Enda's State of the Nation address and Gay Mitchell's presidential campaign in 2011, as well as netting €15,000 for tweaking Health Minister James Reilly's speeches. She also writes regular newspaper columns. Her husband and business partner, Tom Savage, is also the chairman of the state broadcaster RTÉ. The spin doctor had a torrid time in 2012 over RTÉ's handling of the *Prime Time Investigates* libel of Fr Kevin Reynolds. Having thrown RTÉ news chief Ed Mulhall to the wolves by insisting that ultimate responsibility for the programme lay with him, Savage later faced calls to resign. It would later emerge that Prone had advised Fr Reynolds after he had been defamed by RTÉ. Prone and Savage's son Anton Savage is a PR guy too and also works with Today FM as a broadcaster, having replaced Sam Smyth on the Sunday-morning schedule.

Paul Smith

The Trinity-educated Smith served as managing partner of Ernst & Young from 2000 to 2009. Ernst & Young was the auditor of Anglo Irish Bank during the boom and it earned tens of millions in fees for audit and other services. In September 2011, an investigation by former civil servant John Purcell into Ernst & Young's performance as auditor has found that it had cases to answer in relation to the concealment of loans to Sean FitzPatrick and Willie McAteer and also in relation to the €7 billion back-to-back transaction with Irish Life & Permanent in September 2008. Ernst & Young has consistently defended its work at Anglo. The firm has since landed lucrative contracts with NAMA and the state.

Bernard Somers

The younger brother of former NTMA chief Michael Somers is one of the best-known restructuring and insolvency experts in the country. Apart from advising former Anglo boss Sean FitzPatrick, Somers has worked with some real blue-chip names over the years. He is a board member of DCC, which is chaired by former AIB chief executive Michael Buckley. He is joined on the board by former EU commissioners David Byrne and IBI corporate financier Róisín Brennan. Somers has also been a director of Irish Continental Group, rubbing shoulders with former AIB deputy chairman John McGuckian, who stepped down as head of UTV Media in mid-2012.

Michael Somers

The career civil servant became secretary general of the Department of Defence in 1985. Charlie Haughey would later move him to the Department of Finance and thence to the NTMA. Formerly the highest-paid civil servant in the country, Somers used to take home close to €1 million per year as head of the state treasury agency. After he retired in November 2009, Brian Lenihan appointed him as a public-interest director at the banjaxed AIB. He later became the bank's deputy chairman. Since his retirement, Somers has also racked up a serious CV of boardroom posts, including roles at multinational insurer Willis and IFSC-based Hewlett Packard International Bank. He's a member of the Governing Council of the Institute of Directors and a director of St Vincent's Healthcare. For more details, see Chapter 4.

Dick Spring

Red Dick is looking more like pinstriped Dick since his retirement from politics. The former Tánaiste, Minister for Foreign Affairs and Labour Party leader is now a money-making machine. The Kerry man – a rugby player capped seven times by Ireland – is a public-interest director of AIB. The job earned him €59,000 in 2011. Spring, who is entitled to a €121,000 Oireachtas pension, is Brian McCarthy's right-hand man at the Fexco financial services empire. Fexco splashed out a modest €25 million to buy Goodbody stockbrokers from cash-strapped AIB in 2010. Spring was on the AIB board at the time, but would have excused himself from any relevant discussions in order to avoid conflict of interest. He's also involved with the Alder Capital currency-trading fund, which has made good money by shorting the euro. Quite a turnaround for the man who once described currency speculators as 'financial pirates'. The Spring political dynasty continues in Kerry with the success of his nephew Arthur Spring in the 2011 general election.

Ned Sullivan

The bearded Waterford man was part of the marketing team that launched Bailey's Irish Cream on to the world stage, and won the UCD Michael Smurfit Graduate Business School award for the alumnus of the year in 2005. Things haven't gone quite as well for Sullivan since then. The former AWG chief executive joined the board of Anglo Irish Bank in 2001, and became the senior independent director. Sullivan stepped down as a director a few days after the bank was nationalized in 2009. He was also the chairman of McInerney, the listed property firm that went splat under a mountain of debt. Sullivan is chairman of Eircom, which went into examinership in April 2012 creaking under the weight of its debts. He's been the chairman of Greencore since 2003, earning €200,000 for the part-time role in 2011. His old Anglo colleague Sean FitzPatrick joined him on the board of Greencore in 2003. The Smurfit Business School connection brings Sullivan into contact with the likes of Paddy Power's Patrick Kennedy, Valeo's Michael Carey, United Drug's Liam FitzGerald and Davy Stockbrokers' Tony Garry.

Peter Sutherland

The former Fine Gael Attorney General became Ireland's European Commissioner in 1985. He then made headlines for his role at the landmark General Agreement on Trade and Tariffs, which completely revolutionized world trade and opened the door to globalization. The Gonzaga-educated former prop forward was much in demand from the private sector after that coup. He was a chairman of AIB as the bank ploughed headlong into the DIRT scandal. That didn't hold Suds back, and he moved on to become chairman of BP and Goldman Sachs International. He was also a board member of Royal Bank of Scotland, which had to be rescued by the British government. The businessman is hooked in with the secretive Bilderberg Committee, the Trilateral Commission and the European Round Table of Industrialists – all groups made up of some of the most influential and powerful business people in Europe.

Paddy Teahon

The former secretary general of the Department of the Taoiseach has carved out a lucrative career in the private sector since leaving his job as one of the country's most powerful civil servants. Teahon served under three Taoisigh – Haughey, Reynolds and Bruton – and was pivotal in everything from pay talks to the Northern Ireland Peace Process. The state didn't let go of Teahon when he retired, as he was tapped up to spearhead politically driven projects such as the ill-fated Campus and Stadium Ireland Development and the Digital Hub. His unrivalled book of contacts has proved useful to his other employers. The Kerry native became a board director of Johnny Ronan and

Richard Barrett's property development group Treasury Holdings, now one of NAMA's biggest borrowers. Teahon was closely involved in negotiations with NAMA before legal hostilities broke out. Teahon is a director of Merrill Lynch International Bank and his Teahon Consulting 'advises a number of Irish and multinational companies'.

Michael Walsh

Former Department of Finance mandarin Michael Walsh moved to the private sector, hooking up with billionaire Dermot Desmond at NCB and IIU. He became the €100,000-a-year chairman of Michael Fingleton's Irish Nationwide Building Society in 2001, around the time that the tiny financial institution embarked on a crazed lending spree. Walsh resigned in February 2009 as Irish Nationwide imploded. In January 2012, he stepped down as a director of Desmond's IIU as the Central Bank prepared to question his fitness and probity as a financial services director.

Epilogue

Deep inside the Apostolic Palace of the Vatican, separated from the legendary Sistine Chapel only by the Sala Regia, is the lesser known Pauline Chapel. It's the private chapel of the Pope and is not usually open to the millions of tourists trooping through St Peter's and the other Vatican sights. The rather gaudy chapel, built in 1540, features Michelangelo's frescoes depicting the crucifixion of Christ. On 5 July 2009, it reopened after a major five-year restoration project.

On the same day back in Ireland, things were spectacularly grim. UCD academic Morgan Kelly had just scared the bejaysus out of *Irish Times* readers with one of his utterly terrifying pieces about the intensifying economic meltdown. Businesses were closing at a rate of five a day and unemployment had reached the highest levels since the days of the 'Self Aid' unemployment benefit concert in the 1980s and Christy Moore's song 'Ordinary Man' about the impact of losing a job. House prices were plummeting fast and the banking system was utterly trashed. On that day in July, the TASC think tank released a report on the inequities of society. It contained a survey which found that 85 per cent of people polled felt that wealth in Ireland is not distributed equally. Ireland was a nation coming apart at the seams.

When the Vatican authorities decided to embark on the ambitious restoration of the Pauline Chapel back in 2004, they had, despite the Church's great wealth, sought a dig-out. An organization called the Patrons of the Arts in the Vatican Museums was tasked with raising some money for the €9 million project. And who better to tap up than the boisterous Irish, who had been buying up much of Europe's prime real estate funded by the likes of Anglo Irish Bank and Irish Nationwide?

At the ceremony marking the reopening of the chapel, Pope Benedict XVI thanked all of those who had ponied up for the renovations, including the Vatican Museums, the Governorate of Vatican

City State and the Patrons of the Arts in the Vatican Museums. According to a newsletter published by the latter association:

> On Sunday, July 5th, after Holy Mass celebrated by Giovanni Cardinal Lajolo in the Pauline Chapel, the benefactors were able to see the marble plaque bearing their names displayed in the Sacristy of the Papal Chapel. In addition to the plaque, the Patrons of the Arts in the Vatican Museums have created a series of medallions to recognize the spirit of giving of the individual donors. These medallions were bestowed for the first time by Cardinal Lajolo upon benefactors of the Pauline Chapel. They will continue to be awarded to recognize Patrons who make an exceptional donation to the Vatican Museums.

The Patrons of the Arts in the Vatican Museums newsletter noted that there were four classes of donor. The Michelangelo medallion is for benefactors who have handed over $1 million to Vatican museum projects. It is a solid-gold object with the face of Michelangelo on one side and the Vatican coat of arms on the other. The sterling silver Raphael medallion is given to people who have chipped in over $500,000, while the Bernini medallion recognizes donations of $250,000 plus. The final trinket is called the Bramante medallion, a gold-plated medal for donors gifting more than $100,000. Each medallion, 'sculpted and engraved by Italian artists, is accompanied by an elegant calligraphy scroll of thanks and recognition'.

'From what I understand the group you refer to came together by invitation of some international businessmen along with the collaboration of my predecessor,' Fr Mark Haydu, who runs the Patrons of the Arts in the Vatican Museums, told Nick Webb. 'An event was held where he presented the project and our need and from that event, several of those present as well as others who they later contacted, decided to help out to varying degrees.'

A grey marble plaque in the sacristy of the chapel, five feet tall, is inscribed with the names of the benefactors. The list of donors is broken into four separate blocks. In the top block, Irish American hedge fund veteran William Bollinger is named. It must have been a hefty donation.

The second tier of donors includes:

MR PATRICK MCKILLEN

McKillen would become Anglo Irish bank's biggest client and
a major client of NAMA.

MR SEAN MULRYAN

The former stonemason turned homebuilder would borrow
more than a billion from Irish banks before the property
market collapsed.

MR DEREK QUINLAN

The one-time Revenue official turned property speculator is
now one of NAMA's biggest borrowers.

MR JOHN RONAN

The bearded half-owner of Treasury Holdings, known to most
as Johnny, was one of the country's most high-profile
property developers.

MR SEAN FITZPATRICK

The then chief executive of Anglo Irish bank, which would
lend so dangerously that the state would need to give it €30
billion to staunch its losses.

MR DENIS O'BRIEN

The billionaire telecoms and media tycoon, and Ireland's
richest man.

The third tier features:

MR MICHAEL FINGLETON

The boss of Irish Nationwide Building Society, which needed
a €5.4 billion bailout from the taxpayer as it was sunk by its
shocking lending practices.

Acknowledgements

There are so many people to thank that it begs the question did we really write the book ourselves.

Thanks to Michael McLoughlin at Penguin for the vision thing; to the Lionel Messi of editing, Brendan Barrington, for another spectacular exhibition of literary dribbling skills; and to Cliona Lewis, Patricia McVeigh and the rest of the team, without whom none of this would be possible. To journalist Harry Leech, whose meticulous work in the archives helped us to support our rhetoric with detail. To Nuala Walsh for her generosity in giving her free time to impose relative order on a paperchase of chaos. To our editor at the *Sunday Independent*, Anne Harris – a true enlightened despot and one who has our back – and the late Aengus Fanning, who got us mad about stuff. Special thanks to ace reporters Tom Lyons, Louise McBride and Roisin Burke for doing more than their fair share. Huge thanks to others in the *Sunday Independent*, including Danny McConnell, Ronald Quinlan, Shane Fitzsimons, Brendan Keenan, Tony Tormey, Dan White, Max Doyle and John Reynolds, as well as photo editor David Conachy and ace snappers Tony Gavin and Gerry Mooney. Thanks also to Michael Denieffe and all the others at INM who put up with angry phone calls about us.

A big shout out to all the others who have helped or bought pints over the years, including Brian Carey, Aine Coffey, Niall Brady and Martin Fitzpatrick. Also the readers of the *Sunday Independent* and all those people who have provided us with secret files, documents and thumping good stories over the years.

Thanks to Monica McWeeney and Emma Webb for all the support and cups of tea. To Rebecca for putting up with the writing of another book. And the kids Tom, Sarah, Millie and Edward. You'll have to tidy your rooms now.

To Ruth for her superhuman calm as she observed yet another subversive project being cooked up under her own roof.

Index

A&L Goodbody 116, 117, 162, 239
Abbott, Henry 208
ABN Amro 133
ABP Group 235
ACC Bank 125, 253
accountancy firms 118–32 *see also specific companies*
ACS (Asset Covered Securities) Act 77
Adams, Gerry 111, 174
Aer Lingus 55, 60, 69, 117, 133, 235, 255, 256, 267
Aer Rianta 208, 239
Ahern, Bertie 68, 83, 94, 123, 132, 145, 165, 185, 211, 218, 263–4
Ahern, Dermot 145, 200, 222, 227
AIB (Allied Irish Banks) 18, 55, 115, 116, 119, 120–21, 124, 131, 133, 134, 161, 162, 169, 178, 248–9, 250, 261, 264, 265, 272, 273, 274; Allfirst subsidiary 119; and DIRT 45, 56–7; and Doherty 51; and Gleeson 45–7, 48; and Kennedy 48, 49; and Somers 93, 272; and Sutherland 56–7, 274
Airpair partnership 136
Airscape 89
Airspace Investments 168
Alameda County Employees' Retirement Association 124
Alanis 169
alcohol industry 81–3 *see also* C&C Group
Alcohol Products Bill 81
Alcohol Strategy Task Force 81
Alcorn, David 100
Alder Capital 273
Alkermes 62
Allen, Bernard 19, 103–4, 105
Allen, Breda 188
Allen, Kieran 81

Allen, Paul 74–5
Allen & Overy 162
Allfirst 119
Allied Irish Banks *see* AIB
American Chamber of Commerce Ireland 266–7
Amethyst, Operation 215
An Bord Altranais 117
Anchorage Capital 177, 264
Anderson, David 218
Anglo Irish Bank 51–2, 77, 98, 112, 116, 119, 123, 124, 125–7, 129, 131, 133, 135, 137, 139, 142, 143, 157, 164, 241, 246, 256, 259, 264, 266, 271–2, 273, 279; and Drury Communications 72; and Dukes 67–8; and IL&P 19, 29, 50, 124, 126, 127, 236, 271; nationalization 18; and Quinn 67–8
An Post 73, 100, 104, 111, 145, 239, 248
Ansbacher (Cayman) 55; accounts 1–2, 55; Report 55, 243
Aon McDonagh Boland Group 96, 241, 259
Apollo 176, 251
Appleby, Paul 132, 250
Arnold, David 168
Arthur Andersen 237, 241
Arthur Cox 17–18, 72, 112–16, 117–18, 136, 162, 258, 267
Asset Covered Securities (ACS) Act 77
Association of Higher Civil and Public Servants 69
auditors 118–32 *see also specific companies*
Aviva 169
Aylward, Brian 148
Aylward, Liam 186
Aylward, Sean 32

B&I 2
Bacon, Peter 160, 234–5

Baker, James 58
Baldock, Henrietta 133, 134
Ballsbridge 45, 169, 236; Four Seasons
    Hotel 47, 60, 136; Jurys Hotel 116
Ballymore Group 90, 161; Ballymore
    Properties 160, 162, 163, 235;
    Ballymore Residential 65
bank guarantee 7, 12, 17–21, 38
bank loans 9, 112, 127, 133, 135, 168, 176,
    269; and NAMA *see* NAMA (National
    Assets Management Agency)
Bank of Ireland 18, 50, 51, 63, 77–8, 97,
    113, 115, 116, 130, 134, 137, 162, 176, 237,
    238, 255, 256, 260, 261; bonuses 11; and
    Burrows 38–41; and Considine 10–11;
    IBI 73; and Molloy 52–3; state support 11
Bank of Scotland (Ireland) 115, 268–9
bankruptcy 79
Bannon 168
Bannon, James 109, 224
Barclay brothers 112, 122
Barclays Capital 47
Barrett, Gerry 161
Barrett, Richard 128
Barrett, Sean 196
Barrington, Kathleen 67–8, 77
Barry, Tony 243
BAT (British American Tobacco) 41–2,
    117, 237
BCM Hanby Wallace 163
BDO Ireland 167
BDO Simpson Xavier 162, 241
Beacon Medical Group 73, 117
Beauchamps 163
Beausang, William 23
Beef Tribunal 44, 201–2, 203
Begg, David 64, 235
Beggs, John 260
benchmarking 8
Benedict XVI, Pope 277–8
Berkery, Michael 257
betting tax 79–80
Bilderberg Group 45, 59, 274
Bird, Charlie 121
Birmingham, George 209
Birmingham, Mary 169

Blackrock Clinic 117, 235, 261
Blackrock Land International 169–70
Blackstone 134–5
Blaney, Neil 193
Blayney, John 98
Bloxham 172
BNP hedge funds 14
Bohan, Mary 100
Bolger, Ron 4, 235, 261
Bollinger, William 278
Bonner, Kevin 107, 108
Bord Altranais 117
Bord Bia 102–3, 240
Bord Gáis 60, 111, 255
Bord na gCon 101–2
Bord na Móna 52, 73
Boucher, Richie 50–51, 63, 236
Boucher, Simon 224
Bowler, Gillian 236
BP 54, 56, 57–8, 274
Bradshaw, Lar 47, 264
Brady, Patrick 236
Brady, Rory 208
Braiden, Olive 208
Brennan, Larry 172
Brennan, Michael 66
Brennan, Róisín 272
Brennan, Seamus 142
Brennan, Shay 142
Brennock, Mark 72–3
Breslin, Colm 77
Bresnihan, Valerie 224
Briscoe, Ben 188
British American Tobacco (BAT) 41–2,
    117, 237
Broadcasting Authority of Ireland 70, 239
Broadcasting Commission of Ireland 69
Brophy, Ed 241
Brown, Gary 103
Brown, Jim 63
Browne, Harry 189–90, 191
Browne, John, Baron Browne of
    Madingley 57
Browne, Tom 139
Brunker, Eric 137
Bruton, John 43–4, 54, 237, 257

Bruton, Richard 13, 35, 72, 99–100, 237
BSkyB 84
Buckley, Michael 3, 120, 212, 250, 272
Budd, Gardner 229
Budgets: 2006 12; 2007 17; 2009 35; 2010 34, 80
Burger, Carl 63
Burke, Joe 211
Burke, Ray 187
Burrows, Richard 38–43, 50, 237
Burton, Joan 16, 24, 124, 166
Bus Éireann 107
Bush, George W. 190
Business & Finance magazine 50, 126–7
Business Plus magazine 72–3
Byrne, Breffni 237–8
Byrne, David 92, 94–5, 187, 238, 272
Byrne, Eric 188
Byrne, Gay 104, 136, 137
Byrne, Sharon 80
ByrneWallace 162, 163

C&C Group 10, 81, 253, 268
C&D Foods 235
Cabinet DN 237
Cahill, Brendan 238
Callaghan, John 4
Cambridge (financial services group) 3
Cameron, David 84
Campus and Stadium Ireland Development 165, 263, 274
Cantwell, David 157
Cardiff, Kevin 7, 8, 18, 19, 20, 23–7, 28–30, 134, 238–9, 245
Carey, Michael 102, 274
Carey, Pat 100
Carlow-Kilkenny 102, 208
Carlyle 113
Carraig Beag consortium 136
Carroll, Liam 157–8, 161, 268
Carroll, Paul 239
Carswell, Simon 79
Carty, Paul 97–8
Casey, Denis 50, 51, 236
Cassells, Peter 70, 239
Castlelands Construction 180

Cawley, Noel 240
CBRE (CB Richard Ellis) 159, 173–4, 254
Celtic Helicopters 97, 98
Cement Roadstone Holdings *see* CRH
Central Bank 8, 118, 127, 129, 134, 235, 236, 248, 254, 269; 2005 Financial Stability Report 9; and the Nyberg Report 19, 21
Century Homes 122
Certus 242
Chambers, Russell 133
Channel 6 (TV station) 69
Chari, Raj 85
Charleton, Luke 129
Chartered Accountants' Regulatory Board 127
Chartered Land 116, 163
chewing gum levy 76
Childers, Nessa 28, 223
Chinese walls 69, 73, 113, 115, 138
CIÉ 42, 106–9
CIF (Construction Industry Federation) 65, 67
Citibank 246
Citygroup 47
CityJet 40
civil service 30–33; Outside Appointments Board 10; pay 11, 33–5, 91–2, 98–9, 164–5; size 36 *see also specific governmental departments, e.g. Finance, Department of*
Clancy, Seoirse 137–8
Clarke, Derek 29
Clarke, Frank 209, 225
Clifford, Michael 200
Clohessy, Grainne 145, 146
Clune, Terry 128
Coca-Cola 68, 247
Codd-Nolan, Kathleen 224
Codd, Pauline 224
Coffey, Paudie 108
Cogan, Frank 35
Coghlan, Michael 223
Coillte 60, 61, 133, 238
College Partnership 137
Collier, Declan 265

Colliers International 170
Collins, Bernard 240
Collins, Gerry 203, 221
Collins Stewart 141
Commission for Public Service
    Appointments 30
Communications Clinic 74, 271
Company Law Act (1963) 113–14
Conduit Partnership 136, 137
Conlon, Ciaran 240
Conlon, Julian 136
Connolly, Ciaran 30, 32
Connolly, Michael 182
Connolly, Oliver 105
Connolly, Paddy 203
Considine, Tom 8–11
Construction Industry Federation
    (CIF) 65, 67
Conway, Seamus 1
Coolmore Stud 72
Cooney, Hugh 95–6, 241, 259
Cooper, Matt 83
Corcoran, Jody 145–6
Corcoran, Nick 113
corporate donations 88–90
corporate tax 62
Corrigan, John 93–4, 241–2
Cosgrave Developments 161
Costello, Declan 56, 208
Costello, Emer (née Malone) 222
Costello, Joe 222–3
Costello, John A. 114
Coughlan, Mary 146
Coulter, Carol 198, 199, 229
Courts Act (1961) 217
Covanta 75–6
Coveney, Simon 80, 101–2
Cowen, Brian 12, 13, 14–15, 16, 71, 75,
    77–8, 80, 96, 97, 100, 145, 192, 207, 222,
    256, 259; Budgets 12, 17
Cox, Arthur 113–14
Cox, Pat 242
Coyle, John 208
CPL 52, 253
credit crunch 12
Credit Suisse 47

CRH (Cement Roadstone Holdings) 53,
    55, 84, 130, 243, 252, 256, 259, 260, 261,
    264, 266
Criminal Law Amendment Act on
    statutory rape 196–9
Cronin, John 244
Cross, Kevin 223
Crotty, Jerry 62
Crowley, Conor 2–3
Crowley, Laurence 2–3, 4, 39–40, 255
Crowley, Niall 2
Cullen, Martin 69, 76, 85
Cullen, Paul 36, 104
Culliton, Jim 55, 243
Culture Ireland 69
Cunniff, Sarah 136
Cunningham, John 63, 120
Cuomo, Andrew 124
Curtin, Brian 214–18, 226
Cushman & Wakefield 170

D2 Private 168
DAA see Dublin Airport Authority
Daly, Brian 120
Daly, David 167
Daly, Frank 98–9, 131–2, 164, 167, 182,
    244, 250
Daly, Mark 179
Daly, Michael 63, 266
Daniel, Liam 261
D'Arcy, Jon 137
Davern, Don 184
Davern, Michael 184
Davern, Noel 184
Davy Stockbrokers 9–10, 11, 260
Day, Catherine 244–5
DCC 4, 5, 95, 130, 249–50, 256, 272
de Buitlear, Donal 152–3
De Rossa, Proinsias 28
Deenihan, Jimmy 104
Deepwatch Horizon oil spill 57
Deering, Pat 102
Deery, Matthew 189
DeLay, Tom 190–91
Dell, Michael 63
Dell computer company 63, 68, 252, 259

Deloitte & Touche 97, 98, 119, 129–30

Delta Airlines 56

Dempsey, Dermot 222

Denham, Susan 204, 209, 226, 229

Dennison, Kieran 104

Dent, Karen 224

Departments, governmental *see specific departments, e.g. Finance, Department of*

DEPFA 98, 244

Dermot G. O'Donovan 137, 138

Desmond, Barry 25

Desmond, Dermot 50–51, 140, 257, 275

Deutsche Bank 47, 79

Devins, Jimmy 220

Devins, Mary 220

Devlin, Caroline 136

Dew Partnership 137

DHR Communications 70, 239

Diageo 81

Digital Hub Development Agency 70, 239, 274

Dilger, David 3

Dillon Eustace 162–3

Direct Partnership 136–7

DIRT tax scandal 4, 45, 56–7, 119, 121, 125, 253, 261

Dochnal, Marek 243

Doherty, Colm 46, 51, 264

Doherty, Michael 77

Doherty, Moya 128

Donaghy, Eamonn 137

Donatex 161

donations, corporate 88–90

Donlon, Jim 100

Dorgan, Sean 245

Downes, Ronnie 15

Doyle, Cliona 70

Doyle, David 7, 11–12, 18, 23, 25, 33, 34, 245

DP Energy 60

Drennan, John 100

drinks industry 81–3 *see also* C&C Group

Drumm, David 52, 77, 139

Drury, Fintan 71

Drury Communications 71–2, 80, 256

DTZ Sherry FitzGerald 175

Dublin Airport Authority (DAA) 52, 117–18, 259, 267

Dublin Bus 100, 107

Dublin Dental Hospital Board 100

Dublin Docklands Development Authority 122, 128, 161, 264

Dublin Port Tunnel 66

Dukes, Alan 67–8, 245–6

Duleek Limited Partnership 137

Dunlop, Frank 67, 85

Dunne, Ben 44

Dunne, Sean 50, 116, 236

Durcan, Patrick 223

Durkan: Brothers 180; Group 180–81

Eames, Adrian 255

EBA (European Banking Authority) 254

EBS 18, 63, 115, 134, 235, 271

Ecofin conference 69

Economic and Social Research Institute (ESRI) 15, 16, 98, 247–8

Economist magazine 12–13, 55

Edelman Ireland 70–71, 72

Edward Holdings 161

Eircom 53, 133, 135, 165, 252, 261, 273

EirGrid 105

Elan 48, 62, 63, 97, 132, 256, 259, 260, 265

Elderfield, Matthew 127, 254

Eli Lilly 63

Elliot, Mark 128

ENRC 237

Enright, Olwyn 72

Enright, Tom 72

Enterprise, Trade and Employment, Department of 63–4, 69

Enterprise Ireland 53, 84, 261, 265

Entrepreneur of the Year competition 128

Environment, Department for the 85, 86, 123–4

Equality Authority 111

Ericsson 56

Ernst & Young 119, 124–30, 131, 144, 145, 161–2, 253, 271–2

ESB 60, 111, 208, 239

ESRI *see* Economic and Social Research Institute

European Banking Authority (EBA) 254
European Court of Auditors 25–6, 28–30
European People's Party 28
European Round Table of Industrialists 274
European Union (EU) 7, 12, 84; IMF/EU
    bailout 18, 21

Facebook Ireland 84, 267
Farrell, Enda 177
Farrell, Jim 246
Farrell, Pat 76, 77, 246–7
Farren, Ronan 70
FÁS 71, 251–2, 263
Faughnan, Sean 241
FBD Insurance 72, 245
Fennelly, Nial 187
Fexco 273
Fianna Fáil 68–9, 72, 85, 86, 96, 100–101,
    105–6, 111, 114, 123, 142, 145, 184–6, 187,
    188–9, 192, 193, 194, 196, 197, 199, 200, 202,
    203, 204, 207–8, 209, 214, 219, 225, 246
Fianna Fáil–Progressive Democrats
    coalition 198, 201, 209
Finan, Irial 247
Finan, Sean 104
Finance, Department of 7–37, 61, 69, 79,
    83, 93, 114–15, 116, 134, 135; audit of
    appointments 30; bank guarantee 7, 12,
    17–21, 38; economic forecasting 12–17,
    20–21; Implementation Advisory
    Group 8–9; lack of awareness of the
    looming banking crisis 19–21; and the
    Nyberg Report 19, 21; pay 11, 33–6;
    Public Service Management and
    Development 8; severance gratuities
    7–8, 12; and the Wright Report 21–3
Finance Magazine 175
Financial Emergency Measures in the
    Public Interest Act 34
Financial Regulator 8–9, 10, 77, 123, 129, 236,
    265, 269; and the Nyberg Report 19, 21
Financial Times 49, 55
Fine Gael 24, 28, 29–30, 44, 54, 55, 56,
    68–9, 70, 71, 73, 76, 80, 86, 88–90,
    99–100, 101, 102–4, 106, 109, 167, 179,
    194, 242, 249, 262–3, 271

Fine Gael–Labour coalition 101, 106–11,
    222–5, 233
Fingleton, Michael 51, 269, 279
Finlay, Fergus 67
Finlay, Thomas 187
Finnegan, Marian 175–6, 247
Finnerty, Ailish 114
Firstwood Partnership 137
Fiscal Advisory Council 111
FitzGerald, Alexis 116, 244
Fitzgerald, Ann 70
FitzGerald, Garret 54, 55, 223, 249
FitzGerald, John 247–8
Fitzgerald, John 248
FitzGerald, Liam 274
FitzGerald, Mark 248
FitzGerald, Peter 128
Fitzpatrick, Dermot 100
Fitzpatrick, Eileen 94, 99, 248–9
FitzPatrick, Jonathan 168
FitzPatrick, Sean 51–2, 71, 112, 120, 124,
    125, 126, 139, 234, 259, 264, 271, 272,
    273–4, 279
Flannery, Frank 73, 249, 257
Flavin, Jim 4–5, 52, 95, 249–50, 256
Fleishman-Hillard Saunders 71
Fleming, John 180
Flinter, Dan 266
Flood Tribunal 44, 67, 85
Flynn, Donal 60
Flynn, Phil 268–9
Flynn, Turlough 167
Foley, Deirdre 168
Food Industries 3
Forde, Donal 250
Fordmount Group 137–8
Fortress Investment Group 177
Forum Partners 177
Four Seasons Hotel, Ballsbridge 47, 60, 136
Fox, Mildred 188
Foxe, Ken 240
Fraser, Martin 62
Frawley, Adrian 137
Freedom of Information Act 14, 31, 63, 77,
    92, 99, 100, 228
French, Arthur 76

Friary Law 105
Friel, Hugh 259
Friends First 48, 141, 256
FTI Consulting 135
Furlong, Gerard 221
Fyffes 5, 130, 169, 249–50, 255, 256

Gaffney, Phil 107, 108
Gageby, Douglas 209
Gallagher, Jackie 62, 68
Gallagher, Laura 64
Gallagher Shatter 105
Gallaher 117
Gannon, Gerry 172, 183
Gannon Homes 65
Gardaí 52, 215, 269
Garrett, Myra 238, 261
Garry, Tony 274
Garvey, Damien 70
Gashi, Olga 128
GATT (General Agreement on Tariffs and Trade) 56
Geaney, Donal 97, 132
General Agreement on Tariffs and Trade (GATT) 56
Geoghegan, Michael 182, 250–51
Geoghegan Quinn, Máire 25, 145, 205
Gibbons, Conal 221
Gibbons, Hugh 221
Gilmore, Eamon 25–6, 28, 82–3, 111, 222, 223–4
Gleeson, Dermot 44–9, 54, 136, 168, 208, 251
Glennon, Jim 71
Goggin, Brian 39, 49–50, 77–8, 176, 236, 251
Goldman Sachs 17–18, 57, 134; Bank (Europe) 118; International 56, 274
golf 2, 71, 76, 145, 244, 264
Goodbody Stockbrokers 60–61, 249, 273
Goodman, Larry 3, 5, 44, 45, 201, 235, 239, 261; Food Industries 3
Goodman International 3
Goodwin, Sir Fred 58
Google 63
Gordon, Ray 73, 74
Gordon MRM 73
Gorman, Sean 63, 251–2

Gormley, John 66, 75–6, 81, 122
GPA (Guinness Peat Aviation) 55
Grafton Group 72, 130, 236
Gray, Alan 259
Gray, Peter 259
Green Party 85–6, 100–101
Greencore 3, 48, 253, 256, 273
Grehan, Ray 128
Guardian 41–2
Guidelines for Managing Underperformance in the Civil Service 31–2
Guidry, Greg 62
Guiness Peat Aviation (GPA) 55
Guinness, Jennifer 208
Guinness Mahon Cayman Trust 2
Gunne, Pat 254
Gunning, David 60
GVA Donal O Buachalla 170

Hamilton, James 32–3
Hamilton, Liam 201–2, 204, 210, 212, 213, 214, 226
Hamilton, Stephen 136
Hamilton Osborne King 171
Hanafin, Mary 200
Haran, Paul 247, 252
Harbourmaster Capital 135
Harcourt Group 89
Harney, Mary 71, 81, 119, 197
Harrington, Stewart 242
Hartery, Nicky 252
Harvey-Jones, Sir John 55
Haughey, Charles J. 'Charlie' 2, 93, 94, 97, 145, 184, 193, 194, 195, 196, 201, 202, 203, 272
Haughey, Sean 195
Haughey Boland 97
Haydu, Mark 278
Hayward, Tony 57
Health, Department of 72, 81, 82, 83
Health and Safety Authority (HSA) 100
Heaney, Catherine 70
hedge funds 14
Heffernan, Tony 70, 239
Heineken 81
Heneghan, Pat 104

Hennesy, Grainne 270
Henry, Joan 172
Heraty, Anne 52, 253, 256
Herlihy, John 48, 63, 252, 253
Hester, Stephen 79
Hickey, Pat 40
Higgins, Joe 110, 115
Hillery, Brian 98
Hodgkinson, David 124
Hogan, Gerard 198–9
Hogan, John 253
Hogan, Phil 24, 76, 102
Hogan Lovells 162
Holding Cement Polski 243
Hollis, Guy 254
Hollway, Paul 137
Honohan, Patrick 78, 254
Honohan Report 78
Hope, Ann 81
Horan, Con 254
Hourican, John 63
Housing Finance Agency 27
Howlin, Brendan 24, 28, 33, 110, 241
Howlin, Richie 100
HSE (Health Service Executive) 117, 247, 248, 258
Hughes, Austin 260
Hughes, Seamus 221
Hume, John 54
Hunt, Jeremy 83–4
Hunt, Marie 173
Hurley, John 8
HWBC 170
Hynes, Rose 255

IAASA (Irish Auditing and Accounting Supervisory Authority) 120
IAPF *see* Irish Association of Pension Funds
Iarnród Éireann 107
IBEC *see* Irish Business and Employers Confederation
IBF *see* Irish Banking Federation
IBI 73
IBM 266
IBRC 240, 265

ICTU (Irish Congress of Trade Unions) 146, 147
IDA (Industrial Development Authority) 111, 239, 240, 245, 259, 261, 266
IFSC (International Financial Services Centre) 237, 270
IIBOA (Irish Independent Betting Officers' Association) 80
IMF (International Monetary Fund) 7, 12, 265; and Burrows 42–3; European Regional Advisory Group 42–3; IMF/EU bailout 18, 21
Imperial Tobacco 117
Indaver 64
Independent News and Media (INM) 45
Ingersoll Rand 237
Ingram, Bob 63
Ingram, Phil 133
INM (Independent News and Media) 45
Insight Consultants 73, 249
insolvency 79
Institute of Public Administration 85
Institution of Chartered Accountants of Ireland (ICAI) 78, 97–8
Intel 259, 265, 267
International Financial Services Centre (IFSC) 237, 270
International Monetary Fund *see* IMF
International Securities and Trading Corporation (ISTC) 139–41, 142, 266
Irish Aid 70
Irish Association of Pension Funds (IAPF) 146, 148, 149, 151
Irish Auditing and Accounting Supervisory Authority (IAASA) 120
Irish Aviation Authority 97
Irish Bank Resolution Corporation 135
Irish Banking Federation (IBF) 64, 76, 77, 78, 79, 246
Irish Banking system: and the credit crunch 12; crisis and crash 11–12, 19–21, 29, 38, 114–15; nationalization 7; policy shaping 76–9; state guarantee 7, 12, 17–21, 38
Irish Business and Employers Confederation (IBEC) 40, 87, 146

Irish Congress of Trade Unions (ICTU)
146, 147
Irish Continental 2, 272
Irish Distillers 39, 81
Irish economy 7, 8, 9, 12–17; Budgets *see*
Budgets; crash 12–13; Department of
Finance's economic forecasting 12–17,
20–21; IMF/EU bailout 18, 21;
personal debt crisis 79; recession 18
Irish Farmers Association 64
Irish Ferries 84
Irish Glass Bottle site, Ringsend 165,
172, 263
Irish Independent 66, 96, 175, 178, 188,
220–21
Irish Independent Betting Officers'
Association (IIBOA) 80
Irish Insurance Federation 146
Irish Life & Permanent (IL&P) 19, 29, 50,
51, 73, 121, 123, 126, 127, 134, 169, 236,
237–8, 240, 261, 263, 271
Irish Medication Safety Network 69
Irish Nationwide Building Society 18, 51,
119, 121, 123, 128, 129, 244, 269–70,
275, 279
Irish Pensions Board *see* Pensions Board
Irish Sports Association 68
Irish Sports Council 100
Irish Stock Exchange 73, 253
Irish Taxation Institute 78
Irish Times 14, 36, 54, 56, 73, 76, 77–8, 79,
104, 166–7, 191, 193, 194, 198, 199, 203,
210–11, 227, 229, 231–2, 277
ISTC *see* International Securities and
Trading Corporation
Ivory, Pat 64

J. C. Flowers 113
JAAB *see* Judicial Appointments Advisory
Board
Jacob, Michael 255
JEAP 137
Jefferson Smurfit plc 118
Jennings, Austin 77
John Paul Construction 65
John Sisk & Son 65

Johnson, Keenan 224
Johnston, William 137
Jones Lang LaSalle 165, 166, 170–71, 174,
262, 263
Joyce, Brian 247
judges 184–233 *see also individual judges*
Judicial Appointments Advisory Board
(JAAB) 205–8, 219, 221, 224
Judicial Council Bill 226, 227–9
Jupp, Vivienne 107
Jurys Hotel, Ballsbridge 116
Jurys Inns 136
Justice, Department of 30, 32, 65, 69, 111,
197, 213–14, 217, 229

Kane, Archie 53
KBC Bank 163
Keane, Maurice 52, 98, 246, 250, 255–6
Keane, Michael 73
Keane, Ronan 196, 226
Kearns, Eamonn 23, 31
Kearns, Nicholas 231
Keaveney, Cecilia 220
Keaveney, Colm 29
Keena, Colm 73
Kelland Homes 116
Kellegher, Donal 167–8
Kelleher, Robbie 260
Kellogs 72, 84
Kelly, Cyril 210, 211–12, 213, 214
Kelly, Mrs Cyril (Patricia McNamara)
222
Kelly, David 77
Kelly, Declan 135
Kelly, Morgan 14, 277
Kelly, Nicky 188
Kelly, Paddy 139, 163, 169, 183
Kelly, Paul 221–2
Kelly, Peter 158
Kennedy, Brendan 143–4, 155, 156
Kennedy, David 256
Kennedy, Gary 48–9, 246, 253, 256,
259, 265
Kennedy, Geraldine 210–11
Kennedy, Jerome 4, 255
Kennedy, Patrick 130, 256, 259, 274

Kenny, Enda 25–6, 28, 29, 62–3, 71, 75, 86,
    88, 99, 101, 102, 103, 110–11, 114, 134,
    155, 179, 197, 223–4, 231, 240, 249,
    262–3, 264, 268, 271
Kenny, James 76
Kenny, Pat 137
Kenny, Paul 153–4
Kerins, Angela 257
King, Paul 169
Kingspan 72, 95, 122, 238
Knight Frank 170
KPMG 2, 3, 4, 40, 119, 120–22, 129–30,
    131, 137, 158, 161, 163, 267–8
Kragholm, Jens 75

Labour Party 28, 29–30, 66, 84, 90, 101,
    109–10, 204, 205
Lacey, Jim 4, 5
Laemont Developments 137
Laffoy, Mary 197
Lambert Smith Hampton 170
Landy, Vincent 187
Larkin, Celia 70
Lavan, Vivian 194–5
law firms 112–18 *see also specific companies*
Law Society 113, 205, 219, 226
Lawlor, Aine 91
Lawlor, Liam 3, 5, 44
Lawson, Nigel 55
Leamy, Fergal 241
Ledbetter, Peter 136
Lee, George 121, 150
Lehman Brothers 17, 124
Lenihan, Brian 7, 10, 11, 19, 34, 41, 50, 51,
    52, 66, 80, 92, 96, 100, 113, 115, 133, 160,
    182, 211, 234, 244, 246, 248, 267, 272;
    Budgets 34, 35, 80
LHM Casey McGrath 158
Liberty Mutual 68
Lindsay, Alison 218, 223
Lindsay, John 218–19
Lindsay, Pat 218
Lindsay Tribunal 146
Linehan, Hugh 169
Lisbon Treaty 265
Lisney 170

Liveline 137–8, 197
Lloyds Banking Group 121
Lloyds TSB 53
L. M. Rothschild 134
lobbying regulation 84–8
Lombard International Assurance 262
Luas (Dublin tram service) 66
Lucey, Tim 221
Luddy, Enda 157–8
Luxembourg 25; European Court of
    Auditors 25–6, 28–30
Lydon, Don 211, 212
Lynch, Ciaran 107, 108
Lynch, Jack 193, 200
Lynch, John 106
Lynch, Justice 187
Lynch, Philip 257
Lyons, Tom 15, 121, 135

Macalister, Terry 42
McArdle, Pat 257
McArthur, Malcolm 193
McAteer, Willie 51–2, 127, 271
MacBride, Sean 220–21
McCague, Eugene 258
McCann, Carl 255
McCann, Neil 2
McCann, Pat 253
McCann FitzGerald 116, 117, 244
McCartan, Pat 195, 209
McCarthy, Colm 154
McCarthy, Cormac 177, 247, 258
McCarthy, Dermot 10, 11, 33, 34, 62
McCarthy, John 14–15, 258
McCaughey, Gerry 122, 128
McColgan, John 128
McConnell, Danny 15
McConnon, Jim 158–9
McCourt, Declan 265
McCracken Tribunal 97, 145
McCreevy, Charlie 8, 13, 79, 96–7, 132,
    214, 269
McCullagh, Denis 187
McDaid, Jim 220
McDermott, Nigel 113
McDonagh, Brendan 160, 164–5, 166

McDonagh, Ciara-Elena 192
McDonagh, Donagh 186–92
McDonald, Frank 194
McDonald, Mary Lou 26, 28
McDonnell, Conor 112, 113
McDowell, Michael 85, 188, 197, 198, 209, 226–7
McEnery, Brian 167
McEntee, Paddy 215
MacEochaidh, Colm 225
McGann, Gary 52, 139, 241, 256, 259
McGee, Harry 14–15
McGennis, Marian 100
McGilligan, John 208
McGowan, Kieran 259–60, 266
McGrath, Fergal 158
McGrath, Mattie 184–6, 191–2
McGrath, Michael 27–8
McGrath, Paul 16
McGuckian, John 272
McGuinness, John 143, 155, 221
McHugh, Joe 72
McInerney 253, 273
Macken, Fidelma 187
McKerr, Mike 126–7
McKillen, Paddy 112–13, 122, 136, 161, 162, 279
McKillop, Sir Tom 58
Mackin, Martin 62, 68
Mackle, Maria 15–17
McLaughlin, Dan 260
McLaughlin, Kyran 136, 259, 260
McLoughlin, Ray 55
McManamon, Peter 242
McManus, Brigid 33
McManus family 176
MacMenamin, John 209, 225
McNally, Donal 30–31
McNamara, Bernard 183
McNamara, Patricia (Mrs Cyril Kelly) 222
McNamara, Paul 169, 170
McNeive, Paul 171
McNulty, Michael 144–5
McQuaid, Alan 260
McSharry, Gary 114
MacSharry, Heather Ann 260–61, 266

MacSharry, Ray 54, 96, 261
McStay, John 141
Madison Dearborn Partners (MDP) 118
Maher, Anne 261
Mahon, Aidan 152
Mahon Tribunal 2, 123, 218
Main Partnership 136
Mainstream Renewable 84
Mallabraca 113
Mallee, Paul 107, 108
Malone, Gráinne 222, 223
Malone, Joe 194
Malone, Peter 10
Mansergh, Martin 184–5, 186
Maple Partnership 136
Maples and Calder 162
Mara, P. J. 97, 247
Margetson, Ernest 187
Marrinan, Jack 187
Martin, Chris 63
Martin, Kelly 114
Mates, Michael 195
Matheson Ormsby Prentice (MOP) 116, 162, 270
Matthews, Joe 210
Matthews, Sarah 63
Mayo Renewable Power 62
MDP (Madison Dearborn Partners) 118
Meade, Joe 141
Meaney, Phil 101–2
MEAS (Mature Enjoyment of Alcohol in Society) 82–3
Mehigan, Brian 130
Melvin, Ronan 104
Menzies, Gina 104
Mercer 32
Merrill Lynch 17–18, 24, 132–4, 275
Microsoft 68, 242, 259, 267, 270
Milton, Jim 72
Mitchell, Alan 224
Mitchell, Gay 242, 271
Mitchell, Jim 56–7, 203–4
MKC 63, 74, 75
Molloy, Pat 52–3, 261
Molloy, Rody 252
Molony, Ronan 244

Monahan, Phil 2
Monarch Properties 2
Mongey, Iarla 64, 71–2
Mooney, Derek 188
Mooney, Patrick 137
Moran, Carroll 215
Moran, Derek 16
Moran, John 24, 37, 174, 262
Moran, Johnny, hotels 129
Moran, Mary (née Malone) 222
Moran, Matt 262
Morgan Stanley 172, 178
Moriarty Tribunal 97, 243; report 86
Morrissey, Dan 136
Mortell, Mark 71, 262–3
mortgages 9, 14, 79, 258
motor industry 74–5
Mountjoy Prison site 65
Mueller, Christoph 63
Mulcahy, John 165–6, 174, 182, 250, 263
Mulcahy, Tom 55
Mulhall, Ed 271
Mulherin, Michelle 170
Mulryan, Donal 178
Mulryan, Sean 183, 279
Murphy, Gary 85
Murphy, Gerry 63, 134, 135
Murphy, John 63
Murphy, Kevin 51, 263
Murphy, Martin 63, 261
Murphy, Padraig 35
Murphy, Ronan 123, 252, 263–4
Murray, Brian 201
Murray, Joe 72
Murray, John 187, 193–200, 202–3, 208, 227, 231
Murray Consultants 72
Musgrave Group 252
myhome.ie 73, 244

NAMA (National Assets Management Agency) 63, 72, 73, 87, 98, 112, 115, 116, 122, 128, 129, 131–2, 135, 137–8, 158, 159, 160–70, 172–83, 234–5, 238, 239, 244, 250, 254, 262, 263, 267, 268, 272, 275

National Building Agency 100
National Concert Hall 104
National Conference Centre 65
National Consumer Agency (NCA) 69, 70, 111
National Development Corporation 42
National Development Finance Agency 100, 246
National Irish Bank (NIB) 4, 121
National Pension Reserve Fund (NPRF) 96–7, 100, 114, 132, 145, 154, 242, 256
National Roads Authority (NRA) 100
National Treasury Management Agency (NTMA) 9, 10, 19, 24, 27, 73, 91–9, 114, 115, 147, 164, 238, 241, 246
Naughton, Gerry 72
Naughton, Martin 179
NCA (National Consumer Agency) 69, 70, 111
Neary, Patrick 254, 265
Nesbitt, Richard 136
NewERA 94, 111, 249
News Corp 83–4
NIB (National Irish Bank) 4, 121
Nix, Brendan 190
Nolan, Ann 31
Nolan, Terry 62
Noonan, Michael 24, 25–6, 27–8, 44, 79, 96, 114, 134, 135, 154, 155, 161, 163, 167, 170, 174, 250
Northern Rock 17
'note to John Furze' 55
Nowlan, Bill 168
Nowlan, Kevin 168
Nowlan, Rod 168
NPRF *see* National Pension Reserve Fund
NTMA *see* National Treasury Management Agency
Nyberg Report 9, 18–19, 21, 131

O'Brien, Arthur 137
O'Brien, Denis 44, 114, 139, 241, 257, 268, 279
O'Brien, Jim 31
O'Brien, Ronan 241
O'Brien, Tony 10

O'Byrnes, Stephen 62, 74
O'Callaghan, Barry 136
O'Callaghan, Deirdre 104
O'Caoimh, Ronan 136
O'Ceidigh, Padraig 128
O'Connell, Owen 238
O'Connor, Dan 46, 120, 136, 176–7, 264
O'Connor, John 224–5
O'Connor, Pat 225
O'Connor Donal 259, 264–5
Ó Cuív, Éamon 144
ODCE (Office of the Director of
    Corporate Enforcement) 52
O'Dea, Mary 265
O'Donnell, Hugh 218
O'Donnell, John 31
O'Donnell Sweeney 163
O'Donoghue, Breege 10
O'Donoghue, John 207, 211, 213, 215, 220
O'Donoghue, Tadhg 208
O'Donovan, Denis 216, 217
O'Donovan, Patrick 108–9
O'Dowd, Fergus 34
O'Driscoll, Sean 257
O'Dwyer, Fergal 130
O'Dwyer, James 118, 168, 252, 265
OECD (Organisation for Economic
    Co-operation and Development) 15,
    150–51
Office of Public Works (OPW) 64–6
Office of the Director of Corporate
    Enforcement (ODCE) 52
O'Flaherty, Hugh 186, 211, 213, 214
O'Flynn, Joe 255
O'Flynn, Michael 183, 257
O'Hanlon, Rory 95
O'Hara, Jim 265
O'Higgins, Kevin 225
O'Higgins, Michael 190, 191
Oireachtas Committees 74, 106, 109, 110,
    118, 165, 216, 217; Joint Committee on
    Economic Regulatory Affairs 125–6;
    Joint Committee on Finance 166; on
    Transport 106–9
O'Keeffe, Batt 66
O'Kennedy, Michael 85

O'Leary, Dermot 260
O'Leary, Michael 117, 130, 208–9
O'Leary, Olivia 194
O'Leary, Sean 199
O'Mahony, Liam 266
O'Mahony, Tiarnan 139–44, 147, 177, 266
O'Malley, Iseult 225
O'Murchada, Barra 15
O'Neill, Declan 105
O'Neill, Julie 33
O'Neill, Peter 266–7
Operation Amethyst 215
O'Regan, Hugh 129
O'Reilly, Sir Anthony 45
O'Reilly, Emily 92
O'Reilly, Joe 167
O'Reilly, Liam 120
Organisation for Economic Co-operation
    and Development (OECD) 15, 150–51
Ó Ríordáin, Pádraig 115–16, 117–18, 267
O'Riordan, Frank 136, 137
Ormond, Peter 100
O'Rourke, Feargal 123
O'Rourke, Terence 4, 267–8
O'Shea, Eoin 25, 29
O'Sullivan, Carl 137
O'Sullivan, Finian 247
O'Sullivan, Finn 136
O'Toole, Fintan 57
O'Toole, Martin Joe 186
Owen, Nora 207
Owens, Danny 100
Owens, Evelyn 208

P. J. Carroll 42, 117
PAC *see* Public Accounts Committee
Paddy Power bookmakers 80, 130, 177,
    256, 258, 267
Park Developments 162
Parker, Michael 73
Parlon, Tom 64–7
patronage, political *see* political
    patronage
Patterson, Brian 268
Penrose, Willie 223
pension funds 141–56

Pension Shock 150
Pensions Act (1990) 141
Pensions Board 141–50, 155, 261, 266
Performance Management and
    Development System (PMDS) 31
Permanent TSB 14, 73
Pernod Ricard group 39, 40, 81, 237
Perry, John 224
personal retirement savings accounts
    (PRSAs) 153
Pfizer 242, 267
Pharmaceutical Society of Ireland 69
PIRC 42, 130
Pizarro Developments 169
Point Village 116
political lobbying regulation 84–8
political patronage 54, 97, 100–105,
    109–10, 111, 144, 199, 208, 209–10,
    221–5, 232, 233
Pollard, Mark 169
Poolbeg incinerator project 75–6
Potterton, Angus 172
Power, Paddy 259
Pratley, Nils 41–2
Pratt, Maurice 268–9
Price, Sonja 116–17
PricewaterhouseCoopers (PwC) 19, 119,
    123–4, 129–31, 145, 162, 263–4
Prime Time 74, 183, 271
Progressive Democrats 64–5, 71–2, 74, 86,
    201, 214–15
'Project Luke' 123
Prone, Terry 74, 271
property market/industry 9, 11, 12, 15–17,
    157–83, 277
PRSAs (personal retirement savings
    accounts) 153
Public Accounts Committee (PAC) 4, 15,
    19, 27, 28, 45, 56–7, 65, 94, 103, 119,
    143, 155, 253
Public Expenditure, Department of 31–2,
    60, 87
Purcell, Deirdre 269
Purcell, John 127, 271
Purcell, Stan 269–70
Pye, Robert 14

Q4 Public Relations 62, 63, 68–70
quangos 91–111 *see also specific organizations*
Quinlan, Derek 47, 112, 122, 136, 279;
    penthouse 179
Quinlan, Michael 211, 213–14
Quinlan, Ronald 60, 61, 179
Quinlan investors/consortiums
    136–7, 165
Quinlan Private 136, 162
Quinn, Fergal 168
Quinn, Lochlann 45, 59
Quinn, Martina 70
Quinn, Ruairi 75, 85, 103
Quinn, Sean 67, 68, 123, 139, 165
Quinn Group 68
Quinn Insurance 68
Quirke, Liam 270

Rabbitte, Pat 26, 67, 87, 104
rape legislation 196–9
RBS *see* Royal Bank of Scotland
Rea, Luigi 187, 195, 212
Redmond, Mary 118
Redquartz Developments 163
Registration of Lobbyists Bill 84–5
Rehab 73, 257
Reidy, Liam 136
Reilly, James 241, 244, 271
Rellis, Paul 64
Rentokil 40, 237
Research Priorities Report 265
Review Body on Higher Remuneration in
    the Public Sector 10
Reynolds, Albert 83, 96, 97, 184, 201, 202,
    204–5, 246, 259
Reynolds, Kevin 74, 271
Reynolds, Leonie 222
Richardson, Des 83
Ring, Michael 223
Riordan, Ann 270–71
Riordan, David 224
Road Safety Authority (RSA) 104
Robinson, Mary 54, 67, 105, 200, 204
Roche, Dick 76
Rogers, John 216, 217
Rohan, Ali 168

Rohan, Ken 83
Ronan, Johnny 128, 161, 279
Rooney, Dan 75
Rooney, Denis 182, 251
Rosney, Bride 104–5
Ross, Seamus 139
Ross, Shane 94, 110, 143–4,
Ross, Wilbur 63, 236
Rossbank 120
Rothwell, Eamonn 136
Rowan, John 139
Royal Bank of Scotland (RBS) 56, 57, 58,
    63, 79, 133, 274
RSA (Road Safety Authority) 104
RTÉ 17, 54, 66, 67, 74, 91, 112, 121, 122,
    150, 239, 271; *Liveline* 137–8, 197; *Prime
    Time* 74, 183, 271
Ruane, Frances 98
Rusnak, John 119, 264
Russell, Matt 44
Ryan, Anne 210
Ryan, Eamon 248
Ryan, Gerry 197
Ryan, Patrick 195–6
Ryan, Paul 64
Ryan, Shane 122
Ryan, Tony 55
Ryanair 60, 71, 84, 117, 122, 260

Savage, Anton 271
Savage, Tom 74, 271
Savills 172, 180; Commercial 170; plc 168
Schmidt, Eric 63
Schwarzman, Stephen 63, 134
Shannon, Paul 16
Shannon Five 189–90
Shatter, Alan 105, 224
Sheedy, Philip 210–13, 226
Sheehy, Eugene 45, 48, 49–50, 256
Shell 62, 68
Sherry, Michael 137
Sherry FitzGerald 175–6, 248, 265
Sherwin, Sean 188
Shields, Laurence 255
Shipsey, Bill 5, 250
Shortall, Roisin 83

SIPO (Standards in Public Office
    Commission) 61, 86, 89–90
Siteserv 241
SIVs (Structured Investment Vehicles) 140
SKC (Stokes Kennedy Crowley) 1, 2–3,
    241 *see also* KPMG
Slattery, Domhnal 247
Smith, Michael 225
Smith, Paul 125, 271–2
Smithwick, Peter 208
Smurfit, Michael 118
Smurfit Kappa 52, 84, 247, 260, 266
Smyth, Brendan 204
Smyth, Esmond 200–201, 208
Smyth, Leonora 201
Smyth, Noel 161; art collection 183
social welfare payments 12
Society of Actuaries 146
Somers, Bernard 272
Somers, Michael 91–4, 257, 261, 272
Sorrell, Sir Martin 67
Spain, Alex 1–5
Spring, Arthur 273
Spring, Dick 196, 204, 205, 257, 265, 273
Staines, Michael 211–12
Standards in Public Office Commission
    (SIPO) 61, 86, 89–90
State Claims Agency 73
Staunton, Kevin 224
Stewart, Peter 182
Stokes Kennedy Crowley (SKC) 1, 2–3,
    39–40, 241 *see also* KPMG
Strahan, Bryan 118
Strauss-Kahn, Dominique 42
Structured Investment Vehicles (SIVs) 140
Sullivan, Eddie 10
Sullivan, Ned 253, 273–4
Sun 186–7
Sunday Business Post 75, 77, 139–40
Sunday Independent 9, 15, 26, 60, 100, 103,
    121, 135, 145–6, 166, 179, 246, 265
Sunday Times 23, 31, 61, 139, 220
Sunday Tribune 83, 197
Sutherland, Peter 43, 53–9, 118, 257, 274
Sutherland School of Law 59
Sweeney, Brody 102–3

Taaffe, Tony 187
Taggart Holdings 128, 129
Tallon, Geraldine 33
tax 12, 15; betting tax 79–80; corporate
    62; DIRT tax scandal 4, 45, 56–7, 119,
    121, 125, 253, 261; loopholes 122
Teahon, Paddy 274–5
Teahon Consulting 275
Telecom Éireann 60, 72, 235
Temple Bar Properties 145
Tesco 68, 70, 245
Thatcher, Margaret 195
Thornhill, Don 152–3
Thornton Hall prison project 65
Timer Partnership 137
Top Level Appointments Board/
    Commission 9, 252
Torpey, Michael 24
Total Produce 255
Transport, Department of 60, 69, 117
Travelport 47–9, 251
Traynor, Des 2, 55, 97, 243
Treasury Holdings 65, 72, 116–17, 128, 129,
    160, 161, 162, 163, 168, 169, 235, 275
Trilateral Commission 43–4, 45, 47, 59, 274
Tully, Daniel 132
Tunney, Jim 211
Twohig, Caroline 27
Twomey, Enda 77
Tysabri 62

UBS 48
Ulster Bank 14, 63, 79, 115, 116, 157, 244,
    245, 257, 258
United Drug 52, 117
United States of America: American
    Chamber of Commerce Ireland 266–7;
    US Chamber of Commerce 62–3; US
    Securities and Exchange Commission 62
Uruguay 56

Varadkar, Leo 70, 99–100, 101, 103–4, 106,
    109, 117, 267
Vatican, Pauline Chapel 277–8

wage increases, Irish 8
Wall, Frank 194
Wall, Michael 218
Wall Street Journal 55, 56, 270
Walsh, Brian 193
Walsh, Gabrielle 193
Walsh, Joe 11
Walsh, Michael 275
Waterford Wedgwood group 53, 261
Watt, Robert 60
Webb, Nick, *Sunday Independent* 26,
    166, 168
West Properties 178
Whelan, Fergus 147
Whelan, John 74
Whelan, Karl 36
Whelan, Máire 101
Whelan, Pat 51–2
Whelehan, Harry 203–5
whistle-blower legislation 86
White, Michael 223
WHPR (Wilson Hartnell Public
    Relations) 67–8
WikiLeaks 258
Wilkinson, David 158
William Fry 116, 136, 162, 238
Wilson Hartnell Public Relations
    (WHPR) 67–8
Witherell, Brett 135
Witty, Andrew 63
W. K. Nowlan 168–9, 170
Word Perfect Translations 128
Wright, Paddy 96
Wright Report 18, 21–3
Wrigley 76
Wrynn, James 104
Wyeth Medica Ireland 117

Xtra-vision 3, 5

Zoe group 158
Zonegran 62
Zurich Bank 159
Zurich Financial Services 37, 63